The Library as Forum in the Social Media Age

John M. Budd

ROWMAN & LITTLEFIELD
Lanham • Boulder • New York • London

Published by Rowman & Littlefield
An imprint of The Rowman & Littlefield Publishing Group, Inc.
4501 Forbes Boulevard, Suite 200, Lanham, Maryland 20706
www.rowman.com

86-90 Paul Street, London EC2A 4NE

Copyright © 2022 by The Rowman & Littlefield Publishing Group, Inc.

All rights reserved. No part of this book may be reproduced in any form or by any electronic or mechanical means, including information storage and retrieval systems, without written permission from the publisher, except by a reviewer who may quote passages in a review.

British Library Cataloguing in Publication Information Available

Library of Congress Cataloging-in-Publication Data

Names: Budd, John, 1953- author.
Title: The library as forum in the social media age / John M. Budd.
Description: Lanham : Rowman & Littlefield Publishers, [2022] | Includes bibliographical references and index. | Summary: "Libraries may be the last location where civil, serious political discussion can take place. This book details precisely how that vision can be achieved"—Provided by publisher.
Identifiers: LCCN 2021058325 (print) | LCCN 2021058326 (ebook) | ISBN 9781538168356 (cloth) | ISBN 9781538168363 (paperback) | ISBN 9781538168370 (epub)
Subjects: LCSH: Libraries—United States—History. | Libraries—Political aspects—United States. | Libraries and community—United States.
Classification: LCC Z665 .B919 2022 (print) | LCC Z665 (ebook) | DDC 027.073—dc23/eng/20220203
LC record available at https://lccn.loc.gov/2021058325
LC ebook record available at https://lccn.loc.gov/2021058326

Contents

	Preface	v
	Introduction	1
Chapter 1	Libraries, Then and (Mostly) Now	19
Chapter 2	How Do We Talk to One Another?	89
Chapter 3	What Conversations Can Take Place in Libraries (and in What Ways)?	129
	Index	189
	About the Author	193

Preface

On January 6, 2021, many things on the political landscape changed. A number of individuals marched on the US Capitol and then breached the security of the building. At the time of this writing investigations into the breach are ongoing. I mention this event to illustrate the strong need for civil political discourse in this country. Something went seriously wrong in the days leading up to January 6; there was little conversation about the present political state of affairs. Moreover, there was little in the way of discursive practice about differences that exist among people of various ideological (not in the pejorative sense) bents. When there were things said, there may have been little listening; what was said was not attended to, regardless of the partisan political side of the speaker and the listener. The people of the United States should be able to converse about political issues without anger and in the most ethical manner possible. That is, there should be the possibility for calm discussion of points of differences. There should be reason and the rational sharing of ideas. The present work is a response to the need for civil and ethical discourse (and the *ethical* must be emphasized). There must be ways that can be employed that can result in a greater degree of understanding of points of view and the sources of those points of view. It is intended to demonstrate the means by which conversations can be held and guides to the participants and facilitators of such conversations. The means must be detailed and must be achievable. That is why both the conversational method and the philosophical framework are presented to such an extent. Libraries can become spaces where the conversations can take place, and this objective is a major component of the present work. The need, I should emphasize, for this guidance is pressing, and it is my hope that this book will help achieve the end.

Outline of the Book

Chapter 1 will offer a much deeper analysis of libraries, from their history in the United States to the present state. All types of libraries—school, public, and college and university—will be included. The policies and the tenets of their origin will be examined as a prelude to what they are, and what they stand for, today. In part, the standards and guidelines propounded by the American Library Association (ALA) will form a substantial topic of discussion. What the ALA has to say represents, in many cases, official stances of the profession, but this does not mean that there is universal agreement on them or universal adherence to them. The profession and the institutions are complicated, and the statements do not form the be all and end all of practice by professionals or actions within institutions. All that said (and to repeat from earlier), libraries do envision themselves as democratic institutions (even if "democracy" can be a problematic conception).

Chapter 2 will provide an analysis of discourse, including the techniques of discourse as communicative action, the ideologies of discourse, and the ethics that should be a component of discursive practice. Statements about libraries (and librarianship), conservatism, and liberalism will be fodder for examination in this chapter. The scope of analysis requires that the many aspects of discursive theory will be covered. The linguistic conventions of discourse as the mode of communication and as rhetoric must be a component of the chapter. The ideological elements of discursive practice are elements of all the statements mentioned earlier. Discourse ethics, in both the generic and the specialized applications, is also a feature of the analysis, not necessarily because it is ubiquitous but because it should be constitutive of the statements on all the topics under review here.

The last chapter, chapter 3, will return us to the library as a possible ideal commons. All of what precedes this chapter is recapitulated as the content of the civil discourse that a genuine operating commons entails. As will be shown, libraries of all types can be third spaces (other than home and work) where there can be serious and open discussions that affect the body politic. It is recognized that, as Brennan (2016), not everyone will avail herself or himself of the commons, but it can attract many people who want to be informed about the state of the nation today and into the future. The materials and access mechanisms of libraries are integral to the position of commons. Those services can be transcended, though, by being a space where theorists and commentators of the substance discussed in previous chapters can present ideas in meaningful and accessible ways. Ultimately, chapter 3 will offer a means by which the sharing of ideas can flourish; the practical elements of phenomenology will be at the heart of this purpose. This will include sample conversations surrounding several contemporary topics. The samples will display varying opinions on the topics and will demonstrate what the opinions mean for discourse.

There is the possibility for the sharing of political and societal ideas, but much analysis comes before the realization of the objective of sharing. This book is an effort to contribute to the discourse *and* the place of libraries in reaching the goal.

Reference

Brennan, J. (2016). *Against democracy*. Princeton: Princeton University Press.

Introduction

What Is This Book About?

As the preface indicates, there is a pressing need for civil political discourse in the United States. These examples are instructive for us today for a number of reasons: the thoughtfulness of the authors demonstrates the importance of clear thought and expression, the seriousness with which issues are taken shows how the commentary *could* take place, and the time taken to make and validate the points of the commentators illustrates how discourse and conversation might take place today. These are essential elements that can typify political commentary; thoughtfulness rather than raw emotion can carry the day. The importance of serious commentary cannot be overstated. This is an integral portion of the thesis of the present work.

Another important part of the thesis—the *most* important part—is the potential locus for civil political discourse, the library. When I speak of the library, I mean the institution writ large. Just about all libraries, regardless of type or home, can serve as spaces where conversations can occur. Most libraries tend to be politically neutral space where exploration and discovery by individuals can take place. The exploration can take myriad forms, and it is up to libraries to have (or have access to) resources that can enrich the explorer. The discovery side entails that libraries house, and can provide, multiple viewpoints so that the explorers can find those viewpoints and decide what they choose to believe. These services are ingrained in most libraries, and librarians take the services to heart. This is why so many collections of materials are diverse; the explorers can locate those multiple points of view. This is a hallmark of what libraries exist to accomplish.

The present book suggests that there is something else, something beyond what the existence of materials and access can do. Libraries can indeed serve as the locus for civil political conversation. This is, admittedly, a tall order for libraries; it does occur in some instances, but it could be much more ubiquitous and far reaching. It is also something with which libraries may need assistance. For instance, conversation may best be mediated by a specialist, so librarians might need to recruit people who specialize in moderating and facilitating challenging conversations. These individuals, and the librarians, will have to insist upon ethical action by discussants. Chapter 2 details what that means and how it can take place. Discourse ethics is essential for the success of the entire endeavor. Yet more is needed for success to be defined, not in terms of the changing of minds but in terms of understanding and respect for divergent viewpoints. Phenomenology provides a philosophical framework for such understanding. Among other tenets, phenomenology demands the acceptance of the Other as an *other* self. This does not refer necessarily to assuming that we are all alike (far from it) but that individuals have intentions and act upon circumstances through justice and coexistence. Chapter 3 details how phenomenology can guide action. That chapter also includes sample conversations on topics that are of importance today.

Before we explore libraries in some detail in chapter 1, a few ideas about libraries, most of which are not endorsed here, should be presented to share the variety of thought that surrounds libraries. We will return to a summary of this book and its contents at the conclusion of this introduction.

Libraries and the Future I

"We wish to destroy museums, libraries, academies of any sort, and fight against moralism, feminism, and every kind of materialistic self-serving cowardice. . . . Come on then! Set fire to the library shelves!" (Marinetti, 2006, pp. 11, 12). These words, originally written in 1909, express the prototypical anarchist viewpoint toward one symbol of culture—libraries. While anarchists did not achieve the goal of burning libraries, more recent (postmodern?) statements are also hostile to what is seen as a traditional social institution. While not postmodern (this does have an inkling of a grand narrative, albeit a technophilic one), Dillon (2008) presents an almost utopian vision for the present and future: "The Web has already taught people to want this vast and endless sea of information, and they are already building the ships. Every day brings new Internet tools for finding and sharing information. Millions of people who haven't been in a library in years, are now busy helping to build what is, in essence, the new global networked library. We suddenly have millions of new colleagues and this can only be good" (p. 82). Dillon's point of view is very similar to that of the producers of some social media platforms; there is a promise of "friends" with whom one can have meaningful relationships.

Not everyone agrees with the foregoing (perhaps especially not with Marinetti). There are some, maybe many, who take the opposite attitude, expressed by Chiarizio (2013): "Public libraries have played a critical part in the tradition of the United States and remain a critical part of the democratic infrastructure by making materials available to everyone regardless of income or status. As e-books replace physical books, it is important to consider the role that libraries will play going forward." The notion of libraries as part of a democratic infrastructure will be revisited shortly, but it carries some import that deserves attention. Suppose one were to disagree with the claim; on what basis would the disagreement rest? There could be, one supposes, objection to "infrastructure," rejecting a structural foundation for democracy or any political stance or ideology. That would be a mistake; all political ideologies are grounded upon structures that are multifarious and multitype, as we will see. One could reject "democracy" because the current ways of organizing and operating all structures are not, in fact, democratic. That opinion will require some attention. The other component of the quotation—e-books replacing books—has shown itself to be more or less fictional because the sales of books continue to rise, and reading continues to be popular. In fact, a belief in the ubiquity of e-books might be adopted as an argument *against* the flourishing (or even continued existence) of libraries.

Predictions of the "death" or end of libraries are not new (and are not usually as ideological as Marinetti's). Almost four decades ago Thompson (1982)—stating an opinion that was neither new to him nor rare (especially at that time, but still present today)—said, "The age of printing is over. Printing as such is no longer employed in book production. It has been rendered obsolete by the combination of offset-litho [itself virtually obsolete], filmsetting, and computerization. Gone are the tons and tons of printing type" (p. 76). Only the most die-hard Luddite would miss those tons of type. The production processes involved in book production are immensely more efficient and effective. But Thompson is talking about more than production processes. He (1982) further said that "the real attack of the pre-emptive technology . . . will be in the area of *new* information, news information—not *older* material" (p. 96; emphasis added). He (1982) concluded his polemic by adding, "In sum the consensus of the evidence is that the integral form of the new age will be electronic. The book at best will be a partial realization of that form. . . . What then of libraries?" (p. 98). The prediction, viewed from today's lens, is not only mostly inaccurate but can also be seen as quaint. His question, though, is one of the guiding points of the present work. What of libraries? Thompson (1982) was also correct in one of his overarching predictions: libraries could be obsolete if they are not "user friendly." That is true; if libraries do not exist to enrich the lives of their community members, they not only would be obsolete, they probably should be. However, today's libraries of all types and sizes overwhelmingly exist for the benefit of communities. Librarians know this and work to realize that end. What needs to be addressed is: What more can libraries do to be people's genuine "third space"?

At the time of writing, Dillon (2008) suggested,

> Up until fifteen years ago, libraries had a comfortable information monopoly. Libraries were in every university and every town in America. If you wanted authoritative information you had little choice but to go to the library. We were both the Rockefellers and the Microsoft of information. And then, almost before we could even form a committee to discuss the issue, we not only lost that monopoly, but became somewhat bemused bystanders as innovators poured out of every nook and cranny with new ways to find and use information. (p. 72)

The premise is not actually salient; libraries did not have a monopoly, in part because for many years most libraries did not embrace an "informational" essence. Public libraries frequently existed for entertainment and, perhaps, some degree of edification; school libraries served as curricular support more than anything, and even some college libraries were mechanisms of augmentation of course content and teaching. Libraries eventually themselves became nooks and crannies of information, authoritative or not. Also, libraries themselves absorbed the technologies that enhanced access to information, authoritative or not. What most libraries are now are centers—even supercenters—for what people want to discover, learn, know, or believe.

In some instances, fear govern discourse. As Herring (2005) wrote some years ago,

> Threats to the role of the teacher-librarian are quite real. Unless the teacher-librarian acts to counteract these threats, both the teacher-librarian and the school library could be seen as peripheral to the school curriculum and considered an expensive luxury that the school cannot afford. Therefore, to remain a key player who is central to the school curriculum as information literacy and

resources expert, the teacher-librarian cannot argue that the responsibilities of the current role do not allow time for new ones. Embracing, exploiting, and sharing new technologies is an effective way for the teacher-librarian to promote the position's vast contributions to the school, securing the teacher-librarian a place in the history of education that will be a long and positive one. (p. 29)

One might accept, in particular, Herring's warning if one also believes that education is threatened. That said, it cannot be denied that support for school libraries has diminished over the past few decades. There may be rooms occupied by out-of-date materials and not housing a librarian. There may be librarians who work at two, three, or even more libraries in the course of a week or more. There are administrators and teachers who genuinely do not think that the library or the librarian is efficacious any longer. The action and process of learning is such that the thinking should be disabused. Again, discovery is something that has an individual, as well as a group- and teacher-directed, component.

More generally, there are stated opinions that express the coming death of libraries.

> If publishers and authors maintain their tight control on these books after they are scanned, public libraries will still have an important place as a free source for them, even if they can loan out only a few electronic copies at a time. On the other hand, if Google and others can arrange with publishers and authors to allow low-cost downloads of whole books—a likely prospect, seeing that it gives publishers a new way to squeeze revenues from their backlists—then libraries will inevitably recede in importance. It's a simple matter of convenience: free or low-cost access to digital books will make libraries more dispensable. Librarianship isn't about to disappear as a profession. But if librarians want a steady supply of patrons, they'll need to find ways to keep their institutions relevant in the digital age. ("The Death of Libraries?")

Again, the presumption is based on events of some time ago; many details of logistics have been resolved. In fact, libraries are able to expand their services thanks to vendors that have viewed libraries as opportunities and not competitors. For example, the service Kanopy allows libraries to stream films with a library card: "We stream thoughtful entertainment to your preferred device with no fees and no commercials by partnering with public libraries and universities. Everyone from film scholars to casual viewers will discover remarkable and enriching films on Kanopy. Log in with your library membership and enjoy our diverse catalog with new titles added every month" (https://www.kanopy.com/). Because of such services libraries of all types are able to expand their offerings greatly. This is one example of the evolution of what libraries are reaching out to offer their communities.

More recently Walters (2018) examined some particular aspects of academic libraries in particular: "Most such articles fail to distinguish between four distinct practices: (1) acquiring fewer print books, (2) withdrawing books from the collection, (3) moving books to offsite storage, and (4) replacing print books with e-books" (p. 415). These observations are undeniably accurate for a majority of university libraries. Do they signal problems for the libraries? Walters (2018) adds, "If acquisitions funds are reallocated from books to journals, the emphasis of the collection may also shift from book-centric disciplines such as history and literature to the journal-centric STEM disciplines (science, technology, engineering, and math) that have been identified as national priorities for secondary and higher education" (p. 415). Again, he is not incorrect in suggesting that humanities (and some social science) disciplines may have suffered and may continue to suffer with the shift in materials expenditures. The financial difficulties of college and university libraries create a concern on campuses; can the materials and services of the libraries meet the needs of academic communities? Interlibrary loan is mentioned as a potential panacea, but if all libraries are suffering with their budgets, where will the books come from? As we will see in a later chapter, the humanities are criticized these days and are deserving of defense on the basis of their contributions to human knowledge. Meanwhile, college and university budgets are diminishing, and this is symptomatic of the financial crisis of higher education in general. A later chapter will be devoted to education and will include examination of the fiscal problems that higher education faces and the priorities set by institutions.

It is not unusual that recent commentaries on the future of libraries have tended to concentrate on technology and technological influences on information. Writers such as Zastrow (2018) talk about libraries in what is termed a "postliterate" world and claim that "we" (in this case, archivists) are part of the problem. It may be, according to Zastrow, that the world needs to prepare for a dystopian, post-Internet world. "Part of our ongoing mission has always been to help information seekers navigate the existing universe of knowledge, regardless of format. Perhaps we'll even figure out how to make pictorial catalogs to provide access to the post-literates" (Zastrow, 2018, p. 17). It is not likely that we will live in a post-Internet world in our lifetimes, but is postliteracy possible? Could it be that there will (soon) be a decline in reading—not merely in the activity of reading, but in the ability to read? Polan (2018) warns that, "When you are as bombarded by as much information as we are, you end up using sources that don't challenge you, that are reduced in complexity and density, and you read them quickly. You become a less critically analytical person, which makes you more vulnerable to fake news. When it comes to our democracy and how we pick our leaders, we may be handicapped by a failure to give sufficient attention to multiple viewpoints and complex arguments" (p. 18). In a more extreme vein Bruccoli (2007) says, "Books are at risk because reading is at risk. Students don't read books or anything else—probably because their teachers don't require or expect much reading from them. Students are losing the ability to write, because they don't read. Instead of suppressing book reading and discouraging library use, educators—including librarians—should herd students to the library. At gun-point, if necessary" (p. 73). Could his analysis be correct? When it comes to the future and libraries in a technological environment, there may always be the question of money. Shulenburger (2016) reminds readers that those in control still exert powerful influences, regardless of the technological platform: "What we should not do is latch on to 'solutions' that strengthen the power of those who have controlled access to scholarly communications and used that control for their enrichment and to the exclusion of society's benefit" (p. 5). While Shulenberger's attention is narrow, the concern regarding the control, perhaps especially the monetary control, over information could be the most pressing in a world that fears the demise of libraries.

Libraries and the Future II

There is no doubt that there are challenges in the present and future for libraries. Financial resource allocation constitutes one of the biggest challenges, but there are others. As Jones (2015) notes, "an academic library cannot sit back comfortably and assume that society (or its university administration) will support it no matter what" (p. 114). This is a serious concern, especially as society becomes a factor. Can/should society be worried about the future of libraries of all types? Should parents be concerned about their children, their college-age offspring? Should citizens wring their hands over the fate of public libraries? These are no mere existential questions; they have material consequences. One of the people who shares this anxiety is Eric Klinenberg. He (2018b) has expressed his dismay: "Countless elected officials insist that in the 21st century—when so many books are digitized, so much public culture exists online and so often people interact virtually—libraries no longer need the support they once commanded." It may well be that it is just *because* of the technology and social media that libraries must receive support. For one thing, much of the electronic and digital resources that are found in libraries are very expensive; people cannot afford this kind of access. A resource provided by Johns Hopkins University Libraries warns:

> Social media can provide instant news faster than traditional news outlets or sources and can be a great wealth of information, but there is also an ever increasing need to verify and determine accuracy of this information. Here are some items to consider that can help determine authenticity:
>
> - Location of the source—are they in the place they are tweeting or posting about?
> - Network—who is in their network and who follows them? Do I know this account?
> - Content—Can the information be corroborated from other sources?
> - Contextual updates—Do they usually post or tweet on this topic? If so, what did past or updated posts say? Do they fill in more details?
> - Age—What is the age of the account in question? Be wary of recently created accounts.
> - Reliability—Is the source of information reliable? ("Evaluating Information")

Another realization that comes to the fore is that libraries are not a component of markets in the traditional or common sense of the concept (although some disagree). It is true that all libraries make purchases and subscriptions and procure licenses, but they do not (for publicly supported institutions) pass costs on to those who use them. Klinenberg (2018b) points out that in the summer of 2018, *Forbes* magazine published an article suggesting that society no longer needs libraries; retailers like Amazon can meet public demand. Readers of that article objected so strenuously that *Forbes* removed it from its Web site. Not everyone can avail herself of a retail outlet to gain access to all the information, news, and entertainment she might want or need. For example, parents of millions of students cannot afford to buy what their children require to keep up with what is covered in courses. Moreover, many citizens cannot afford to purchase books, magazines, etc. The idea that retail outlets can meet people's information needs is, first of all, ignorant. It is also dangerously foolish. The thinking behind it is that everyone is at least upper middle class, that everyone has substantial disposable income. It is also foolish in that it presumes that people can gain access to *all* informational resources; that individuals can purchase what libraries pay—sometimes—millions of dollars for. The author obviously is unknowing or has an ideological bent that eschews awareness of the needs of most of the people in the United States.

Klinenberg has extended his argument in a recent book titled *Palaces for the People*. In this book he begins with a long essay on libraries and their impact on society in general and on depressed and underrepresented areas. He speaks of libraries and other social structures as an essential kind of *infrastructure* for society, a structure that can enable people to improve social difficulties, rather than just physical challenges. As he (2018a) writes, "'Infrastructure' is not a term conventionally used to describe the underpinnings of social life. But this is a consequential oversight, because the built environment—and not just cultural preferences of the existence of voluntary organizations—influences the breadth and depth of our association" (pp. 15–16). He is correct to use the term; there is a structural component of social activity. That structure is necessary to many people who lack the customary personal structures of safe housing, safe schools, places to get food, etc. There are millions of people who need the infrastructure that may be invisible to many but is a necessary part of life for others. Klinenberg (2018a) continues, "But when the social infrastructure gets degraded, the consequences are unmistakable. People reduce the time they spend in public settings and hunker down in their safe houses, Social networks weaken. Crime rises. . . . Distrust rises and civic participation wanes" (p. 21).

Klinenberg (2018a) emphasizes that, in most communities, entrance is free to public libraries and everyone is welcome. (Be assured that many cities and towns have rules for behavior; in general, if visitors are not disruptive, there are no problems with them using the collections, access, and facilities.) For those who qualify for library cards the services of the libraries are free of charge. Libraries can also provide communities for people; Klinenberg (2018a) notes that in 2016 more than twelve million people in the United States who are aged sixty-five and older live alone. The space, materials, access to information, and services (especially those aimed at that age group) can be a welcome alternative to staying in one's own home. Being among others is a benefit that may be underappreciated. (This can become the difference between *social* and social *media*.) Things like readers advisory services can also be another desirable benefit that the library can offer. The library, for everyone, can be a safe space—respite from loneliness. The same can hold true for school and college and university libraries; being around other people, even as one engages in one's own activities, can be healthy. The library, as a free place to go, can be a *third space*. That space can be attractive to millions of people of all ages across the country. Klinenberg (2018a) makes a vital point that relates to the foregoing: "Libraries are not the kinds of institutions that most social scientists, policy makers, and community leaders usually bring up when they discuss social capital and how to build it. . . . But social infrastructure provides the setting and context for social participation, and the library is among the most critical forms of social infrastructure that we have. It is also one of the most undervalued" (p. 32). If one wants to examine that last claim, one can look at the funding per resident for the library and compare that funding to peer cities and towns. That is actually a very telling measure when it comes to assessing a community's social infrastructure.

The reader can note that the word "services" recurs here. That recurrence is deliberate. Librarians interact with the visitors to libraries of all types and sizes in any number of ways. It is almost the epitome of an open society. One definition holds that an open society is "a society characterized by a flexible structure, freedom of belief, and wide dissemination of information" (https://en.oxforddictionaries.com/definition/us/open_society). As will be shown in the second chapter, this definition typifies the library. Be assured, libraries do not constitute a utopia, but libraries are built on fairly long-standing foundations of freedom and openness. The people who work to assist visitors are dedicated to creating a welcoming space, a collection that represents discovery, knowledge, and replenishment. While there are walls in some communities, libraries—especially public libraries—are free to all. More will be said later, but the Carnegie Library beneficence led to hundreds of towns being endowed with public libraries (see Van Slyck, 1996).

What Comes Next

Before continuing, it must be realized by everyone that the vast majority of libraries within the United States are public institutions. Among other things, that realization means that most libraries are supported by public funds, be they direct taxation, taxation for public schools, or state support for higher education. These libraries are *public*; their funding comes from the people and the institutions exist for the people. That alone does not make them democratic; their actions and policies do that. While many libraries do have codes of conduct, those stated codes tend to be in place in order to preserve the most effective experiences for everyone who wants to avail themselves of the information, entertainment, access, and services that the libraries of all types have to offer. It also must be said that libraries tend to be political institutions; they exist according to political guidelines (or even rules) and they can also be *politicized* as they go about providing information and services to diverse communities. Moreover, it is argued by a number of people that libraries are both established and operate as democratic institutions. That is a claim that cries for close examination on both counts. It is also an open question whether libraries *should* operate as democratic institutions. The foregoing realities necessitate analysis of the public and political elements of libraries' existence.

This is a good time to elucidate the purpose of this book. Everyone wants to believe something. Almost everyone wants information on which to base beliefs (and by "information" I mean the kinds of narratives that can give shape to thoughts and beliefs). Many people want knowledge; they want some warrant for their beliefs. Others seek truth. In the simplest terms, this book aims to be an examination of serious definitions and depictions of conservatism and liberalism. In part this will be a historical journey because neither idea comes to us fully formed at the present time. Each ideology (see the discussion shortly for some excursus into what ideology means and how it is used here) has a long past and takes on many twists and turns. That is to say, there is no such thing as a conservative or a liberal orthodoxy. The serious thinkers taken up here have different concentrations and pathways to some ultimate(?) idea. Each has a perspective, a point of view. Further, each can draw from the past as it exists at the time the thinker is writing. That past helps to shape thought so that, to use just one example, Edmund Burke's "history" is not the same as, say, Michael Sandel's. What will follow includes an examination of libraries and the history that renders them what they are today (diverse as they are). A description of the book's contents concludes this introduction. A unifying theme for the work is borrowed from Alex Callinicos (2006). In his extremely thoughtful work on what constitutes critique, he asks, "how is transcendence possible?" (p. 1). To clarify the question, he (2006) adds, "Transcendence in the sense in which I am interested in it embraces in particular innovation in the social, political, and intellectual realms. How are we able to go beyond the limits set by existing practices and beliefs and produce something new?" (p. 1). As is the case for Callinicos, the purpose here is to produce something new. That something new is a pathway to sympathetic civil discourse about the state of affairs in which we find ourselves. That is indeed a tall order. And it will not be a simple task, if adopted.

The "something new" is dependent upon our cognitive processes—their powers and their limitations. A great deal can be said about this (and more *will* be said as we travel through the exploration here). For now, some summarizing points will suffice. Steven Sloman and Philip Fernbach (2017) write about the shortcomings of the knowledge bases that each of us rely upon. They emphasize the ability to comprehend what it is we do *not* know, along with how to seek that missing knowledge within intellectual and cultural communities. When they approach thinking about politics, they (2017) quickly recognize some of the drawbacks of communities of thought:

> This is how a community of knowledge can become dangerous: The people we talk to are influenced by us and—truth be told—we are influenced by them. When group members don't know much but share a position, members of the group can reinforce one another's sense of understanding, leading everyone to feel like their position is justified and their mission is clear, even when there is no real expertise to give it solid support. (p. 173)

Sloman and Fernbach (2017) stress that causal explanation is the most reliable means to sound conclusions. When people talk about political issues and policies, however, they tend not to be engaged in causal explanation. Emotion and passions are more likely to govern thought and action. (As we will see in chapter 2, this is the mode of thought that David Hume claims rules our thinking and acting.) The authors do provide considerable depth into what comprises causal explanation; there is not time and space to delve deeply into their ideas here, but the work is highly recommended. They (2017) do conclude their excursus on politics by saying, "This discussion yields a variety of lessons about out political culture. One is simply a confirmation of an obvious fact about our political discourse: It's remarkably shallow" (p. 187).

It is also useful here to depict what this book is *not*. While there are popular works on politics and current affairs by commentators that have decided agendas, those kinds of works will not be discussed. This includes writings from the left and the right. By way of example, a recent book by Ann Coulter (2018) will not be delved into deeply. She (2018), for example, says, "Don't feel sorry for [the media]. They had plenty of opportunities to do the right thing. They chose not to. The press no longer provides news. . . . Once venerated outposts of journalism have imploded under Trump, reducing their value to nothing. . . . Reporters say, *you'll be sorry when you can't get the truth!* They seem not to realize that we don't feel like we're getting it now" (p. 217; emphasis in original). On the other hand, John Nichols (2017) writes,

> Something is broken in America. The structures that were meant to protect and preserve the republic have been undermined. The American experiment has been rendered vulnerable by the excesses of partisanship that manifest themselves not just in Trumpism but in the acquiescence to Trumpism by congressional charlatans who have traded away their consciences in order to align themselves with an unconscionable president. (p. 9)

These kinds of polemical barbs have no place here. To repeat, serious and intelligent thought will be examined; it is there that we can learn, locate information, and find reasons for our beliefs.

What Are Some Political Influences?

Liberty

The body of this book will entail an examination of libraries within the political milieu. In order to accomplish this objective, a glance here at some political influences can help set the tone for what will come. Because libraries in the United States emerged in some important ways from the classical liberal tradition (a tradition that, readers should be reminded, precedes the party and partisan politics of the past several decades), the liberal tradition cries for examination. The examination here will be quite brief. While many sources can, and will, be invoked, a reasonable starting place is with John Stuart Mill. Mill (2007) and his views on the liberty an individual should be able to enjoy are quite well known. He (2007) made the point of recognizing "the nature and limits of the power which can be legitimately exercised by society over the individual" (p. 63). Society, of course, includes the government. Mill did also state that there must be limitations to individual liberty; no one should be able to impose upon another, causing harm or even inconvenience to the other. That said, every individual should be free (and indeed has a responsibility) to exercise free choice. That freedom requires the application of intellect and judgment. So liberty, in this classical sense, means being free from imposing the will of society and government and also necessitates the discrimination and moral governance of free choice, within certain limits. Mill's ideas will be explored in much greater depth in chapter 3.

Classical liberalism is certainly not dead, but the political world has morphed in many ways. Not only that, liberalism as it has been passed down through generations has its critics. One of the more forceful of the recent critics is Patrick Deneen. He (2018) writes, "Nearly every one of the promises that were made by the architects and creators of liberalism has been shattered. . . . Liberalism has failed—not because it fell short, but because it was true to itself. It has failed because it has succeeded" (pp. 2–3). He (2018) maintains that liberalism has failed in part because it has succeeded in making the populace simultaneously more individualist and more statist. There is a substantial and increasing sense not merely of self but of a particular kind of selfhood that seeks to valorize "otherness" as a measure of self. This selfhood is, in Deneen's eyes, eliminative; it corrodes the common sharing and economic fate to which everyone is party. He criticizes progressivism as the putative sole direction of liberalism's purpose, as well as conservatism's wish that it is the path to America's rise through the Constitution's source as resistance to liberalism's advance. Both of the ideologies are, according to Deneen, today's branches of liberalism. They actually have a substantive set of connections. Deneen's argument will require considerably more study and explication. Suffice it to say for now that the distinctions between political right and political left are numerous and complex. Deneen does offer some cogent observations regarding the differences, but there will be opportunities to critique his ideas (being cognizant that "critique" is not used here as a synonym for "criticism").

There has been a voluminous amount written on liberty. Os Guinness (2018) has a unique point of view that will require substantial exploration in chapter 2. He (2018) begins by writing, "The great American republic is in the throes of its gravest crisis since the Civil War, a crisis that threatens its greatness, its freedom, and its character. . . . The Left sees only the danger of the Right, and the Right the danger of the Left, so extremism confirms and compounds extremism" (p. 1). He questions what, exactly, *is* the freedom that America stands for? His argument is complex and frequently draws on religious scriptures (from many sources) to illustrate both where things have gone awry and the directions that liberty should take. There will be a number of readers who will question his reliance on religious thought, words, and practices, and their views will be considered along with those of Guinness. At the heart of his thesis is the claim that, today, the revolution of 1789 (the French Revolution) holds sway over the grounding of the revolution of 1776. The world's embrace of the tenets of the French Revolution, in fact, has influenced thought and action within US politics and policies. Equally important to Guinness is the relationship between negative and positive freedom, both of which are essential, although more attention in policy is paid to the negative. The ideas Guinness (2018) espouses are to be taken seriously, as should critiques of his position.

One additional thinker will be mentioned briefly here (he cannot be ignored)—Isaiah Berlin. He (2002) makes a point that should not be forgotten: "The doctrine [of liberty] is comparatively modern. There seems to be scarcely any discussion of individual liberty as a conscious political ideal . . . in the ancient world" (p. 176). In his deep analysis of the origins and nature of liberty, Berlin (2002) adds, "It is that liberty . . . is not incompatible with some kinds of autocracy, or at any rate with the absence of self-government. Liberty in this sense is principally concerned with areas of control, not with its source" (p. 176). He (2002) notes that individual freedom is not arbitrary; therefore there will inevitably be instances of conflict and disagreement; liberty is not utopian. With relation to a concern that is close to the hearts of librarians, Berlin (2002) asserts that the elimination of censorship is an infringement upon personal liberty; laws against censorship "are fundamental needs of men as men, in a good (or, indeed, any) society" (p. 215). Berlin

(2002) includes a discourse on modern political ideas, which are as cogent and essential as just about any presented. It will be no surprise that Berlin's thought will be examined further.

Democracy
Democracy is a good thing, is it not? Well, that depends on which theorist one pays attention to. And it depends on which elements of democracy are featured. For example, Ronald Dworkin focuses on human dignity and what democracy can assure toward that end. He (2006) says that when it comes to dignity, "The first principle—which I shall call the principle of intrinsic value—holds that each human life has a special kind of objective value" (p. 9). He follows that up: "The second principle—the principle of personal responsibility—holds that each person has a special responsibility for realizing the success of his own life, a responsibility that includes exercising his judgment about what kind of life would be successful for him" (p. 10). Dworkin (2006) is, for the most part, sanguine about the prospects for democracy, but he warns that there are at least two paths that democracy can take—the majoritarian path, which rests on governance by the greatest number of people, and the partnership path, by which people govern themselves by participating, in partnership, in the full operation of the enterprise. In his (2006) work he makes some particular recommendations for the future of democracy in the United States, including recommendations about the judiciary at the highest level.

While democracy may still be regarded as positive by many, there are some aspects of politics today that will have effects—positive and negative—upon the body politic. One of these forces is identity politics, which is an intensely complex notion and set of actions by people. Amy Gutmann (2003) is one who sees the existence of the identities that people own and is of the opinion that democracy should take account of this factor: "*Democratic politics is bound up with both how people identify themselves and what they therefore want.* For this to be true, identity groups must be politically relevant and worthy of our careful attention" (p. 15; emphasis in original). The positive element of such a realization, according to Gutmann, is when identity groups argue for rights and justice. When that is not the case, identity politics can take on a more decidedly negative aspect. The quest for justice is the positive with regard to identity in American politics. Care must be taken, however, that justice is indeed the end goal and that the practice of politics always keeps justice in the forefront.

Not everyone is a fan of democracy, though. (Plato will be discussed later.) Jason Brennan (2016) is a forceful critical voice in opposition to democracy as it is practiced in the United States today. Among other things, Brennan (2016) maintains that a decline in political participation is not negative: "This decline in political engagement is a *good start*, but we still have a long way to go. We should hope for even less participation, not more. Ideally, politics would occupy only a small portion of the average person's attention" (p. 3). His stance is that the majority of people are apathetic about politics and, so, should not burden themselves with the nuances of this complex world. Another (rather small) portion of the population is fervent, sometimes even fanatical about politics, to the point that it constitutes an emotional disturbance. The smallest group is constituted by those who exercise rationality and seek information and knowledge about political processes and outcomes. He (2016) states what, to many, would be a minority viewpoint in that he sees "democracy's value as *purely* instrumental; the only reason to favor democracy over any other political system is that it is more effective at producing just results" (p. 11). Brennan is not the only theorist to adopt such an idea of democracy; for that reason alone it is worth exploring.

Populism
There are some positive ideas regarding populism, but the negative ones are more numerous. Does it have its origins in the United States? That is something of an open question, but John Lukacs (2005) connects populism to American history: "The evolving history of the democratization of the world is well-nigh inseparable from the Americanization of the world. Not identical, but inseparable" (p. 5). He (2005) continues, "Our question is how traditional democracy can exist much longer, when traditional liberalism has decayed" (p. 6). Lukacs (2005), in his examination of the effects of populism on democracy, maintains that ideological thinking has replaced statesmanship in discourse and politics. Pragmatism appears to have disappeared. "Ideology" will not be delved into at this time, but there will be definitions and discussion in chapter 2. Lukacs invokes the idea that originated with Alexis de Tocqueville—the tyranny of the majority—as an outcome of pluralism, saying that the phenomenon actually slows the sharing and consideration of ideas. In summary, Lukacs (2005) expresses a fear for the future of democracy due to a rise of fear that populism brings about.

The connection between democracy and populism is not unique to Lukacs. As Mudde and Kaltwasser (2017) observe, "We position populism first and foremost within the context of liberal democracy. . . . Theoretically, populism is most fundamentally juxtaposed to liberal democracy than to democracy per se or to any other model of democracy" (pp. 1–2). They (2017) recognize a sometimes stated ideal of populism as a struggle between the "people" (*vox populi*) against a corrupt elite but hasten to add that the ideal is seldom, if ever, realized in fact (and according to the actual will of the people). They (2017) conclude, "Populism is part of democracy. Rather than the mirror image of democracy, however, populism is the (bad) conscience of liberal democracy. In a world that is dominated by democracy and liberalism, populism has essentially become an illiberal democratic response to undemocratic liberalism" (p. 116).

Paul Taggart (2000) will have a final word in the introduction to this topic:

> I approach these problems in these pages by exploring six key themes that run through populism:
>
> - populists as hostile to representative politics;
> - populists identifying themselves with an idealized heartland within the community they favour;
> - populism as an ideology lacking core values;
> - populism as a powerful reaction to a sense of extreme crisis;
> - populism as containing fundamental dilemmas that make it self-limiting;
> - populism as a chameleon, adopting the colours of its environment. (p. 2)

It becomes evident that populism, as idea and as action, must be addressed in the coming pages, primarily as a pathological political ideology.

References

Berlin, I. (2002). *Liberty*. H. Hardy (Ed.). Oxford: Oxford University Press.
Brennan, J. (2016). *Against democracy*. Princeton: Princeton University Press.
Bruccoli, M. J. (2007). The end of books and the death of libraries. *Against the Grain* 31(1), https://docs.lib.purdue.edu/cgi/viewcontent.cgi?referer=https://www.google.com/&httpsredir=1&article=5252&context=atg.
Callinicos, A. (2006). *The resources of critique*. Cambridge: Polity Press.
Chiarizio, M. (2013). An American tragedy: E-books, licenses, and the end of public lending libraries? *Vanderbilt Law Review* 66(2), 615–44.
Coulter, A. (2018). *Resistance is futile: How the Trump-hating left lost its collective mind*. New York: Sentinel.
The death of libraries? (2005). *MIT Technology Review*, https://www.technologyreview.com/s/404030/the-death-of-libraries/.
Deneen, P. J. (2018). *Why liberalism failed*. New Haven: Yale University Press.

Dillon, D. (2008). A world infinite and accessible: Digital ubiquity, the adaptable library, and the end of information. *Journal of Library Administration* 48(1), 69–83.

Dworkin, R. (2006). *Is democracy possible here? Principles for a new political debate.* Princeton: Princeton University Press.

Evaluating information. (2018). Johns Hopkins University Libraries, https://guides.library.jhu.edu/evaluate/social-media.

Guinness, O. (2018). *Last call for liberty: How America's genius for freedom has become its greatest threat.* Downers Grove, IL: IVP Books.

Gutmann, A. (2003). *Identity in democracy.* Princeton: Princeton University Press.

Herring, J. F. (2005). The end of the teacher-librarian. *Teacher Librarian* 33(1), 26–29.

Jones, W. (2015). Deciding crises in academic libraries. *MediaTropes* 5(2), 111–14.

Klinenberg, E. (2018a). *Palaces for the people: How social infrastructure can help fight inequality, polarization, and the decline of civic life.* New York: Crown.

Klinenberg, E. (2018b). To restore civil society, start with the library. *New York Times*, https://www.nytimes.com/2018/09/08/opinion/sunday/civil-society-library.html.

Lukacs, J. (2005). *Democracy and populism: Fear and hatred.* New Haven: Yale University Press.

Marinetti, F. T. (2006). *Critical writings.* New edition. D. Thompson (Trans.). New York: Farrar, Straus and Giroux.

Mill, J. S. (2007). *On liberty.* M. B. Mathias (Ed.). New York: Pearson Longman.

Mudde, C., and Kaltwasser, C. R. (2017). *Populism: A very short introduction.* Oxford: Oxford University Press.

Nichols, J. (2017). *Horsemen of the Trumpocalypse: A field guide to the most dangerous people in America.* New York: Nation Books.

Polan, S. (2018). The future of reading. *Psychology Today* 51(4), 18–19.

Shulenburger, D. (2016). Substituting article processing charges for subscriptions: The cure is worse than the disease. https://www.arl.org/storage/documents/substituting-apcs-for-subscriptions-20july2016.pdf.

Sloman, S., and Fernbach, P. (2017). *The knowledge illusion: The myth of individual thought and the power of collective wisdom.* New York: Penguin Random House.

Taggart, P. (2000). *Populism.* Buckingham: Open University Press.

Thompson, J. (1982). *The end of libraries.* London: Clive Bingley.

Van Slyck, A. A. (1996). *Free to all: Carnegie libraries, American culture, 1890–1920.* Chicago: University of Chicago Press.

Walters, H. W. (2018). The death and migration of book collections in academic libraries. *Portal: Libraries and the Academy* 18(3), 415–22.

Zastrow, J. (2018). Keepers of knowledge in a post-literate future. *Computers in Libraries* 38(7), 15–18.

CHAPTER ONE

~

Libraries, Then and (Mostly) Now

It should probably be recognized right off the bat that libraries in the United States (of just about all types) are products of a classical liberal ethos. George Smith (2013) offers an insightful basis for the thinking that is behind this liberalism: "how people view their own interests will ultimately depend on their beliefs about human nature, social interaction, the proper roles of coercion and persuasion, and a host of other abstract issues" (pp. 1–2). (Spoiler alert: What Smith has to say applies to libraries of all types in the nineteenth century in particular, but does seep into the twentieth century.) It should be noted that, in the nineteenth century there began to be a kind of rift between what some called "old" liberals. The differences between "old" and "new" liberals was, at times, not necessarily radical, and over time the distinctions blurred (see Smith, 2013, pp. 4–25). The changes will be addressed, especially, in the discussion of public libraries shortly. The rise of libraries occurred in the nineteenth century, when the spirit of classical liberalism (particularly the notion that freedom and liberty should be at the heart of governance) arose with the likes of John Stuart Mill; his father, James; and others. Richard Epstein (2003) makes the absolutely essential point that (both the right and the left) "place an enormous stress on the importance of deliberative democracy, but often give no clue as to the proper subjects of deliberation, nor the arguments that should carry the day in these deliberations" (p. 8). He puts his finger on the very purpose of this book. The spirit Smith speaks of took hold on both sides of the Atlantic, but, in this chapter, the focus of attention will be on the United States.

In the introduction, Eric Klinenberg was quoted as saying the libraries are places to gather and that everyone is welcome. This is a fact that cannot be overstated. In keeping with the sentiment, Susan Pinker (2014) concludes her book by suggesting four principles that will enhance the "village effect" related to bringing people together:

> Principle 1. Live in a community where you know and talk to your neighbors.
>
> Principle 2. Build real human contact into your workday. Save email for logistics. Use phone or face time for more nuanced interaction.
>
> Principle 3. Create a village of diverse relationships. Build in social contact with members of the "village" the way you work in meals and exercise.
>
> Principle 4. Everyone needs close human contact. Adjust the ratio of your face-to-face to screen communication according to your temperament, just as you adjust how much and what you eat according to your appetite. (pp. 268–73)

Wayne Wiegand (2015) cites Pinker as someone who has cogent ideas about the interactions that are possible in libraries. Her principles are fitting for the idea set forth here of the commons; the contact people have with one another helps people to get to know one another in very genuine senses and allows for civil conversations to hold sway. Her words need to be taken seriously.

In order to understand how libraries got to their present state, some historical background is necessary. This is not a history lesson; the background will be treated in brief, but extensive historical studies will be mentioned and cited. As will be the case with future chapters as well, there is a fairly high level of selectivity applied to the background and present state of libraries. For good or ill, it is not possible to present exhaustive treatises on libraries, politics, discourse, and commons. That said, the objective here is to meld all of the topics together in a coherent and cohesive whole. The background will be followed by some discussion of the state of libraries and some key issues in which libraries and librarianship are involved. The chapter is not an exhaustive lesson on libraries and librarianship; it is a prelude of what is to follow, which are the serious conservative and liberal viewpoints, conversations on difficult topics, and the possibility for libraries to become genuine commons.

Background

College and University Libraries

It would be a gross exaggeration to say that the history of libraries in the United States mirrors the general history of the country. This is not to say that there were no libraries in colonial and postcolonial times. The early libraries were small, poorly structured, and almost entirely dependent upon philanthropy. Plus, they tended to be associated with colleges in the very early days. The primary example is that of Harvard College. The college got its start in 1636, very soon after the Bay Colony was settled. The beginning, as Louis Shores (1963) documents, was when the colony's general court voted to

> give four hundred Pounds towards a school or College, whereof two hundred Pounds shall be paid next year, and two hundred Pounds when the work is finished, and the next Court to appoint where and what building. (p. 1)

Two year later, John Harvard willed £779.17.2 in cash and more than three hundred books to the college (Shores, 1963, p. 11). The bequest was sufficient for the college to be named for him. The growth of both the college and its library proceeded very slowly for quite some time. There were some students, studying primarily for the ministry, and some money and books donated to the library over the next several decades. Shores (1963) notes that "the first administrative milestone is passed in 1667 with the appointment of the first librarian, Solomon Stoddard, and the legislation of the first set of rules and regulations" (p. 13). Actually, a better description of Stoddard's work would be "keeper of the books" and enforcer of the rules. The first library catalog was not printed until 1723 though (Shores, 1963, p. 14).

The regulations of the Harvard College library were very limiting and strict. The 1667 regulations state in part:

1. No person not resident in the Colledge, except an Overseer shall borrow a book out of the Library.
2. No Schollar in the Colledge, under a Senior Sophister shall borrow a book out of the Library.
3. No one under master pf Aer (unless it be a fellow) shall borrow a book without the allowance of the Praesident. (Shores, 1963, pp. 181–82)

The laws were amended in 1740.

It should be noted that Shores (1963) provides an admirable sketch of the remaining eight institutions' libraries founded during colonial time: William and Mary, Yale, Princeton, Columbia, Pennsylvania, Brown, Rutgers, and Dartmouth. The experiences of these colleges were not dissimilar to those of Harvard. As Shores (1963) reports, "In 1701, Sir John Davie sent 160 to 170 volumes to [Yale]. Then came a series of donations to the library that made College history"; Jeremiah Dummer influenced people to donate, and "about 800 valuable books were received from a group of prominent literary and public men" (p. 23). Because the colonies, through much of the eighteenth century, had limited printing apparatus, donations of works from Europe typified collection building for the libraries. It should also be noted that some institutions' libraries suffered from fires (notably William and Mary), one lost volumes in a move from Saybrook, Connecticut, to New Haven (Yale), and others fell prey to occupations during the Revolutionary War (such as Princeton and Columbia). By 1800 the colonial colleges did have libraries that were more or less operational but were very small and were filled principally through donations.

It stands to reason that the faculty of the colonial colleges were educated, to a considerable extent, in England (particularly at Cambridge). Arthur Hamlin (1981) explains, "Instruction at Cambridge, as later at Harvard, William and Mary, and the other colonial colleges, was based on the seven liberal arts as laid out by Martianus Capella in the fifth century. These were the Trivium of Grammar, Rhetoric, and Logic, and the Quadrivium of Music, Arithmetic, Geometry, and Astronomy" (p. 7). Hamlin (1981) also notes the exceptional growth of the Yale library in 1733; it benefited from the gift of about a thousand volumes given by Bishop George Berkeley (p. 15). Such notable gifts made a big difference in the libraries, not only of Yale but of all the colonial libraries.

The period that extends into the nineteenth century is referred to by Lee Shiflett (1981) as that of the classical college. There was a growth in the number of colleges in large part because of the westward spread of the population: "Between 1790 and the 1820s, the trans-Allegheny population increased from about 100,000 to over two million with many families making two or three moves in a brief time" (Shiflett, 1981, p. 3). The settlers tended to establish churches (sometimes by conflicting Protestant sects), and along with the churches came the building of small denominational colleges, intended to prepare young men for the various ministries. Because they did tend to be small and sectarian, a number closed as populations continued the westward movement.

The growing pains of colleges were not limited to the founding and closing of some colleges; they extended to the very purpose of some of the mature colleges. Shiflett (1981) observes that at Brown president Francis Wayland strove to reform the curriculum, placing his own position on the line in the process. In 1850 Brown adopted an electoral model with alternative courses leading to degrees. That reform was not successful, though, and counter-reforms followed in the 1850s. Shiflett (1981) does add that "perhaps the most important document of this period was the Yale Report of 1828. The report was designed to end criticism of the classical system and to curb attempts at the radical reform of substituting modern language for Latin and Greek. Its wide dissemination and authoritative origin gave it a high degree of acceptability" (Shiflett, 1981, pp. 12–13).

With rare exceptions (see Stoddard at Harvard), faculty tended to serve the added functions of librarians. Because the collections were small and the opening hours of the libraries were few (usually only a few hours a week), faculty members—frequently junior faculty who did receive a small additional stipend—served as keepers of the books. Shiflett (1981) writes, "The professor-librarians of the nineteenth-century American college have become a commonplace in the mythos of American librarianship. . . . [F]or the most part, professors were the group who were available and who were reliable enough to be entrusted with what represented a major portion of the college's wealth" (p. 35). Given the limited operating hours, the limitations on who would be able to check out books, and the small collections, it was also common during the classical college period for there to be only accession lists of books and few full-blown library catalogs (save for the larger collections of the more mature colleges).

Frederick Rudolph (1962) sums up the state of affairs in the aftermath of the Yale Report: "By sending out enthusiastic young graduates to found colleges in the barbaric West and South and by training clergymen to become college presidents, Yale and Princeton, in a way that the University of Virginia was not, were in a position to define what the American college would be" (p. 161). Rudolph (1962) also offers a perspective on the exclusion faced by women:

> The failure of coeducation and of separate women's colleges to make much headway before 1860 should be viewed in the context of those other educational reforms which also remained essentially blacked until after the war. . . . The movement for higher education for women . . . would suffer from the essential poverty of the collegiate foundations and from the widespread suspicion of the class- and sectarian-conscious colleges. (p. 312)

For a very brief pre–Civil War summary of colleges and their libraries, see Budd (2018); for details, refer to Shiflett (1981) and Hamlin (1981).

In 1876 the US Bureau of Education produced a massive study and survey of libraries under the title *Public Libraries in the United States of America: Their History, Condition, and Management*. It must be mentioned that "public" in this work is writ large; it refers to all types of libraries (traditional public, college, social, etc.) that are accessible to at least some members of the public. A large portion of the book consists of essays on these various types of libraries. The chapter on college libraries is composed by the editors of the volume. It is notable that, at the outset of the essay, the authors (US Department of the Interior, 1876) write, "A library may be rich in choice works, but if the rules of its management are such that these works can be approached only by a select few and under restrictions as to use, or under other embarrassing regulations, their value is but slight" (p. 60). These words constitute a not-subtle criticism of the state of college libraries at the time, where (see the regulations mentioned earlier) there were indeed restrictions on use and even opening hours during which books could be read were not at all uncommon. The critique does not stop there (US Department of the Interior, 1876):

> as has already been hinted . . . few colleges have possessed funds to build up libraries on a scientific plan. Their collections consist largely of the voluntary gifts of many individuals, and hence are usually of a miscellaneous character. Comparatively few of the patrons of our colleges in the past have appreciated the essential importance of ample and well selected libraries, Recently, however, more liberal views have prevailed in this respect. This, with fewer restrictions as to expenditure, will enable college officers to select with greater discrimination and more definite purpose. (p. 62)

To illustrate the criticisms, Hamlin (1981) points out that for a substantial period (roughly the 1840s to the Civil War) students took it upon themselves to establish their own literary societies and to charge themselves fees so that books could be selected and purchased. For example, at the University of North Carolina, the Dialectic and Philanthropic Society owned many more books than did the university library. Thomas Harding (1971) estimates that in 1849 the society owned 8,800 books, while the institutional collection was just 3,500. Hamlin (1981) elaborates on the situation:

> The student who was largely dependent on these association libraries in the nineteenth century had certain advantages over his successors in later ages. For one thing, books, students, and indeed librarians were mostly sheltered under the same roof. Meetings were held in the room that housed the collection. . . . Then to they were *his* [sic] books. He and his friends selected and paid for them. How much better, therefore, they must have seemed than the contents of the

institutional bookstack. . . . It was only as change in institutional emphasis cam after the Civil War that the importance of the societies and their libraries began to decline. (p. 40; emphasis in original)

In time, most of the collections of the societies were absorbed into the college and university libraries and added to the institutional collections.

In the middle of the Civil War a monumental (for higher education) piece of legislation was passed and signed—the Morrill Act of 1862. This legislation was officially known as the Land Grant College Act of 1862. The principal purpose was to enhance agricultural education in all states. "Each state was given public lands or scrip equaling 30,000 acres for each senator and representative according to the apportionment of 1860" (Budd, 2018, p. 26). Some western states complained that the less agrarian but more populous northern and Atlantic seaboard states would benefit disproportionally. That said, some northern states did not have sufficient public lands and accepted scrip instead of acreage. The states handled the disposition of the act somewhat differently. "Some, such as Wisconsin, Minnesota, North Carolina, and Missouri, gave the land-grant responsibilities to existing state universities. A few—Oklahoma, Texas, South Dakota, and Washington—established new colleges that would immediately be competitors with the existing universities for state funding" (Budd, 2018, p. 26). A second act was passed in 1890, and a provision of that act was that no applicant could be denied admission on the basis of race. However, a number of states established "separate but equal" institutions. The ramifications of the acts are still with us, and a great amount of agricultural extension and research takes place at land grant universities.

A major year in the history of higher education and libraries was 1876. In addition to the publication of *Public Libraries in the United States of America* (which included Charles Ammi Cutter's *Rules for a Dictionary Catalog*), this was the year the American Library Association was founded at the meeting of librarians from many states. Further, it was the founding year of the Johns Hopkins University, a different type of institution. The first president of the university, Daniel Coit Gilman, "insisted that the work at Johns Hopkins should be at the graduate level; undergraduate instruction should be left to other institutions" (Shiflett, 1981, p. 84). Johns Hopkins was built upon the German seminar model, and library organization followed suit. The collection was developed to support research activities. Gilman himself said,

> It is the business of a university to advance knowledge; every professor must be a student. No history is so remote that it can be neglected; no law of

mathematics is so hidden that it may not be sought out; no problem in respect to physics is so difficult that it must be shunned. No love of ease, no dread of labor, no fear of consequences, no desire for wealth, will divert a band of well-chosen professors from uniting their forces in the prosecution of study. (Gilman, 1898, p. 55; quoted in Shiflett, 1981, p. 85)

Johns Hopkins was intentionally modeled on the dual principles of *lehrfreiheit* (the freedom to teach) and *lernfreiheit* (the freedom to learn).

The noble beginnings of the university as Johns Hopkins represented had its adherents in the nineteenth century, but with the university movement came the nascent bureaucratic institution. This tendency was railed against by, among others, Thorstein Veblen (1923) and Abraham Flexner (1930). More will be said about the corporate and bureaucratic tendencies later (and they apply to libraries of all types as well as to higher education).

The last quarter of the nineteenth century saw substantial growth of many colleges and universities. A number of colleges, most particularly sectarian-affiliated colleges in small towns or rural areas, remained undersized, with few students and very small libraries. Hamlin (1981) provides what may be the most comprehensive data on collection sizes. One appendix demonstrates collection sizes for select institutions in 1849 (pp. 230–31). One can contrast those data with information on library holdings and numbers of doctoral degrees awarded from 1876 to 1975, presented in another appendix (pp. 232–37). Not everyone was enamored of the university movement; William James (1903) published an essay titled "The Ph.D. Octopus." Budd (2018) summarizes James's opinion: "The doctorate, said James, was a vanity; it was a symbol of the overspecialization of the student, who would then carry that excess into a faculty post—and be applauded for it" (p. 29). On the other hand, Shiflett (1981) observes, "Spencerian social Darwinism dominated the thought of America's middle class through the end of the nineteenth century, teaching it that the betterment of society was inevitable and that social wrongs would be corrected in the natural order of things" (p. 60). This idea of progress was a pervasive and powerful one.

The twentieth century was one of expanded (but not uninterrupted) growth for higher education and its libraries. One measure of expansion was the entry of the federal government in funding university research. In the early part of the century the US government began expending several millions of dollars to support research. Later in the century, especially post–World War II, agencies including the National Science Foundation and the National Institutes of Health were spending billions of dollars in an effort to "win" the Cold War. Add to these agencies the expenditures of the US

Department of Defense and other agencies and the research monies have exceeded $100 billion. As the chapter proceeds, more will be said about research and funding. Naturally, universities having larger libraries acted in support of the beginnings and growth of research activity. As we will see, this means, in part, great attention to the journal literature, which had its beginning, on a very small scale, in the seventeenth century.

Prior to the growth of the twentieth century came both education for, and the professionalization of, librarianship. Hamlin (1981) quotes Professor Otis Robinson of the University of Rochester in an 1876 response to Samuel Swett Green:

> A librarian should be much more than a keeper of books; he [sic] should be an educator. . . . The relation which Mr. Green has presented ought especially to be established between the college librarian and the student readers. No such librarian is fit for his place unless he holds himself to some degree responsible for the library education of the students. . . . It is his province to direct very much of their general reading; and especially in their investigation of subjects, he should be their guide and friend. (pp. 123–24)

Robinson's admonition may be one of the first arguments for information literacy as a library function. It should be noted that Green and Robinson were exceptional in their attention to students and their learning. As Shiflett (1981) says, "The myopic view of the functions of the library by the new full-time caretakers and their intellectual limitations did little to establish an aura of respect for the librarian's position in the institutions" (p. 167). It seems apparent that there was considerable variance of experience in college libraries in the later nineteenth century.

The growth of the first part of the twentieth century was limited, of course, by the Great Depression. There were financial, and other, limitations relating to who could attend colleges and universities, as well as to the growth of libraries during the 1930s (especially). After World War II, though, there was the impetus for financial and population growth. When it comes to higher education, the 1948 GI Bill of Rights made (and stills makes) it possible for many veterans to avail themselves of college educations. It should be noted that, even before World War II, library collections did increase greatly, due in part to the small size from which most institutions began. Fremont Rider (1944) made bold predictions of future growth, based primarily on emerging technology, specifically microcards. He (1944) predicted that

> the Yale Library will, in 2040 [one hundred years later than the data he worked with], have approximately 200,000,000 volumes, which will occupy over 6,000

miles of shelving. Its card catalog file—if it then has a card catalog—will consist of nearly three-quarters of a million catalog drawers, which will of themselves occupy not less than eight acres of space. New material will be coming in at the rate of 12,000,000 volumes a year; and the cataloging of this new material will require a cataloging staff of over six thousand persons. (p. 12)

Needless to say, Rider's extrapolations from the past levels of growth were tremendously exaggerated. As Budd (2018) adds, "There remains . . . the reality that library collections [and access to information] are dynamic, and their expansion . . . is a sore predicament . . . for libraries dealing with matters of finance, space, selection, and so on" (p. 32).

Post–World War II higher education, and libraries, experienced alarming growth through the 1970s. Contributing to the growth were several pieces of federal legislation passed after the Soviet launching of the satellite Sputnik. Sensing that the United States was falling behind its global rival in science and technology, Congress had the foresight to enact such legislation as the National Defense Education Act in 1958 and, subsequently, the Higher Education Act of 1965. Other acts will be discussed further on that had immensely influential histories. Beginning in the 1980s, the pace of growth began to slow, for social, political, and financial reasons (not the least of which was an ultimate slowing in population growth, immigrants excepted). There was also the recession of the 1970s, the minor recession around the year 2000, and what some refer to as the Great Recession beginning in 2007 and lasting for several years. Much more could be said about the present state of higher education (which definitely affects libraries), such as the decline in state funding for public higher education, but this component of the background will suffice for the time being.

Public Libraries

If one wants to be a stickler, "public" libraries—in the sense of community libraries supported by the public at large—are a nineteenth-century creation. However, libraries accessible to members of the public have a longer and a rich history. For example, the original Harvard College library was considered a "public" library, even though, as President Henry Dunster stated in 1645, "the public library in the College is yet defective in all manner of books" (quoted in Chaplin, 1872, p. 80). As is mentioned earlier, the Harvard College library depended upon donations of books and money to build (quite slowly at first) a collection that was, for many years, less than adequate for the instructional needs of the institution. Also, it is apparent that Harvard was not alone in its reliance on the generosity of donors. There was little mechanism in the colonies for the production of books, so what made their way into libraries everywhere was once the property of well-off individuals or the results of some infrequent purchasing trips to Europe.

Jesse Shera (1949) notes that the town of New Haven was also the beneficiary of a bequest of books from Theophilus Eaton (p. 24): "certain books lately belonging to my brother, Mr. Samuel Eaton, intended for the use of a college, and appraised, as I take, to about, or near, twenty pounds" (quoted in Dexter, 1918, p. 223). Eaton's gift of 1656 was intended to be used by the townspeople. Eventually, the books were passed along to Yale. As was the case of Harvard, what was to be Yale College was also used by the public, to an extent. Elsewhere in New England, in Concord, Massachusetts, to be specific, a collection of books was acquired in 1672 to be administered by the town (Shera, 1949, p. 25). This was a rarity, not just in New England but throughout the colonies. It was not possible, at that time, to be able to speak of a public library "movement" yet.

What might be said to be the beginning of the movement occurred in the late seventeenth, early eighteenth centuries. The Reverend Thomas Bray, representing England's Society for the Propagation of the Gospel in Foreign Parts, traveled to the colonies and established parochial libraries in the colonies, primarily in Maryland. A total of thirty-nine libraries were established to enable Christians in the colonies to gain access to scripture and theology. These were aimed principally toward clergymen, so that they would have access to works on religion and would be able to enhance their ministries. Charles Laugher (1973) concludes his history of Bray's work by saying,

> Originally, [Bray] had planned to provide [parochial] libraries for all of the parishes in Maryland, but as he learned of the extensive cultural poverty of the people in the colonies, he enlarged his plans to provide for one large library in the chief city of each province, the provincial or general library, and a smaller collection, the parochial library, for each of the colonial parishes. A third type of library, the layman's library, would contain books which could be loaned by the minister, and a large collection of pious books and tracts which would be given free to the people. (p. 76)

In the aftermath of Thomas Bray beginning his work, some other notable events took place. Shera (1949) reports that "three other town book collections were established in New England before library history entered a new phase" (p. 29). He says that Oxford, Lancaster, and East Sudbury, Massachusetts, were given book collections for public use. As Shera (1949) says, "By the beginning of the fourth decade of the eighteenth century the public library movement in New England, if indeed it could as yet be so called, had ended its first phase" (p. 30). What would come next would be somewhat different in kind but would reach a more substantial population.

There were some categories of libraries that would come to the fore in the eighteenth century—social, subscription, and circulating libraries. These types had some features in common, but the subscription libraries charged some sort of fee for services. This could take the form of an annual fee, which would allow for the use of the collection for the duration of the fee period, or a use fee, according to which borrowers were charged when they were loaned a book or magazine issue. (At times the two fee models would be combined by a particular library.) The common purpose of these libraries was to enable members of a community to have access to reading materials. It could be said that the most famous of these was the Library Company of Philadelphia, established by Benjamin Franklin and others. Franklin (1964) himself described the beginnings in 1731:

> And now I set foot my first Project of a public Nature, that for a Subscription Library. I drew up the Proposals, got them put into form by our greater Scrivener [Charles] Brockden, and by the help of my friends in the Junto [a debating society also known as the Leather Apron Club, founded in 1727], procur'd Fifty Subscribers of 40s. each to begin with and 10s. a Year for 50 Years, the term our Company was to continue. We afterwards obtain'd a Charter, the Company being increas'd to 100. (p. 130)

The Library Company's collection had modest beginnings (about forty-five volumes in 1732), but it grew thanks to the subscription fees charged to the members. The Library Company of Philadelphia continues to exist as a nonprofit organization (see https://librarycompany.org/).

The Library Company's founding was a major event in the history of public libraries and was emulated in other towns and cities quite quickly. Wayne Wiegand (2015) remarks on the noteworthiness of Franklin's creation:

> In two respects the Library Company served as a forerunner of the American public library. First, it assumed a position in a colonial public culture with older social institutions like the church, and newer social institutions such as bookstores, taverns, post offices, and coffeehouses where colonists began to develop a public interest. Second, by collecting materials "suited to the tastes and purses of young tradesmen," Franklin identified value in the Library with work, not leisure. In 1732, information addressing work was commonly referred to as "useful knowledge." (p. 8)

The Library Company's collection was indeed broad and far reaching and aimed at the edification of its members. (I should add here that Wiegand's [2015] book may be the finest history of public libraries in the United States. Being readable and fraught with stories of library users, it is almost certainly the one book readers should turn to for a general history.)

The choice of reading matter available to people became quite common in both social and subscription libraries. Shera (1949) illustrates the degree of choice in presenting a list of contents of the Redwood Library, endowed by a gift in 1747 from Abraham Redwood for a library in Newport, Rhode Island. The contents included such topics as belles lettres, science, ancient and modern history, theology and philosophy, law, biography, and more (p. 39). Shera (1949) adds that "the works of the French philosophers Montesquieu, Voltaire, Rousseau, and the Encyclopedists, as well as the latest scientific and historical treatises from Great Britain, were purchased by the colonists with promptness at prices that were generally reasonable" (p. 47). It appears that reading, especially for purposes of personal enlightenment, was a feature of some importance among the population of the colonists.

While the subscription library was an important development in colonial times, the growth of the social library was at least as important for the people. Shera (1949) points out that between 1731 and 1780 a total of fifty-one social libraries were established in New England (p. 55). The social library differed from the subscription library (at least) inasmuch as the latter was a common law incorporation, and the members did not own the library or its stock. Shera (1949) does make an important distinction that identifies something of a peculiarity in colonial law though:

> In the beginning, corporate existence was not a matter of precise definition; it arose in response to immediate circumstances and was molded and modified according to the economic, geographic, and social environment. The corporation was an instrument for the accomplishment of a specific purpose. . . . Until 1684 Massachusetts was itself a corporation deriving authority from a crown charter, and the New England town a corporation which, from the earliest period . . . had powers associated with a corporation. (p. 64)

I mention this distinction to demonstrate the differences between "then" and "now."

Shera (1949) marks the enormous post-1780 growth in social libraries throughout New England. Whereas by 1800 there were 333 such institutions, by 1850 there were 1,064 (and it must be emphasized that he limits his analysis to New England) (p. 69). He (1949) writes, "Evidence of the vitality of the social library movement at the turn of the nineteenth century is to be found not only in the enactment of general permissive legislation providing for the establishment of such libraries but also in the eagerness with which local booksellers competed for social library patronage" (p. 70). In terms of the tastes of the reading population, it should also be noted that the period of the "social library movement" also marked a decided rise in the popularity of reading fiction. As we will see, the rising popularity of novels among the public is something of a bone of contention when genuine *public* libraries come to the fore.

Speaking of *public* libraries, that movement had its beginnings in the first third of the nineteenth century. As Shera (1949) says, "The public library is in every sense an institutional descendant of the social library, but in its governmental relationships it represents an innovation" (p. 161). At first some smaller towns, like Peterborough, New Hampshire, developed public support systems for their libraries (which did indeed tend to grow from social and other types of collections). Shera (1949) quotes from an 1834 report on the new library: "In the short time the Library has been in operation it is pleased to observe that the books have been called for in no inconsiderable numbers, and read with satisfaction, as we believe" (p. 164). Other towns also developed publicly supported libraries in New England in the 1830s and 1840s.

The first library that should be spoken of in some detail is the Boston Public Library, which, naturally, served a large population. That library was greatly anticipated well before its opening. Sidney Ditzion (1947) observes that "a meeting of the young men of Boston in April 1841 hailed the proposed institution as a destroyer of class distinctions, sectional antagonisms, and international ill will" (p. 6). That was something of an unusual sentiment, given that the forces behind the establishment of the Boston Public Library were the city's elite, the Brahmins. These men (note the gender reference) included Francis Wayland, Edward Everett, George Ticknor, and others of the intellectual and power class. Ditzion (1947) notes, "Underlying Ticknor's program for free schools and free libraries was a deep concern for the preservation and enhancement of our republican institutions on the foundation of an intelligent populace" (p. 16). The official authorization to found a public library in Boston was signed by the governor of Massachusetts on March 18, 1848 (see Shera, 1949, p. 175). Members of the library's board of trustees were elected on May 24, 1852. Shortly after that date, on July 6, the first report of the trustees was issued. (For those who have a particular interest in the Boston Public Library, Shera [1949] adds the entirety of the report, see pp. 267–90.)

By way of illustration of the attitudes of the founding Brahmins, Everett wrote to Ticknor on July 26, 1852,

> The extensive circulation of new and popular works is a feature of a public library which I have not hitherto contemplated. It deserves to be well weighed, and I shall be happy hereafter to confer with you on the subject. I cannot deny that my views have, since my younger days, undergone some change as to the practicability of freely loaning books at home from large public libraries. Those who have been connected with the administration of such libraries are apt to get discouraged by the loss and damage resulting from the loan of books. My present impressions are in favour of making the amplest provision in the library for the use of the books there. (Quoted in Whitehill, 1956, p. 25)

Walter Muir Whitehill (1956) points out the rapid growth in the library's collection in its first few years, from 9,688 in 1853 to 70,851 in 1858 (p. 57). In that brief period the Boston Public Library became one of the largest in the country.

It seems apparent that there is a paradox in the original rhetoric related to the Boston Public Library. On the one hand we have Everett's reluctance to allow the borrowing of books (perhaps out of a concern deriving from some distrust of the public). On the other hand, Ditzion (1947) writes, "The old subscription libraries were failing, [Ticknor] declared, because they were not adapted to the practical wants of the country. . . . The old idea of Benjamin Franklin that young men would profit more from books that they had to make sacrifices to get was inconsistent with the mid-nineteenth-century idea of democracy" (p. 21). Debate over these two viewpoints and the Boston Public Library continued for some time. For example, Charlie Hurt and Jerry McGovern (1991) suggest that the geographic location of the library rendered it all but inaccessible to a substantial portion of the population (especially immigrants from Ireland). The founding of the Boston Public Library may have to be seen within the context of the paradox through a historical lens.

It has been mentioned that the Boston Public Library was founded upon a presumption that the institution would elevate the population by means of the provision of "good reading." A few years after the founding Justin Winsor expressed skepticism that the public's desire for popular fiction would abate. Patrick Williams (1988) reports that, in 1871, "Winsor was not very optimistic. He spoke of a 'fair chance' that novel readers might seek better books and acknowledged that readers 'sometimes' advance to higher levels. But he was clearly skeptical about the taste-elevation theory that represented the official position of the Boston Public Library" (p. 7). Williams (1988) adds, "That position was restated in 1878 in the report of the committee that audited library operations" (p. 7). Williams (1988) goes on to address fiction reading by quoting Samuel Swett Green (from an address to the ALA Conference in 1876):

> Our libraries are established for the whole community. Their existence can only be justified, and money raised by taxation for their support, when large portions of the community receive benefit from them. . . . There is another consideration. . . . Popular libraries are not established merely for instruction. It is meant that they should give entertainment also. They are regarded s a means of keeping order in the community be giving people a harmless source of recreation. (p. 16)

Green would prove to be in the minority of librarians for some time to come.

There would be changes in the state of libraries and in the work that takes place in them. Williams (1988) notes that, "By 1900, state library commissions had been created in seventeen states. By 1910, there were thirty-five" (p. 29). Williams (1988) also states that, "in 1886, William F. Poole surveyed 108 libraries. Librarians at fifty-three reported that they gave personal assistance to readers. . . . In 1891, the phrase 'reference work' first appeared in *Library Journal*. From 1896 on, reference work was included as a regular part of ALA conference programs" (pp. 29–30). In addition to the services provided to those who came into libraries, there was the beginning, in the late nineteenth century, of what could be called "outreach." To an extent, the outreach services were aimed at the more rural areas. What was referred to as "home libraries" of up to ten books were loaned to households; frequently wagons loaded with books made rounds from libraries to home to deliver and retrieve books. Within towns and cities greater effort was made to reach out to children in order to provide both services and reading materials. Libraries, certainly by the turn of the twentieth century, were becoming active community centers where safe places could be assured for members of communities to read and, in many instances, to learn. Williams (1988) claims that, "By 1916, the missionary era was over. The faith that has created it [coinciding, to a considerable degree, with the larger Progressive Movement] had lost its vigor. The public library community was faced with the task of reconstructing the purpose for the institution in its charge" (p. 35). By 1916 the world was in the throes of the Great War, and the United States would soon enter the fray.

During the period of the late nineteenth to early twentieth centuries a remarkable development in public libraries occurred. By that time, tax support for public libraries was entrenched, but there was still great potential for growth both in numbers of libraries and in their quality. Libraries of all types (and sizes) relied upon philanthropy for development, but beginning about 1890 a philanthropic storm swept over communities. Readers with some familiarity with the period know that this time marked the beginning of Andrew Carnegie's program for the spread of public libraries in the United States. The most complete work describing this period of philanthropy is that of Abigail Van Slyke (1995). Throughout the book she emphasizes that, while the money disseminated was Carnegie's, the distribution was largely handled through his corporation. The business model and handling through staff members enabled considerable scope for the project, especially in numbers of communities affected. Van Slyke (1995) notes that, "By 1917, Carnegie had promised 1,679 libraries to 1,412 towns at a cost well over $41 million" (p. 22).

Van Slyke (1995) echoes the thoughts of many within the profession of librarianship as she writes, "The traditional understanding of the library as a treasure house, protecting its books from untrustworthy readers, was falling out of currency. Increasingly, the library profession sought to use the public library to bring readers and books together, rather than to keep them apart" (p. 25). A "myth" that has been passed down about the Carnegie Corporation is that there was a very limited selection of building designs available to towns and cities. On the other hand, Van Slyke (1995) says, "the implication that Carnegie imposed [a] design on reluctant beneficiaries is not supported by archival evidence. . . . In reality, library design under the Carnegie program was affected by a broad range of social, cultural, and economic trends at the turn of the century" (p. 45). In short, towns and cities chose the most effective design for their communities and for needs of services. It must be understood that the philanthropy of Carnegie was limited, primarily to the physical structure of the building. The towns and cities had to accept certain responsibilities, particularly when it came to providing an initial collection for the library, an ongoing materials budget, plus support for staffing of the library. These were not trivial responsibilities, and a number of communities balked at the costs associated with the philanthropy. Van Slyke (1995) describes,

> It is also wrong to assume that a Carnegie library meant to local communities what it meant to Carnegie, or even that a Carnegie library meant the same thing for all elements of a given community. In large city and small town alike, the Carnegie library was rarely the product of a spontaneous, universal, community spirit. Rather, Carnegie's requirement that elected representatives lend

official approval and tax-financed support to each library inadvertently forced confrontations between groups with divergent attitudes toward culture and its role in American life. (p. 64)

Van Slyke (1995) discusses the cultural pressure and the economic responsibility in great detail; there is no need to repeat her superior analysis here. Further, her book is copiously illustrated with photographs of libraries, floor plans, and even varieties of furniture. For more on the impact of Carnegie's program and the involvement of town and city officials, do consult Van Slyke's work. Her conclusion, especially coming from someone whose specialization is in architecture and women's studies, is noteworthy:

> Carnegie libraries . . . are by definition cultural institutions, Yet, they are also social institutions. They not only store and organize human knowledge, they mediate and shape human interaction as well. Taken as a group, Carnegie libraries demonstrate vividly that these two functions sometimes come into conflict. . . . A compromise between these two functions, Carnegie libraries built in small towns across the United States embody a planning variety barely hinted at by the similar classical motifs that grace their facades. (p. 159)

For an "internal" (that is, from with the profession of librarianship) view of Carnegie's program, one can turn to George Bobinski (1969). He ultimately warns us that "one must be careful not to give Carnegie philanthropy all of the credit for the growth of the public library" (p. 192). He (1969) provides data on how many non-Carnegie libraries existed in 1923 (more than the Carnegie-endowed ones) and how many millions of people were served by those libraries (pp. 192–93). He also offers in an appendix a list of all the towns and cities receiving Carnegie grants and the amount of each grant (pp. 207–42).

In the aftermath, both of the Carnegie philanthropy aimed at towns and cities and of World War I, William Learned (1924) (on the staff of the Carnegie Foundation for the Advancement of Teaching) wrote a book intended to examine the foundation's charge and the success of that charge—the diffusion of knowledge and understanding among the people of the United States—as promoted by public libraries. In surveying the knowledge landscape, he observed, "There are everywhere indications that our American society is on the eve of a much more thoroughgoing organization of its intelligence service than has hitherto been attempted. . . . The ultimate nature of an organization calculated to make knowledge wieldy and appropriable for general use must of course be determined by industrious experimentation" (pp. 7–8). Learned (1924) anticipated that the organization would have to include materials and knowledge in forms other than print. For him, it is the public library that can provide the necessary organization, and the accompanying apparatus—including services devoted to the diffusion of knowledge—to the public at large. Learned's (1924) work is seldom read today but was, in some respects, prescient in its dedication to the goal of knowledge growth and informational services that remain of essential importance in public libraries.

There have been several works written about some individuals and groups that have had substantial impacts on the background of libraries and librarianship. This book will not go into great detail regarding the persons and groups, but a couple of works will be recommended. One, which mentions several individuals, is Dee Garrison's *Apostles of Culture* (2003). Garrison also includes a perceptive and necessary critique of the feminization of librarianship, which had both beneficial and (especially) deleterious financial ramifications. Another to recommend is Wayne Wiegand's *Irrepressible Reformer* (1996), a critical biography of Melvil Dewey. Because Dewey's influence on the profession remains, Wiegand's book is essential for an understanding of the man and his influence.

Interlude: Education for Librarianship

The last quarter of the nineteenth century, however, signaled the growth both of graduate and *professional* education. The period marked the establishment of professional programs in universities plus the founding of professional associations aimed at fostering standards for members of the profession. Recall that the American Library Association was begun in 1876. And there was a meeting of librarians earlier, in 1853 (of course events intervened before there could be another formal gathering). There was a sort of dichotomy within librarianship prior to the later nineteenth century. Large libraries tended to be led by scholar-librarians such as Justin Winsor and William Frederick Poole. In smaller college and public libraries there were devoted amateurs who, by and large, wanted to provide good reading to patrons. At times there could be apprenticeships, whereby novice library workers could learn from more experienced personnel. Formal education would come about in time. The first educational program was begun by Melvil Dewey, first at Columbia in 1987, and then moved to the New York State Library in Albany shortly thereafter. In fact, as Carl White (1976) points out, "Melvil Dewey called the course which opened at Columbia in 1887 a 'systematic apprenticeship'" (p. 24). (Note: White provides a comprehensive background on apprenticeships [pp. 10–60].)

The origins of education for librarianship were based, in large part, on practical training, along with some general study. At Albany, the principal degree offered was the Bachelor of Library Science (BLS). Dewey relied on a distinguished (especially for a time when there was little in the way of formal education) cadre of colleagues, probably the most notable of whom was Mary Salome Cutler Fairchild, who inaugurated a reading course within the Albany school curriculum, aimed at introducing students to the best literature to be held in libraries. Dewey's program attracted a number of people and the overwhelming makeup of the student body was female. Librarianship was considered an appropriate and admirable profession for, particularly unmarried, women at the time. Before long many women would begin to make it a lifelong profession.

In the aftermath of the founding of the first program by Dewey, several additional schools and programs were established. Pratt Institute founded a school in 1890, the Armor Institute of Technology began in 1893 (and transferred to the University of Illinois at Urbana–Champaign in 1897), Simmons College established a school in 1902, the University of Wisconsin Library School began in 1906, and Syracuse University founded its school in 1908. Other programs at Western Reserve University (1904), the New York Public Library in 1911, as well as the Carnegie schools in Pittsburgh (1901) and Atlanta (1905) also had nascent beginnings in the early days (see White, 1976, pp. 105–6). White (1976) suggests, "The library school triumphed because of two factors: its course of study was longer and more thorough than the summer school's; its training was not, like the training class, geared to a particular library" (p. 106). The Association of American Library Schools (AALS) grew out of an American Library Association Round Table. AASL soon, with member input, set up standards for education. Its successor group, the Association for Library and Information Science Education (ALISE), still contributes to standards established by the ALA's Office for Accreditation (along with the Committee on Accreditation [COA]).

In the 1920s Charles C. Williamson (1971) published two reports commissioned by the Carnegie Foundation on the state of library education at that time. He visited many extant programs and reached a set of conclusions. One of his conclusions is reserved for curricula: "There is little agreement among the schools as to the relative importance of the different subjects in the curriculum. About half the student's times is devoted to four subjects—cataloguing, book selection, reference work, and classification. But even to these major subjects some schools give two or three times as many hours of instruction as others do" (p. 136). He (1971) also evaluated the teaching faculties of the schools and found them wanting; only 32 percent in 1921 were college graduates, for example (p. 138). He (1971) cited the main cause of deficiency for each school was inadequate funding (only a couple of schools had independent budgets) (p. 140). In summary, the existing schools at that time were not considered to be up to the challenge of training professional librarians for all of the libraries that needed them.

Continuing the Carnegie Foundation's support for education, the group dedicated a fund of $1 million to a new school that would ostensibly move the educational landscape forward in curricular, student recruitment, and inquiry matters. For an extremely thorough examination of the founding and early years of the University of Chicago's Graduate Library School, see John V. Richardson's work *The Spirit of Inquiry*. The newly established Board of Education for Librarianship (BEL) included in its 1924/25 *Annual Report* a set of proposed standards:

Advanced Graduate Library School

An integral part of a university which meets the standards for graduate study laid down by the Association of American Universities

Requires for entrance a college degree and the successful completion of an approved one-year professional curriculum

Grants a master's degree for the satisfactory completion of one year of further professional study; and the Ph.D. degree under the university regulations governing the granting of that degree. (p. 15)

It is evident that these standards would constitute a new and different model for education for librarianship.

Richardson (1982) mentions that "the biggest advance, in some people's minds, for the University of Chicago's chances to get the advanced library school was the appointment of [Ernest D.] Burton to the position of acting president upon [Harry P.] Judson's retirement in 1923" (p. 26). Richardson proceeds to detail the establishment of the Graduate Library School and to offer profiles of the early administrators of the program. There were criticisms from without in the first years of the program; some people who were prominent in the profession believed that Chicago was not holding up its end of the bargain with respect to the Carnegie grant. What was perceived to be missing was training for the practice of librarianship. Richardson (1982) provides a list of the course offerings (with course titles) for the academic years 1928/29–1932/33 (pp. 78–79). This list gives an insight into the nature of the school and what the students were exposed to as part of their studies. The list of courses includes what might be considered traditional experiences but also transcended the status quo with such courses as "The History of Scholarship." Richardson (1982) writes that, "By late 1929, Douglas Waples was able to articulate further distinctions between the broadly understood 'library science' (better known today as *librarianship*) and the new 'library *science*.' Basically, 'library science' was to him a human science or humanistic pursuit which lacked content or subject matter *per se*" (p. 145). (It should be noted that "science" essentially originated as an ideology [in the strict sense of the word] in the Enlightenment, but the latter part of the nineteenth century articulated the distinction between *naturwissenschaften*, or natural science, and *geisteswissenschaften*, or human science.) Faculty at the Graduate Library School, by and large, intended to proffer the development of a natural science. An early faculty member of the Graduate Library School, Peirce Butler, aptly summarizes the attitude of Chicago: "It will make an equal difference in the quality of his training whether the school looks upon his future activity as the administration of a public trust or as the correct supervision of a routine procedure" (Butler, 1961 [1933], pp. 103–4).

There will be more to say about the contemporary state of education later; for a snapshot of the state of affairs in the 1980s, refer to the collection of essays edited by Herbert White (1986), which includes assess relating various types of libraries.

Libraries and Librarianship

An examination of librarianship as a professional tends to flow from the state of education for the profession. One of the earliest commentators, Pierce Butler (at the Chicago Graduate Library School), proffered some rather scathing criticism of the contemporary state of preparation (1933) and a vision for the future. Among the first things he (1961 [1933]) wrote was, "Unlike his colleagues in other fields of social activity the librarian is strangely uninterested in the theoretical aspects of his profession" (p. xi). He (1961 [1933]) followed that comment up with one of his most quoted statements: "The librarian apparently stands alone in the simplicity of his pragmatism: a rationalization of each immediate technical process by itself seems to satisfy his intellectual interest" (pp. xi–xii). In his work on Peirce Butler, John Richardson (1992) observes, "During the summer of 1931, librarianship experienced a crisis in the source of authority, a crisis which pitted 'genteel amateurism' against the 'new professionalism'" (p. 83). Butler clearly desired the development of a genuine science of librarianship and set forth a program for reaching that intellectual aim. Space prevents an extremely detailed analysis of Butler's treatise; thanks to Richardson's work, we have that analysis. Those who wish to comprehend Butler's background and his deep rationales for his critique should turn to Richardson.

Among the points made by Butler is that the focus of the profession should not be on books themselves without any understanding of what they actually represent: "Books are mere records of knowledge" (Butler, 1961 [1933], p. 43). One could replace "books" with a term like "informing objects" without sacrificing his point. It is the knowledge/information, rather than the container, that deserves attention. Butler (1961 [1933]) elaborated on his point: "The book is not, in fact, the opinion, or the feeling itself, it is only the record of the author's knowledge that he had thus perceived and felt" (p. 43). For Butler there are not only scientific (generally speaking) and sociological elements, there are also psychological ones. He (1961 [1933]) said, "No knowledge can produce action [and this, for him, was a very important extension] until it is animated by an emotional element" (p. 55). When one reads, one is attempting to appropriate the knowledge contained in the book. Add to these components the "historical problem," as Butler put it. This problem is inherent in the purpose of the library and a source of enlightenment that can be applied by the individual within his [sic] role in the state. "The promulgation of reliable information to the electorate is a fundamental element in the modern theory of democracy" (Butler, 1961 [1933], p. 81). His words echo the essential theme of this book and make the connection between libraries (and librarianship) and the commons explicit.

Years later, Jesse Shera (1976) also wrote an introduction to the profession; its purpose and tone are quite different from Butler's, but it contains thoughts worth sharing in this context. Shera (1976) presents a graphic model to depict his idea of culture. The triangle has scholarship and physical equipment at the sides and social organization as the base (p. 44). Primary in social organization is "institutions," which include the family, law, and religion. Next come "agencies," which include libraries. Institutions "give rise to their respective subordinate agencies or instrumentalities.... The library, then, along with the school, the college, the news media, and other manifestations of the 'knowledge industry,' is one of the agencies through which the institution of education exerts its influence" (Shera, 1976, p. 45). One might take issue with his taxonomy, but the description does make sense, and it does not diminish the library. He proposes a new way of thinking, social epistemology, to define what libraries are engaged in doing; the new way of thinking approaches the knowledge of knowledge. "How knowledge has been developed and augmented has long been a subject of study, particularly by the philosophers; but how knowledge has been coordinated, integrated, and put to work, still remains an almost unrecognized field of inquiry"

(Shera, 1976, p. 49). Interestingly, in the aftermath of Shera usage, philosophers such as Steve Fuller and Alvin Goldman have taken up the program of social epistemology (the details of which transcend the gist of this chapter).

More than three decades ago, there was a small flurry of activity in the literature (mainly from individuals affiliated with the Baltimore County Public Library [BCPL]) around the matter of selection and demand. The preferred means of managing collections could be summed up as the idea of "give 'em what they want," signaling meeting the explicit and implicit demands of library users. (Note: I employ the term "library users" here rather than community members because demand arises from the activities, such as circulation, of those who actually come into the library.) Nora Rawlinson (1990) stated, "Simply put, BCPL is run with the assumption that the taxpayers provide money in order to find the materials they want at their library" (p. 77). The objective of the management style is to optimize turnover, or the numbers of circulations per item in the collection. (It should be noted that turnover is a gross measure, based on the collection at large, *and* an individual measure used to evaluate individual titles in the collection.) Rawlinson (1990) observes that, for "popular" authors (those with proven circulation histories), no reviews are needed to make a purchase decision. In some cases, though, they can be swayed by positive reviews, especially of new authors (p. 78).

The then-director of BCPL, Charles Robinson, developed the description of the mission of the library. He (1989) wrote, "In simple terms, the public library is an educational institution in the broadest possible meaning of that term, but it is *not* an academic institution (p. 147; emphasis in original). Throughout his article he stresses his latter point; the academic library exists for preservation, while the public library exists for circulation. He (1989) says that "failure to manage with an eye toward the basic mission, will bring more of the fuzzy, sentimental, institution- and book-centered thinking so inimical to the interests of the public and the library" (p. 152). In critiquing Robinson's position, I (2001) wrote,

> On the face of it his claim may appear to have merit; a democratic aim may be to have the materials that people want now. On the other hand, abandoning any sort of preservation is ahistorical in a couple of ways. It ignores a longstanding purpose that was included in the missions of many public libraries in the nineteenth century of helping people learn about many subjects. The existence of academic libraries (which, according to Robinson, are solely charged with archival responsibilities) does not necessarily constitute accessibility of information that fosters learning. Further, Robinson's claim assumes that the material that may be in the public library today should not be there tomorrow. The ahistorical nature of the claims skews the argument. Robinson's discourse

emphasizes service to the people and responsiveness to need while eliminating some portion of the population and ignoring some needs in favor of others. (p. 507)

What about those who do not enter the library? Can it be that they balk at entering *because* the library does not have the materials and texts that they want and need? When it comes to "purpose," such questions should be asked. Robinson's response is ideological.

To wrap up this section we can turn to Michael Buckland, who gives us some important matters to consider. He (1988) has said,

> How does one know whether one library is better than another, or that a given library is currently improving or degenerating? Can there be a single usable measure of library goodness? If so, what is it? If not, why not? One *can* concoct measures of library goodness, but their credibility is undermined by the number of arbitrary assumptions that have to be made to piece the parts together. (p. 241)

Buckland (1988) notes that quality and value are notoriously difficult outcomes to measure and that, when there are efforts to measure them, they are reduced to instrumentalities. As an aside, Buckland (2017) has written a superior treatise on information in general; this work does have direct relevance to anyone who would consider what libraries are and what they do.

More Recent Issues: Censorship

Robert Darnton (2014) writes, "Where is north in cyberspace? We have no compass to get our bearings in the uncharted ether beyond the Gutenberg galaxy, and the difficulty is not simply cartographical and technological. *It is moral and political.* In the early days of the Internet, cyberspace seemed to be free and open. Now it is being fought over, divided up, and closed off behind protective barriers" (p. 13; emphasis added). (Darnton provides a masterful picture of censorship as practiced in Bourbon France, British India, and communist East Germany.)

Censorship is indeed a moral and political matter. It always has been. Moreover, censorship has been with us just about since the beginnings of human communication. In keeping with the theme of this chapter, the emphasis will be on the nature and practice of censorship in American libraries. As is evident from the foregoing, censoring was rather commonplace in the nineteenth century, during the rise of libraries of all types. Fiction, as has been noted, had been excluded from library collection on several bases, not the least of which is that it was not considered "uplifting" reading. It did not contribute to the growth of useful knowledge. In extreme cases, fiction was vilified in general; more often, *some* fiction by writers of note would be (frequently grudgingly) included in collection, while popular writers, such as Mrs. E. D. E. N. Southworth, would by and large be excluded. When libraries were beginning to be more "enlightened," some would allow the circulation by patrons of *two* books—one being a fiction title. The restrictions on what was held by libraries was not limited to fiction titles though. Wayne Wiegand (1989) points out, "Recent scholarship has demonstrated that librarians exercised a conservative attitude towards the political and cultural tenor of the collections they built for public consumption until the fourth decade of the twentieth century" (p. 95).

The events of World War I provide a lesson regarding what censorship can mean, both to libraries and to society at large. Wiegand (1989) concludes his detailed study by saying, "Like teachers, social workers, and university faculty (to name but a few groups whose social functions were heavily influenced by Progressive Era reform activities) public librarians became caught up in the wartime hysteria and tended to follow the crowd" (p. 134). He documents that numerous public libraries across the country willingly discarded, even burned books that were deemed to be pro-German. These included propaganda materials that espoused sympathy with Germany and even the German wartime cause, but it also included pacifist literature that dated from the period immediately preceding the US entry into the war (1914–1917). Further, German grammars and dictionaries, as well as sheet music by German composers, were removed and sometimes burned. Many libraries used the US Army's index of banned books as deselection tools (Wiegand, 1989, p. 101). In what may be the most telling instance, Wiegand relates the tale of M. Louise Hunt, assistant at the Library Association of Portland, Oregon, who

> refused to buy any of the Liberty Loan Bonds that the federal government was issuing to finance the war. By the time the hue and cry subsided, members of the local community calling for her resignation from the library included bankers, educators, ministers, powerful civic groups, and important politicians and community leaders. The incident marks two characteristics of the wartime hysteria: the pressure to conform, and the price of resisting conformity. . . . Hunt's response was simple and direct. She refused to buy bonds because she did not believe in war. . . . [P]ublic reaction continued, and ultimately forced Hunt to submit her resignation on 15 April [1918]. (pp. 55–57)

The wartime period was not one upon which the library community can gaze with pride.

Things changed somewhat during the time between the world wars. For one thing, the library community became sufficiently concerned with censorship and challenges to materials that they saw fit to take action. There was popular concern in the 1930s regarding both fascism and communism. Censoring of literary works and other materials continued during this time. As Louise Robbins (1996) points out, the critically acclaimed Steinbeck novel *The Grapes of Wrath* "was vilified from the floor of the United States Congress in 1940 by Oklahoma Congressman Lyle Boren and banned in libraries across the country. . . . Its implicit criticism of the treatment of migrant laborers . . . caused the greatest outcry" (pp. 12–13). At about the same time, the American Library Association Council was drafting the association's first "Library Bill of Rights." The text of that document reads,

> Today indications in many parts of the world point to growing intolerance, suppression of free speech, and censorship affecting the rights of minorities and individuals. Mindful of this, the Council of the American Library Association publicly affirms its belief in the following basic policies which should govern the services of free public libraries:
>
> 1. Books and other reading matter selected for purchase from the public funds should be chosen because of value and interest to people of the community, and in no case should the selection be influenced by the race or nationality or the political or religious views of the writers.
> 2. As far as available material permits, all sides of questions on which differences of opinions exist should be represented fairly and adequately in the books and other reading matter purchased for public use.
> 3. The library as an institution to educate for democratic living should especially welcome the use of its meeting rooms for socially useful and cultural activities and the discussion of current public questions. Library meeting rooms should be available on equal terms to all groups in the community regardless of their beliefs or affiliations. (Robbins, 1996, pp. 13–14)

Censorship continued, and continues. Robbins (1996) provides an exhaustive history of such censorship and challenges to library materials from the time of the first version of the Library Bill of Rights through 1969. Her work should be consulted as one of the most instructive texts available.

Robbins (1996) demonstrates that the Library Bill of Rights went through subsequent iterations as censoring activities continued and, in some important ways, expanded. The latest version of the Library Bill of Rights has been amended by the American Library Association Council as of January 29, 2019. This version reads,

> The American Library Association affirms that all libraries are forums for information and ideas, and that the following basic policies should guide their services.
>
> I. Books and other library resources should be provided for the interest, information, and enlightenment of all people of the community the library serves. Materials should not be excluded because of the origin, background, or views of those contributing to their creation.
> II. Libraries should provide materials and information presenting all points of view on current and historical issues. Materials should not be proscribed or removed because of partisan or doctrinal disapproval.
> III. Libraries should challenge censorship in the fulfillment of their responsibility to provide information and enlightenment.
> IV. Libraries should cooperate with all persons and groups concerned with resisting abridgment of free expression and free access to ideas.
> V. A person's right to use a library should not be denied or abridged because of origin, age, background, or views.
> VI. Libraries which make exhibit spaces and meeting rooms available to the public they serve should make such facilities available on an equitable basis, regardless of the beliefs or affiliations of individuals or groups requesting their use.
> VII. All people, regardless of origin, age, background, or views, possess a right to privacy and confidentiality in their library use. Libraries should advocate for, educate about, and protect people's privacy, safeguarding all library use data, including personally identifiable information. (http://www.ala.org/advocacy/intfreedom/librarybill)

It is readily apparent that the Library Bill of Rights has evolved substantially over time. The present iteration is a combination of negative ("materials shall *not* be excluded") and positive ("libraries *should* cooperate with all persons and groups") ethical stances. Many libraries claim to follow the Library Bill of Rights (even to adhere to its tenets), but in practice strict adherence may be a difficult goal to achieve.

After the passage of the Library Bill of Rights and up to the US entry into World War II, there was a growing anti-Communist sentiment. Before the attack on Pearl Harbor, there were actions that citizens and police forces began to take to stamp out the spread and circulation of Communist literature. As Shirley and Wayne Wiegand (2007) report, "Shortly after noon on August 17 [1940]—a hot, sunny Saturday three weeks after [Detective John

Wade] Webb's visit—the Oklahoma City Police initiated a series of raids on the Progressive Book Store, the local office of the Communist Party, and five private homes" (p. 4). Police arresting individuals even told protesting arrestees that they make their own Constitution in Oklahoma City (Wiegand and Wiegand, 2007, p. 5). "Within five hours [the arrestees] had been carted off to jail without being told the charges against them. All were held incommunicado and under false names supplied by the police so relatives could not trace them to jail" (Wiegand and Wiegand, 2007, p. 9). The Communist Party had been growing in Oklahoma from 1917; the party also saw growth in other states, which prompted a major congressional action: the Special Committee on Un-American Activities (known as HUAC) was authorized by the US House of Representative in May 1938 (see Wiegand and Wiegand, 2007, p. 37). That began a lengthy and ugly period in US history, culminating in the 1950s. Wiegand and Wiegand (2007) paint the full picture of the formal attacks on Communism in the Midwest, with, as is evident from the foregoing, emphasis on Oklahoma.

Censorship during the World War II period through the 1950s was active across the nation. Cindy Mediavilla (1997) notes that "California Library Association (CLA) President John D. Henderson (1941) predicted that the 1940s would make a time" of a battle relating to books and ideas (p. 331). There were efforts aimed at schools as well as libraries that met with some success during the 1940s. The CLA fought ferociously against the censorship efforts in libraries and schools, and their fight did result in some success at retaining materials in libraries and saving some curricula and materials in schools. David Berninghausen (1953), who was a warrior for intellectual freedom, acknowledged that the CLA was a leader in establishing strong intellectual freedom committees in the country and that, "in fact, the national group learning much from California's experiences" (p. 816). Berninghausen, who was also a champion of the Library Bill of Rights (especially the 1948 and later versions), believed in the fundamental stance that it represented:

> In Berninghausen's view, the Library Bill of Rights (1948–) served both to codify and standardize a purist moral stance on intellectual freedom by which impartiality and "neutrality" on non-library issues served as the central principle of the profession. The concept of "social responsibility" that emerged in the context of librarianship in the late 1960s was, in Berninghausen's opinion, a New Left tactic that threatened ALA's traditional "neutrality" and purpose. (Samek, 2001, p. 4)

The "neutrality" matter has not been one of universal popularity, particularly, as Toni Samek (2001) points out, from the period of some unrest and questioning of the status quo.

Meanwhile, specific libraries have stories to be told and, fortunately, there are documents that relate their experiences. For example, the New York Public Library (NYPL) had to fight against anti-Communist backlash. Stephen Francoeur (2011) notes that John Mackenzie Cory, head of the NYPL Circulation Department, "called himself 'an extremist against any form of censorship' who 'often would like to go even beyond the Library Bill of Rights,' because 'yielding to any pressure—even pressure to suppress a book that is abhorrent to you—creates problems which may make it difficult not to submit to other pressures'" (pp. 140–41). Francoeur (2011) reports that the period from 1945 to 1955 was particularly trying (p. 141). He adds, "The first major library censorship battles in the post-war era began in 1947, a year that marked a dramatic increase in anti-communism efforts on the national level. In March, President Harry Truman promulgated the 'Truman Doctrine' that advocated a policy of aggressive containment to confront the growth of communism worldwide" (p. 143). At that time Truman issued Executive Order 9835, requiring loyalty oaths by federal employees. (By way of personal aside, I should say that when I assumed my first state job, I had to take a loyalty oath. This was in 1978 in Louisiana.) Francoeur states that, "Although the [NYPL] did not discard controversial materials in the collection, it did take them out of the spotlight. In response to the 'redhunting' challenge, librarians apparently engaged in defensive ambiguity" (p. 144). Francoeur (2011) concludes, "The NYPL was fortunate that the direct attacks made upon it in the 1940s and the 1950s were not sustained. Many libraries in the 1940s and the 1950s expended considerable time defending themselves from pressure groups, dealing with loyalty oath programmes [sic], and moving to closed stacks items that had been objected to as 'subversive' or 'anti-American'" (p. 156).

The Library of Congress (LC) also faced challenges during the period in question. As Louise Robbins (1994) writes, "The uneasy wartime alliance with the Soviets has dissolved, European colonial powers were losing their dominions, the United Nations was struggling into existence, and the menacing power of the atom had been unleashed" (p. 366). With the loyalty oath under enforcement and the review of some LC personnel taking place, there was considerable tension (including whether some employees would be able to keep their jobs). Four of the LC employees who were not cleared by the FBI resigned or left the library (Robbins, 1994, p. 372). It was not just Communists who came under fire; gay workers were also persecuted. "The purge of homosexuals did not get the same attention from the Librarian's Conference as did the Loyalty Program, perhaps because it was seen as just another facet of that program" (Robbins, 1994, p. 376). Robbins says, "Eventually the loyalty issue waned, although investigations persisted. Political tempers cooled after 1956, aided in part by McCarthy's 1954 censure by the Senate and by Supreme Court decisions that put some limits of the federal government's investigative and punitive powers" (p. 381). This time, of course, did not end censorship forever and always, but it did mark the culmination of large-scale federal efforts to censor and to control employees.

Lester Asheim (1953) wrote a classic article in the midst of the anti-Communist and censorship turmoil, ostensibly to provide a rationale for the selection of materials once and for all. It is a paper that is still cited today. He (1953) sums up his argument early in the article:

> The real question of censorship versus selection arises when the librarian, exercising his own judgment, decides against a book which has every legal right to representation on his shelves. In other words, we should not have been concerned with the librarian who refused to buy *Ulysses* for his library before 1933—but we do have an interest in his refusal after the courts cleared it for general circulation in the United States. (p. 63)

While admitting that there can be subjective decision processes at work, the matter of censorship and selection is not particularly subtle or elusive. He delineates some criteria upon which decisions can, and should, be based, and ultimately says,

> The major characteristic which makes for the all-important difference [between censorship and selection] seems to me to be this: that the selector's approach is positive, while that of the censor is negative. This is no mere verbal quibble; it transforms the entire act and the steps included in it. For the selector, the important thing is to find reasons to keep the book. . . . For the censor, on the other hand, the important thing is to find reasons to reject the book. . . . An inevitable consequence of the negative approach is that it leads to the use of isolated parts rather than the complete whole upon which to base a judgment. (p. 66)

Based on Asheim's argument, it is by no means censorship when an elementary school librarian does *not* purchase a college-level physics book for the collection.

Speaking of school libraries, there are some particular matters that are in effect. It almost goes without saying that parents of elementary school children sometimes take on roles of protection, barring their children from what they may see as dangerous or pernicious ideas. Some themes, such as sexual awakening, homosexuality, religion, and race, tend to arise in the school library setting. Nancy Kravitz (2002) provides a thoroughgoing examination of the events that school librarians must face, including the handling of challenges to materials by parents or others. Her work is seminal in demonstrating just how some materials can come under fire and especially what librarians should do by ways of policies and actions in responding to censorship. Perhaps of particular note, she includes school textbooks in the mix. She offers a historical portrait of censorship and then chronicles some specific challenges and the outcomes of deliberations. She (2002) also cites some case law of import, such as *Pico v. Board of Education, Island Trees Free School District*, which had its beginnings with the attempted removal of eleven books from the school library (pp. 59–62). The case reached the US Supreme Court, where a plurality of justices ruled that the censors had partisan motives.

The *Pico* case was very complex and generated quite a lot of judicial commentary. Fortunately, Donald Dunn (1984) provides an exhaustive background and analysis of the case, its predecessors, and the Supreme Court justices' opinions. He (1984) states at the outset of his examination, "The Court was unable to arrive at a majority opinion in *Pico*. Rather, the Justices produced a plurality opinion, including seven separate opinions, focusing on a variety of issues and aspects of the case" (p. 435). The background on other cases (including some that decided in favor of removal of materials) that, in some ways, led up to *Pico* is invaluable for anyone who cares to delve into censorship arbitration. Dunn (1984) summarizes, "The plurality opinion . . . illustrates the fractured nature of the Court's attempt to wrestle with the complex substantive First Amendment issues. Although the plurality provided some standards of review, these standards fell short of offering clearly articulated guidelines to apply in such controversial and complicated cases. In the immediate aftermath of the Supreme Court's holding, the complications and confusion continued" (p. 452). So, in this important case, no firm conclusion was reached, although the school board did vote by six to one to return books to the shelves, a minor victory that did not quell challenges or censorship efforts elsewhere.

Public libraries have also been the focus of censorship attention in the past . . . and present. In Loudoun County, Virginia, the library board attempted to impose filtering software on library computers. As A. Glick (1998) reports, "In a preliminary ruling in the closely watched lawsuit against Loudoun County (VA) Public Library, U.S. District Court Judge Leonie M. Brinkema on April 7 denied the library's motion to dismiss the case, rejecting its argument that the First Amendment doesn't apply to library decisions on whether to give access to internet information" (p. 22). Glick notes that the ruling does not offer an ultimate settlement in the case. Amanda Ferguson (1999) says in a later piece, "In the first major ruling on the use of Internet filtering software in libraries, U.S. District Court Judge Leonie Brinkema declared the Loudoun County (VA) Library policy requiring Internet filtering software on all public terminals unconstitutional" (p. 17). The national and local library communities were very pleased with the ruling.

Intellectual freedom and opposition to censorship can be boiled down to some essential points, which Eliza Dresang (2006) enumerates: "freedom to think and believe what one will, freedom to express one's thoughts and beliefs in unrestricted manners and means, and freedom to access information and ideas regardless of the content or viewpoints of the author(s) or the age, background, or beliefs of the receiver" (p. 169). Emily Knox (2015) has conducted numerous interviews with librarians to determine reasons for challenges and efforts at censorship. The data and information emanating from her study are too voluminous to mention here, but power relations do arise in her study. As she (2015) says, "In keeping with their professional ethics, information professionals should always be wary when individuals argue that certain materials from the public sphere, especially when such requests are made on behalf of people who have little political agency of their own" (p. 44). Knox's work is definitely instructive and is one of the genuine research-based analyses into challenges and censorship. She (2015) concludes, "It is hoped that the analysis in this book can help us understand the sometimes inscrutable actions and emotions that surround books, reading, knowledge, and power" (p. 139).

Jennifer Elaine Steele (2018) employs gatekeeping theory in her examination of censorship (in its many forms). The theory was proposed by Kurt Lewin (1947), who makes the connection between gatekeeping and mass communication and says that gatekeeping "holds not only for food channels [his initial study] but also for the traveling of a news item through certain communication channels in a group" (p. 145). Steele (2018) adds that the theory is useful for explaining the flow through channels of information and the spread to the public (p. 232). In elaborating on the use of Lewin's theory, Steele (2018) says that "a key component of Lewin's model was his concept of gates. Gates are decision points along communication channels, which come in the form of people, policies, or other forces. At each gate, information is either allowed to flow, or stop" (p. 234). The concept of gates appears to fit well with an analysis of censorship because there are several stages at which a gate can be open or at which it can shut down. The gatekeepers are people who can exercise volition in allowing information to be passed along or be halted. Perhaps of most importance is her (2018) explication of positive and negative forces affecting gatekeeping:

> The concept of forces addresses the notion that there are factors that influence whether information is allowed to flow through a gate or is stopped at the gate. These factors influence gatekeepers' decision-making on gate control. Factors are either positive in nature supporting continuing flow through the gate or negative in nature resulting in closure of the gate and impedance of information flow. (p. 236)

When censorship does occur, the negative forces on the parts of individuals hold sway.

It rather stands to reason that the majority of censorship issues, including challenges to materials and efforts to ban books, occur primarily in school and public libraries. Children and young adults frequent those libraries, although some challengers do so to keep some politically based materials out of the libraries. All this does not mean that college and university libraries do not experience censorship. Robert Bukoff (1995) conducted a survey of a sample of college libraries (with enrollments of 5,000 or fewer) to determine if there were any instances of challenges, censorship, or other actions (including stealing or mutilating materials) from 1988 to 1994. He notes, "Of the 68 responding librarians, 25 libraries (37%) recorded 38 instances of censorship, oftentimes multiple cases within a single library; eleven libraries (16%) fell into the latter category" (p. 397). He (1995) found that the occurrences were more frequent at religious institutions than nondenominational ones. He (1995) summarizes the types of instances that occurred during the time period:

> Eleven individual libraries (16% of the total respondents) reported a request to remove material from their collections; 14 libraries (21%) encountered problems with anonymous tampering, mutilation, or destruction with library computer hardware and library-sponsored bulletin boards, while four libraries (6%) recorded formal challenges that did not require the removal of material from the collection. (p. 399)

The sample size was not large, but the frequency of events does indicate that college libraries, just as do public and school ones, experience efforts aimed at censorship.

Graham Peace (1997) also tackles the issue on a broader scale—censorship in the academic world. He (1997) initially observes, "The issue is not restricted to simply pornography and graphic sex; racist propaganda, anti-religious newsgroups, and instructions for making bombs are all easily available via the electronic medium [including in libraries]" (pp. 35–36). He (1997) does admit that concerns about pornography arise frequently and that there are people—faculty and administrators, for example—who are sympathetic to the concerns. A difficulty arises when some students and faculty are conducting legitimate inquiry into, for example, social impacts of widespread pornographic images as part of their research. Peace (1997) mentions the then-recent passage of the Communications Decency Act (a component of the larger Telecommunications Act of 1996, see https://www.congress.gov/104/plaws/publ104/PLAW-104publ104.pdf) and the influence it can have on the actions of viewing questionable materials via the Internet. It should be noted that those legitimate research activities have not been subject to the act. Peace (1997), who is a member of the faculty of a school of business, does mention libraries and librarians. He (1997) concludes, "Different people have different tastes and each person's views should be given equal consideration, *when feasible*. . . . Libraries are providers of information to a community and generally supported by that community" (p. 38; emphasis added). Peace (1997) ultimately makes a distinction between materials and information that are protected by the First Amendment and those which are not. For material not so protected, "A university must be careful to balance the legal and the moral issues. If the information is deemed to be morally acceptable, a case can be made for allowing access, despite the lack of any legal requirement to do so" (p. 43). The viewing of child pornography, for instance, brings the law into stark relief, regardless of the type of library.

Just a few words will be said about hate speech at this point because the hate speech policies and reactions do ultimately have an impact on libraries. For one thing, as Robert Labaree (1994) points out, there can be tension between the policies and the Library Bill of Rights. He (1994) asks, "Is there a fundamental conflict between the Library Bill of Rights' support of free speech (library ideology) and a college or university's institutional regulation of hate speech?" (p. 372). He (1994) also notes, "A panel appointed by the United States Commission on Civil Rights highlighted four categories of causes for increased hate crimes: (1) deficiencies on college campuses that exacerbate existing tensions; (2) society's failure to keep up with change; (3) competition for limited resources; and (4) extremist speakers" (p. 373). The point Labaree makes is a cogent one: the Library Bill of Rights speaks out against censorship, but higher education institutions have increasingly instituted policies against speech and action (and have been holding individuals responsible for them). More recently, and with some extremists seeking to speak on university campuses, there have been incidents of protests that have, at the time, included violence. One such event centered on the scheduled appearance at the University of California, Berkeley, of controversial speaker and writer Milo Yiannopoulos. He attempted to speak on the campus in February 2017, but protests (some of the protesters smashed windows and set fires) caused the cancelation of the event (see https://www.washingtonpost.com/news/grade-point/wp/2017/09/23/uc-berkeley-says-free-speech-week-is-canceled-milo-yiannopoulos-says-hes-still-coming-to-campus/). Interestingly, according to the University Library's catalog, Berkeley does not own a copy of Yiannopoulos's book *Dangerous*. Further, the MOBIOUS (see https://mobiusconsortium.org/) Consortium catalog indicates that only one university library within the group owns the book.

More Recent Issues: Activism and Ethics

These two issues are, though seemingly incongruous, related. They are motivated by the attempt to discover the "right" thing to do. The motivation can lead individuals in different directions but should be discussed within the same section. This portion of the book will begin with activism. If one goes back to the beginnings of the Library Bill of Rights, activism has a substantial past. The real beginnings, though, tend to mirror activism in general in the United States all the way. Among the earlier instances of activism is Sanford Berman's (1993 [1971]) critique of (especially) Library of Congress Subject Headings that are racist, sexist, xenophobic, etc. His examples are very telling of attitudes toward many social issues. Other individuals have focused their attention on specific issues. For example, E. J. Josey (1987) has addressed the civil rights movement and how librarianship fits into it. As he wrote at the time, "We have come a long way in librarianship; nevertheless we have a long way to go. In the 110-year history of the American Library Association, only two persons of African descent have served as president. In the fifty state libraries of the land, there is only one Black state librarians" (p. 19).

Berman's cause has been picked by others. For example, Amber Billey, Emily Drabinski, and K. R. Roberto (2014) examine a particular information organizational scheme to determine the treatment of gender in description and organization of information. They (2014) note,

> Our critique of RDA [Resource Development and Analysis] 9.7 is grounded in queer theory, a field that provides a useful theoretical frame for rethinking the stable, fixed categories and systems of naming that characterize library knowledge organization schemes. Queer theory is particularly useful for under-

standing new ways of conceptualizing sex and gender that challenge LC and NACO's narrow articulation of these complex identities. (p. 414)

The authors (2014) conclude, "Binary gender is a central organizing feature of contemporary life, but it need not always be so. Indeed, the work of queer theorists and queer people has made gender as much a site of contestation as it is a site of identity. . . . The value of RDA is that it gives catalogers increased agency in terms of resource description and enables next generation catalogers with improved retrieval capabilities" (p. 420). The contested nature of sex and gender is of special import because it deals, as the authors state, both with personal and with group identity plus the need to organize information for effective use. Emily Drabinski (2013) summarizes the challenge to information organization within the larger social milieu: "The problems of bias in library classification structures and subject language are, from a queer perspective, problems endemic to the knowledge organization project itself. If social categories and names are understood as embedded in contingencies of space, time, and discourse, then bias is inextricable from the process of classification and cataloging" (p. 108). Safiya Noble (2018) has examined the structures of, and results emanating from, search engines. She writes,

> This book is about the power of algorithms in the age of neoliberalism and the ways those digital decisions reinforce oppressive social relationships and enact new models of racial profiling, which I have termed *technological redlining*. By making visible the ways that capital, race, and gender are factors in creating unequal conditions, I am bringing light to various forms of technological redlining that are on the rise. (p. 1; emphasis in original)

It should be noted that ALA now has what is called the Spectrum Scholarship: "Through the Spectrum Scholarship Program, the American Library Association affirms its commitment to diversity and inclusion by seeking the broadest participation of new generations of racially and ethnically diverse librarians to position ALA to provide leadership in the transformation of libraries and library services" (http://www.ala.org/advocacy/spectrum).

In a similar vein, Kay Ann Cassell (1987) spoke of the struggle of women in librarianship. As she said, "The Task Force on Women promoted its interest in helping women find better job and salary situations through their programming at American Library Association conferences. Many programs were related to the employment field and especially to legal rights for women including affirmative action and how to file complaints" (p. 24). She concluded by writing, "Once the breakthrough recognition that librarianship was a feminine profession was made, identifying the problems was an easy step for feminist librarians. But solving these problems has not been so easy" (p. 28). Indeed, there could be greater representation by women in managerial positions, particularly directorships. In the areas of race and women's issues, activism may still be required by librarians.

The most complete work on activism, especially official and unofficial ALA activism, is by Toni Samek (2001). She begins with a critique of the treatment of alternative press materials in mainstream library collections: "First, because library users did not have adequate access to the products of the alternative press, they did not have access to the viewpoints expressed therein. . . . Second, because the alternative press was not being adequately preserved as part of the cultural record, many voices from the 1960s would be lost to future generations. Third, because of the absence of alternative perspectives, the mainstream media was over-represented in library collections" (p. 2). The most cogent point in the book is Samek's (2001) statement, "The idea of the library's playing a part in the crafting of the nation's culture through the process of collection development helps illustrate how institutions shape culture and ideology. One of the key characteristics of hegemony, for example, is that power is distributed across a network of civil institutions" (p. 31). As an aside, Douglas Raber (2003) discusses the Gramscian concept of hegemony as he posits that (fitting Antonio Gramsci) librarians are "organic intellectuals" who exercise some hegemonic power over culture. As he (2003) says, "They are the organizers of capitalist hegemony and its culture, and they play central strategic and ideological roles in the superstructure, that reproduces capitalist relations of production" (p. 44). Raber describes not the activist librarian, who tilts against hegemonic ideology, but the status quo. His thoughts are particularly cogent here.

It is difficult to summarize the extent of Samek's work here, but she does go into great detail into the founding and the work of the ALA Social Responsibilities Round Table (SRRT). The current purpose statement of SRRT is,

> The Social Responsibilities Round Tables (SRRT) is a unit within the American Library Association. It works to make ALA more democratic and to establish progressive priorities not only for the Association but also for the entire profession. Concern for human and economic rights was an important element in the founding of SRRT and remains an urgent concern today. SRRT believes that libraries and librarians must recognize and help solve social problems and inequities in order to carry out their mandate to work for the common good and bolster democracy.
>
> Since 1969, members of the Social Responsibilities Round Table (SRRT) have worked to make the American Library Association (ALA) more demo-

cratic. They have also worked to promote a more progressive agenda. In doing so, SRRT has provided a home within ALA for progressive librarians, library workers, and supporters who agree to promote social responsibility as a core value of librarianship. (http://www.ala.org/rt/srrt/)

Samek (2001) notes that the SRRT began by asking some serious questions that members believed needed immediate attention: "(1) What did social responsibility mean? (2) What were the group's social responsibilities? (3) What were the social problems of the library and of librarians? (4) What were the functions of the round table? (5) What were the priorities of the round table? (6) What was to be done next? And (7) How would a relationship with other round tables be established?" (pp. 54–55). The round table that SRRT was most concerned with was the Intellectual Freedom Round Table (IFRT), specifically how to reconcile some apparent differences between SRRT and IFRT. That issue would prove to be a difficult one to resolve.

There were some actions that the SRRT sponsored and attempted to gain support for that Samek (2001) describes and that Douglas Raber (2007) elaborates upon. A principal impetus behind SRRT was change—change in the ways the profession viewed the major matters facing life in a democracy, including war and peace, race, women's issues, fair labor practices, etc. Those who advocated a progressive future for librarianship faced an uphill battle in society at large and especially within ALA as an institution. As Raber (2007) notes, "The idea for a committee to study these issues and to recommend change arose from both the membership and the leadership of the association, and a resolution establishing the Activities Committee on New Directions for the ALA (ACONDA) was easily passed on June 25, 1969" (p. 681). Raber (2007) illustrates the charge of ACONDA, which included such things as reinterpreting ALA's philosophy, setting priorities for action, and taking a fresh look at the organizational structure of ALA (p. 682). There were mixed hopes and expectations for ACONDA (see Raber, 2007, p. 683), but the work of the committee continued apace. Raber (2007) cites the final recommendation on social responsibility by ACONDA (p. 686):

(1) Define the broad social responsibilities of ALA in terms of (a) the contribution that librarianship can make in ameliorating or even solving the critical problems of society, (b) support all efforts to help inform and educate the people of the Unites States on these problems and to encourage them to read the many views on, and the facts regarding, each problem, and (c) the willingness of ALA to take a position for the guid-

ance and support of its members on current critical issues. (ACONDA, Final Report)

Part (b) of the report is a meaningful summarization of the purpose behind the present book. As democratic institutions, libraries have this responsibility and must take it to heart in the future. Unfortunately, when ALA membership was asked to consider the final report, the "meeting ran between fourteen and fifteen hours long, motions were made to table the report; refer it to a membership mail vote; and accept it as an interim report only" (Raber, 2007, p. 689). Further unfortunate happenstance had the 1972 ALA meeting accepting business as usual, and the committee and its report were relegated to the past. SRRT continues its activities, but this opportunity for an activist stance by the profession was missed.

Another example of activism will be presented here (although this marks neither the full summary nor the end of activism). At the 1988 ALA Annual Meeting a debate was held between John Swan and Noel Peattie. An expansion of their positions was published in 1989. Swan (1989) begins by enumerating four key issues that should be considered at the outset of the debate:

First. The marketplace of ideas is itself a profound and enduring idea, but it is also a flawed and distorted mechanism. . . .

Second. There are such things as dangerous and pernicious ideas—not merely lies, but damned lies. . . .

Third. Librarians, like everyone except nihilists, complete cynics and the utterly value-free, will always try to conduct their business guided by some operative notion of the truth, some devotion to accuracy over inaccuracy, honesty over dishonesty, humane and life-affirming values over the reverse.

Fourth. Librarians, like everyone else without exception, will always conduct their business encircled by more or less severe limitations of time, budget, space, opportunity, and or vision. (pp. 15–16)

He (1989) then refutes some of the premises and claims that the most effective means of ensuring freedom of information is the provision of the widest access to ideas, even if they contain no truth. His (1989) position can be summed up here (in the interest of space) in one sentence: "The worst falsehoods, the damnedest lies, have their origins not in ideas but in pathologies, and suppressing symptoms does not cure the disease" (p. 18). He admits to adopting a libertarian stance and advocates "tolerance of the intolerable" (p. 21).

Peattie (1989) adopts a less libertarian and more truth-based position. He (1989) asserts his stance with some numbered points as well:

> First, to say that intellectual freedom is ill-defined is not to dismiss intellectual freedom as not worth defending. . . . A second problem lies in the nature of truth, and competing theories of truth, with attendant questions such as the "liar's paradox," and problems purely philosophical in nature. . . . A third problem . . . , is whether a historical revisionist, such as [a Holocaust denier] or even a Nazi or neo-Nazi, is deliberately propagating a falsehood, or is simply a pathological person with a bizarre desire to believe something that isn't so—namely that the Holocaust didn't happen. (p. 39)

Peattie, among other things, distinguishes between a moral debate (he uses abortion as his example) and a factual debate (such as the existence of the Holocaust). The first is open to question and library collections can, and should, have alternative positions available. The second, for Peattie, is not open to debate, so a library including untrue claims is problematic. This viewpoint is opposed to libertarianism and so is opposed to Swan. Peattie (1989) says, "I prize highly the freedom to read, but I prize more highly the freedom to know; and I want to know that what I read is in some sense 'so'" (p. 95). The debate has not ended with Swan and Peattie and remains a thorny issue for the profession.

While Swan and Peattie make cogent arguments (that do have some similar elements), there is the matter of the provision of information services in libraries. Some years ago, I (2011) suggested that, when it comes to *information* (as distinct from people's reading preferences), there should be a theoretical premise that can guide us. So here is a suggestion for the readers' consideration:

> **Definition:** *Information* is meaningful communicative action that aims at truth claims and conditions.
>
> **Statement of Theory:** *Information* is comprised of those communicative actions (and *only* those communicative actions) that can be evaluated by a population—defined as the intended or potential hearers of the communication—as meaningful. Meaning is not limited to pure semantics, but includes context and history within evaluation. Further, information is true in that there is warrant for the communicative action, that this action includes no deliberate deception or omission, has inherent evaluative components, provides evidentiary justification, and is fundamental to ethics. (Budd, 2011, p. 70; emphasis in original)

These are very stringent criteria and, it must be stated, they *do not embrace everything that every library exists to provide*. The obvious example is that a research library will include obvious lies so that those lies can be studied. (Public libraries may well include such materials and texts as well.) What is meant by this theory is that there are claims and works that aim to be *informative* and should adhere to the theoretical statement. This also means that I tend to find myself in substantive agreement with Peattie and am subject to similar critique.

One more instance (and this is by no means the last word on activism) relates to the fundamental statement of neutrality, as evidenced by the Library Bill of Rights. As was mentioned earlier, many, many libraries state that they adhere to the tenets of the Library Bill of Rights; that may imply that these libraries adopt neutrality as an ideology (in the generic sense). The neutrality stance would be similar to that of the libertarians; what is *said* is worthy of consideration. This is the classical liberal position. According to it, the treatise of a Holocaust denier would have a place in a library's collection, presumably as long as works about the Holocaust as a historical event were also included. Some do not agree with the neutrality doctrine though. Mark Rosenzweig (2008), for one, says,

> The origins of the ideas of impartiality and neutrality . . . , are perhaps more connected to the historical process of institutional rationalization and bureaucratization (of which the new [nineteenth- and early-twentieth-century] librarians were enthusiastic exponents) than to a preoccupation with intellectual freedom. If we have become more democratic, more concerned with equity and social justice, it has been because of a political process and not because of a hewing to imaginary first principles of neutrality. (p. 6)

Robert Jensen (2008) puts the picture even more starkly: "The liberal, pluralist, and democratic features of the system are constantly in tension with capitalism and the state (which typically serves the interests of capital)" (p. 89). Jensen may be setting up straw men in his dichotomy. There is a tension that should be recognized, though, and the Swan and Peattie (1989) debate provides a signal of it. It can be expressed as a question: Are the ideologies of the Intellectual Freedom Round Table and the Social Responsibilities Round Table in concert or in opposition? That is not a rhetorical question; members of the profession and of the institution of ALA grapple with the matter continuously. Even if the question is answered, the heart of the argument is not resolved; what should be the position of librarianship?

The gist of this book is an effort to respond to that latter question, and we will return to it in the final chapter.

A turn to the ethical imperatives of the profession is not an abandonment of (it is suggested here that it is not even a leap from) activism. The attention to ethics is a concrete way to bring the profession of librarianship into relief. The place to start is ALA's Code of Ethics:

> As members of the American Library Association, we recognize the importance of codifying and making known to the profession and to the general public the ethical principles that guide the work of librarians, other professionals providing information services, library trustees and library staffs.
>
> Ethical dilemmas occur when values are in conflict. The American Library Association Code of Ethics states the values to which we are committed, and embodies the ethical responsibilities of the profession in this changing information environment.
>
> We significantly influence or control the selection, organization, preservation, and dissemination of information. In a political system grounded in an informed citizenry, we are members of a profession explicitly committed to intellectual freedom and the freedom of access to information. We have a special obligation to ensure the free flow of information and ideas to present and future generations.
>
> The principles of this Code are expressed in broad statements to guide ethical decision making. These statements provide a framework; they cannot and do not dictate conduct to cover particular situations.
>
> I. We provide the highest level of service to all library users through appropriate and usefully organized resources; equitable service policies; equitable access; and accurate, unbiased, and courteous responses to all requests.
> II. We uphold the principles of intellectual freedom and resist all efforts to censor library resources.
> III. We protect each library user's right to privacy and confidentiality with respect to information sought or received and resources consulted, borrowed, acquired or transmitted.
> IV. We recognize and respect intellectual property rights.
> V. We treat co-workers and other colleagues with respect, fairness and good faith, and advocate conditions of employment that safeguard the rights and welfare of all employees of our institutions.
> VI. We do not advance private interests at the expense of library users, colleagues, or our employing institutions.
> VII. We distinguish between our personal convictions and professional duties and do not allow our personal beliefs to interfere with fair rep-

resentation of the aims of our institutions or the provision of access to their information resources.

VIII. We strive for excellence in the profession by maintaining and enhancing our own knowledge and skills, by encouraging the professional development of co-workers, and by fostering the aspirations of potential members of the profession. (http://www.ala.org/united/sites /ala.org.united/files/content/trustees/orgtools/policies/ALA-code-of -ethics.pdf)

It seems appropriate here to continue with a discussion of ethics (within the context of this work) by invoking the words of Adriaan Peperzak (2004): "Ethics cannot be separated from politics" (p. 21). Indeed, the ethical decisions we make, the ethical "events" that we face, tend to be fraught with political meaning and intention. For this reason, the extended description of John Rawls's (2001) system of social cooperation is appropriate here:

> The central organizing idea of social cooperation has at least three essential features:
>
> a) Social cooperation is distinct from merely socially coordinated activity. . . . Rather, social cooperation is guided by publicly recognized rules and procedures that those cooperating accept as appropriate to regulate their conduct.
> b) The idea of cooperation includes the idea of fair terms of cooperation: these are terms each participant may reasonably accept, and should accept, provided that everyone else likewise accepts them.
> c) The idea of cooperation also includes the idea of each participant's rational advantage, or good. The idea of rational advantage specifies what it is that those engaged in cooperation are seeking to advance from the standpoint of their own good. (p. 6)

Ethical action demands cooperation; in the ideal world, all parties (as Rawls says) are committed to cooperation. One way to look at this is envisioning the entire professional community adhering to the letter and the spirit of the code of ethics. Through that action, all members of libraries' communities can rely on the ethics of the professionals.

I have tried to address the practice of ethics within the context of a rich literature in the profession. As I (2006) wrote, "The derivation of a formal, consistent, agreed-upon practical and normative ethics is no mean feat. In actuality, librarianship has, in many ways and over many years, aimed at this goal. . . . A foundation built upon rights does not deny consequences, welfare, or duty, but it does couch ethics in terms of the well-being of everyone in the community" (p. 266). John Burgess (2019) presents the issue succinctly, especially with regard to "information" ethics: "If, figuratively speaking, ethics is the story of what it means to be good and all the ways humans remain bad, the *information ethics* is the story of the good that can be accomplished with information, and all the ways it may be used to harm. . . . The story of information plays out within individuals, among persons, in communities, and even between people and their creations, from social institutions to artificially intelligent machines" (p. 1; emphasis in original). Robert Hauptman has repeatedly noted that ethics can sometimes degenerate to personal preferences and/or disputes about beliefs (most notably in Hauptman, 2002). It is vital to remember that ethics is based on the foregoing ideas, such as social cooperation, and agreed-upon standards of action.

Here is a more personal take on ethics. Librarianship is continuously marked by the presence of ethical events. By "ethical events" I mean the challenges that can face librarians as part of their professional work. There is a common thread that runs throughout the events that face librarians—realism. It must be noted, though, that the realist stance does *not* imply that there is a naturalized ethics ("naturalized" implying the ethics must follow the rules and methods of the natural sciences). In fact, naturalized ethics is rejected. Kevin DeLapp (2013) states, "The view that moral values exist in a way that is causally and evidentially (though not conceptually) independent from the beliefs of anyone and everyone . . . such that evidence and beliefs do not determine or constitute those values, though they may adequately and reliably measure or reflect them" (p. 17). Jonathan Dancy (1993) maintains that it is not solely a belief that motivates one toward a specific action but rather the fact that underlies beliefs. That means that there are such things as ethical facts that influence beliefs and, thus, *action*. As Shafer-Landau (2003) writes, "Moral realism is the theory that moral judgements [sic] enjoy a special sort of objectivity: such judgements, when true, are so independently of what any human being, anywhere, in any circumstance whatever, thinks of them" (p. 2). To elaborate on an earlier point, a naturalist attitude stems from the belief that all is emitted from the natural sciences, so nothing at all is mysterious. Nonnaturalism—Shafer-Landau's position and mine—holds that science and ethics are different, with unique origins and applications. There are such things as moral reasons and obligations—practical reasons—insofar as belief that an *action* is wrong or good is sufficient reason either to refrain from it or engage in it. This is at the heart of the realism of ethical *action*.

Librarianship: Critical Approaches

As is the case throughout this book, the discussion of critical approaches to libraries and librarianship is selective. Various types and instances of critique are presented here.

It is appropriate that this section begin with the words and thoughts of Patrick Wilson, whose works were both erudite and informative. Howard White (2019) describes Wilson's work: "He used philosophical reflection and thought experiments rather than empirical techniques to arrive at . . . descriptions, but in so doing he drew extensively on empirical research by others" (p. 279). White (2019) adds a remark that aptly summarizes attention to Wilson: "For his breadth of vision alone, Wilson is inexhaustibly re-readable" (p. 303). I will admit that a purpose for recalling Wilson's work is the introduction of his thought to a new generation. White (2019) offers a lengthy examination of Wilson's contributions (which are substantial) to the field of knowledge organization (which is primarily expressed in Wilson's [1968] book *Two Kinds of Power*). Because of this, the concentration here will be on other of Wilson's writings.

Wilson (1977) begins his book *Public Knowledge, Private Ignorance* by saying, "Scholarly and scientific inquiry is a public enterprise, with a public goal, that of adding to or improving the public stock of knowledge" (p. 3). He adds, though, that only a small amount of what is published makes its way into public knowledge; while there is an enormous amount of documentation produced, only a smattering can be incorporated into formal and informal knowledge. This is only one aspect of a large problem related to knowledge growth. There is also the assimilation of what *is* read and (one hopes) evaluated. "Acquisition of knowledge is more than simply the acquisition of understanding of a new statement or story, and the tests for knowledge must be more extensive than the tests for understanding. But the crucial point is that the former include the latter" (Wilson, 1977, p. 8). The demonstration of possessing knowledge is grounded in the ability to express the ideas in words and actions. That is at the heart both of the general, or formal, possession of knowledge and of the individual possession of knowledge. Examinations in schools, when they succeed, demand that respondents be able to state, for example, scientific laws but to explain what they mean and to relate applications of the laws. To the extent that this occurs, public knowledge does grow. Wilson does note that the knowledge base does change over time, as new discoveries and new interpretations are made; therefore, public knowledge is not static.

Public knowledge is most often possessed by the members of specialized, expert, learned groups, most of whom are active in adding to new discoveries and interpretations. This is not to say that the layperson does not and cannot share in the possession of such knowledge, but the layperson usually does not have the time and wherewithal to *be* a scholar or scientist. Wilson anticipated some people's ideas by stating, "The loss of fidelity that summaries of knowledge undergo with the passage of time can be avoided if, instead of publishing one's summary as a document, one maintains it as a file and works continuously to revise it" (p. 28). The radical nature of this suggestion is evident when one considers that state of the academic rewards structure whereby an individual progress to tenure and through the academic ranks by demonstrating *more*—more publications, more conference presentations, more external support for research. As most readers are aware, this suggestion has not been followed. The presumption is that scientists' and scholars' progress is marked by subsequent publications. The difficulty, as Wilson avers, is that each document is a static representation that lasts forever, even if new discoveries are made. This predicament puts a great deal of pressure on the bibliographic record; one must be knowledgeable in order to search the record and to make the most effective use of it. Those who can make use of that record can then, as Wilson (1977) puts it, use it "as a basis for the pursuit of more knowledge" (p. 34).

Beyond the bibliographic record, as Wilson (1977) notes, are personal bodies of knowledge, and these are resources that are used extensively:

> There is nothing surprising in the fact that people figure so largely as sources of information and advice in almost everyone's information gathering system. If one's sources were chosen on purely technical grounds, personal sources would often be preferred, for people have advantages as information sources that impersonal sources lack. . . . They are supple and adaptive sources of information, as documentary sources are not. Anything a personal informant or adviser might tell us could be part of a documentary record, but documents do not organize themselves and rewrite themselves on demand to fit new questions. (pp. 39–40)

Even in the cases of scholars and scientists, a major resource is the knowledge base of someone else. People turn to others to come to know more and to understand what is known. The reasons (to reduce things to only two) are twofold: other people have knowledge that each of us do not have (and so we can come to know more through the interactions with others), and no one has the time and inclination to spend all of one's time searching the documentary record. The latter element is a major limitation to information gathering that can then be used to enhance one's knowledge and understanding. Wilson again anticipates what we now know as a problem—if one cannot pursue the entirety of the documentary record, one may be selective in gathering information. That limitation can lead to difficulties that will be discussed in chapter 3.

Wilson concludes his investigation with a look at libraries, and it is a critical look. He (1977) writes, "To a great extent, communal libraries [those serving a specific community] . . . serve simply as places in which to consult, or from which to borrow, copies of documents with which one is already acquainted" (p. 85). One may disagree with Wilson on this point; individuals seek to affirm those things with which they have an awareness. Some may examine knowledge that is new to them and use the record to explore the knowledge base. What assistance is provided, according to Wilson (1977), can be categorized as "bibliographical assistance, question answering, and selection assistance" (p. 100). Wilson (1977) concludes with a recommendation that is based upon his definition of public knowledge and the relief to private ignorance: "That the stock of public knowledge is, and should be treated as, a common possession, the use and benefits of which should be available not to a restricted few but to mankind generally, is a plausible axiom for information policy. Knowledge should be available to all, and the more needed, the more readily available" (p. 121).

In his last book (*Second-Hand Knowledge*), Wilson (1983) says that there are metaphors and ways of look at personal knowledge to which we should be alerted. For example, he (1983) writes, "Seeing stands for understanding and for learning in general: the way things look to me, from my point of view, from where I stand, is the way I understand things to be" (p. 3). He quickly adds, "We have to beware thinking that all the different partial perspectives provided by different conceptual approaches to the world can somehow be coordinated and merged to arrive at a single, consistent, total view of the world. . . . Experience teaches, but not much" (pp. 7, 9). His major concern in this book is the determination of cognitive authority. Toward this end, Wilson (1983) speaks of a major limitation to firsthand knowledge: "Most important is the basic rule that we can experience of the social world depends on our social location: our location in time and space and in the network of social relationships" (p. 5). In other words, where we stand affects what we see, whereas "the phrase *second hand* is especially appropriate in suggesting second best, not so good as first hand; for in an obvious way, finding out by being told differs from finding out by seeing or hearing or living through an experience" (Wilson, 1983, p. 10; emphasis in original).

In elaborating on cognitive authority, Wilson (1983) expounds, "Cognitive authority is influence on one's thoughts that one would consciously recognize as proper. . . . [It] is clearly related to credibility. The authority's influence on us is thought proper because he is thought credible, worthy of belief. The notion of credibility has two main components: competence and trustworthiness" (p. 15). Although he does not mention Wilson, Alvin Goldman (2002) tacitly draws from Wilson's position: the problem entails

> how laypersons should evaluate the testimony of experts and decide which of two or more rival experts is most credible. It is of practical importance because in a complex, highly specialized world people are constantly confronted with situations in which, as comparative novices . . . , they must turn to putative experts for intellectual guidance or assistance. It is of theoretical interest because the appropriate epistemic considerations are far from transparent; and it is not clear how far the problems lead to insurmountable skeptical quandaries. (p. 139)

It is clear that Wilson's work had some influence on Goldman (and others), and the very idea of cognitive authority is an enduring one.

Wilson (1983) summarizes by examining information retrieval and librarianship in light of cognitive authority and sees some problematic areas. For one thing, in the documentary record, older items are rendered obsolete when newer work makes corrections and updates. This notion essentially includes the belief (that I hold as well) that knowledge (in general) is fallible and corrigible: it can be incorrect, but it can be corrected. In practical terms, Wilson (1983) observes, "The obvious basis for recognizing the cognitive authority of a text is the cognitive authority of its author" (p. 166), when someone has established a tradition or record of producing knowledge and of being worth attending to. Even this carries difficulties. An individual may be biased in favor of certain speakers/writers and against others. This is a matter that will be discussed in later chapters.

When it comes to the structures of institutions, there are some challenges, according to Wilson (1983). For example, "The question of cognitive authority can be rephrased as one of quality control: can those professionally responsible for information storage and retrieval act as quality controllers?" (p. 171). What, then, are the abilities of those in the institutions, and how much reliance can be placed on them? Wilson (1983) concludes with skepticism regarding librarians' abilities to act as, as he puts it, authorities on authorities. He (1983) states, "It looks as if the librarian has no claim to be taken as an authority on authorities after all" (p. 182). Not long after Wilson (1983) published his book Peter Hernon and Charles McClure (1986) conducted an extensive unobtrusive study wherein librarians were asked fact-based questions (answers to which, at times, were best answered by referring questioners to other departments in the libraries). They (1986) found that "personnel from the 26 libraries correctly answered 241 (61.8 percent) of the questions" (p. 38). While this work is not irrefutable evidence that Wilson is correct, it should be taken into consideration. Several decades have passed since all of these writings; it is an open question whether librarians can function as authorities on authorities . . . or even if they should. As White noted, Wilson still needs to be read closely and seriously.

I will exercise authorial discretion here and will present a particular strain of critique that I have written about. Nearly three decades ago I (1995) wrote a piece that offered a discussion of a problem that has plagued librarianship (and information science) for many years: "Possibly by accident but more likely by subtle or overt intention, there is an epistemology that governs thought and work in library and information science, whether it is realized or accepted. The governing epistemology is that which we commonly call positivism, and its ascendance has resulted in both a philosophical stance and a mode of behavior" (p. 295). By way of example, Herbert Goldhor (1972) is quoted as articulating such an epistemological stance: "A scientific law is the statement of a universal, invariant relationship between two or more variables. . . . The formulation of such laws is the goal of research" (pp. 9–10). Others are quoted as saying some things that are quite similar. I present evidence that conflicts with such ideas, and refer to John Searle (1984) as basking this notion: "The radical discontinuity between the social sciences and the natural sciences doesn't come from the fact that there is only a disjunctive connection of social and physical phenomena"; rather, it "derives from the intrinsically mental character of social and psychological phenomena" (p. 84). The distinction cannot be overstated; social phenomena are not limited to a relatively small set of discreet "variables"; they are extremely complex and frequently strike at the identities of individuals and groups (see the earlier discussion on the nature of bias in classification of information).

To counter the positivistic epistemology (which is still extant), I (1995) offer an alternative:

> It is proposed here that hermeneutical phenomenology supplant positivism as . . . a foundation. I hasten to note that this foundation is not a method or set of methods (in fact, the concept of "method" is a deceptively problematic one), nor is it a set of problems to be addressed. Rather, it is a description of a mental state and the public expression of that state. It is a stance, a position—one that

opens the inquirer to possibilities instead of barricading avenues. It is also a vocabulary, a means of expression, a way of describing and explaining. (p. 304)

The first element of the proposal is hermeneutics, which Richard Palmer (1969) describes as a means of determining what moves from manifest content to meaning to what he calls "latent or hidden meaning"; it is a system of discovering significance hovering beneath the manifest content (pp. 43–44). In brief, "Phenomenology is the study of human experience and of the ways things present themselves to us in and through such experience" (Sokolowski, 2000, p. 2). While this is a succinct definition, it must be acknowledged that each of us experiences things both on our own (a sort of psychological solitude) and as a group (however small or large). Therefore, experience is personal (the *I* has the experience) *and* it is shared in a way that helps create understanding, albeit an incomplete understanding (in somewhat technical terms, each of us shares experience with *thou*, with the other).

More needs to be said about phenomenology because the proposition here is that it can provide a serious contribution to epistemology in LIS. We can turn to the concise definition provide by Jean-François Lyotard (1991):

> The term signifies a study of "phenomena," that is to say, of that which appears to consciousness, that which is "given." It needs to explore the given—"the thing itself" which one perceives, of what one thinks and speaks—without constructing hypotheses concerning either the relationship which binds this phenomena to the being of which it is phenomena, or the relationship which unites it with the I for which it is the phenomena. (pp. 32–33)

Inherent in Lyotard's words, and as has been stated by many, we must remember that consciousness is consciousness *of* something; consciousness is directed; it has a purpose. The notion is relation to the "given," to the world that is apparent to our perception. We perceive the world as it is and then reach an understanding of our perception. As Edmund Husserl (1962) adds, "We must . . . be clear . . . that there is no question here of a relation between a psychological event—called experience (Erlebnis)—and some other real existent (Dasein)—called Object—or of a psychological connexion [sic] obtaining between the one and the other in objective reality" (p. 108; § 36).

While much more can (and possibly should) be said about phenomenology, a bit more explication is useful here. For example, Maurice Merleau-Ponty (1962) states, "The phenomenological world is not pure being, but the sense which is revealed where the paths of my various experiences intersect, and also where my own and other people's intersect and engage each other like gears" (p. xx). Husserl (1970), in the last work published in his lifetime, emphasizes that phenomenology is an antipositivist approach; it opens up experience and perception to being itself, with the reduction to a limited set of "facts" or variables. M. M. Bakhtin (1986) expands on the applicability of phenomenology: "A human act is a potential text and can be understood (as a human act and not a physical action) only in the dialogic context of its time (as a rejoinder, as a semantic position, as a system of motives)" (p. 107). To sum up this brief discussion, we can turn to the profound words of Paul Ricoeur (1992), what is important focus on "'ethical intention' as *aiming at the 'good life' with and for others, in just institutions*" (p. 172; emphasis in original). We must remember that libraries should function as "just institutions" and should adhere to all that Ricoeur says.

Another critical approach to the profession is expressed by Ronald Day. Day's complete works are broad in scope; this section will focus on two of his writings that address the subject in today's electronically mediated communication. He (2011) writes in one journal article, "I would like to argue for the importance of viewing subjects and meaningful objects as *co-determined* by social, cultural, and physical affordances and *co-emergent* out of those relationships through expressive powers mediated by mutual efforts" (p. 78; emphasis in original). Day's work can be labeled (what I call) conceptual; that is, it definitely has practical ramifications, but the presentation is couched in more abstract terms. So the meaning for praxis must be sussed out by close reading of his work. This is by no means a criticism because many of my own writings contain similar characteristics. One thing that can be said about Day's work on subjects and objects of communication is that it is antipositivist. He says that mechanistic approaches to causes and effects are not effective analytical tools and do not begin to capture the complex intellective, social, political, economic, and other features of the communicative action.

He uses some examples in his article that illustrate his opposition to positivist thought and suggestion. For one thing, he finds Warren Weaver's communication model to be deterministic and incapable of absorbing subtlety into the process. One the other hand, Day (2011) sees much merit in David Blair's (2006) appropriation of Wittgenstein, especially the employment of language tools and tokens as a model for information exchange (p. 80). In this piece Day emphasizes the role of affordances, or formal causes (principally for action), in particular ways. Because he uses the concept and praxis of affordances in many of his writings, a fairly lengthy quotation (2011) seems to be appropriate:

> There are three advantages to describing causation formally. First, there is much less temptation than with mechanistic causation to attempt to follow

a causal chain back to an illusory initial cause (today, as in much of modern science, the temptation is to reduce social and cultural causes to a physical cause). Along with this is the ability in working with formal causes to describe single actions in terms of non-chained multiple causes of the three types of affordances (e.g., meaningful speech as co-determined by mouth movements, cultural forms of spoken language, and social norms). Last, causes are described as that which allows or "affords" *affects*, rather than a force that necessarily determines *effects*. (p. 81; emphasis in original)

The last advantage may be the most important; it is necessary for a formal cause related to human communication to embrace the personal, the emotive, as well as the cultural, political (as well as technical), and other factors. While he doesn't mention Wittgenstein in this passage, Wittgenstein's thought is apparent throughout.

Day (2011) draws from the French psychoanalyst Jacques Lacan to assist with the examination of one very heavily cited idea, Nicholas Belkin's hypothesis of Anomalous States of Knowledge (ASK). As Day (2011) states, "Unlike need in Belkin's ASK model, need in Lacan's work does not belong to a subject's cognitive state, but rather, it belongs to the condition of the subject in a symbolic order" (p. 82). This notion is vital to Day's program. While the "cognitive turn" (which, it should be mentioned, has enjoyed substantial popularity) carries deterministic assumptions, limited as it is to a *particular* idea of cognition and cognitive action, there is much more that goes into the actions of people when it comes to such things as seeking information (a term that Day recognizes as fraught). Day (2011) does not mention phenomenology in this piece, but the gist of the idea is present nonetheless. For instance, he (2011) says, "The object is not just a 'mere thing,' but it is something through which the subject 'becomes'—i.e., it is meaningful for the subject" (p. 84). Ultimately, the upshot is that the idea of the "user," the seeker and employer of information, is flawed in some important ways. What Day (2011) offers is something of a corrective to that problematic idea.

Day (2014) expands upon the aforementioned ideas and expands the scope of his intellectual program in a recent book. He provides a bit of a summary by saying, "As we will examine . . . , historically and epistemically we are moving from the classificatory and naming functions of documentary structures to the assignment of personal and documentary identity as a *function* and a *product* of sociotechnical systems" (p. 35; emphasis in original). This plan expands upon his article and also introduces much more (too much to address here; suffice it to say that this book is highly recommended to everyone who seeks a broader and deeper understanding of documentation and the evolution from the early days of documentation to the socially, culturally, politically, and economically richer state of information today). It is necessary here to introduce a lengthy passage from Day's (2014) book:

> Humans develop experientially, and this gives them a broad range for learning and adaptation that no machine has yet been able to duplicate as a designed agent. Accordingly, even though post-coordinate, as compared to pre-coordinate, indexing may be seen as an approach that gives the user more freedom for finding the information that he or she wants, it is the transformation of the person into a user (and moreover as a specific type of user, through the selection and narrowing of information choices, often within tasks) that has always been the tool of librarians, ontologists, and search engine designers for raising relevancy scores for searches. This is true whether one is discussing library collection development, classification and cataloging, reader advisory services . . . , special collections, recommending systems, Boolean searching, and even link-analysis search engines, such as Google's PageRank. The notion of the user may differ in scale between all these, but the transformation of persons into users is an essential part of modern information systems. (p. 46)

Day (2014) emphasizes the transformative in the evolution of information systems, again denying mechanistic notions and stressing that there are multiple facets that add complexity to what it means to be a user (subject) and what it means to seek information for specific purposes (that can themselves be transformed). He (2014) writes that "it isn't just 'science' that modern documentary techniques and technologies and documentalists serve and lead, but rather, ideology and political economy, as these are embedded in both professional and everyday use" (p. 63). The insinuation of ideology leads Day into his drawing from Hegel's dialectical methods. He incorporates the idea and method to examine the emergence both of subjects and of objects over time and through newly applied technical developments. Day is no technological determinist, but he is quick to recognize that technology "emerges" *along with* the subject. He mentions that there are sociocultural *and* technical logics that influence to codevelopment of technologies and humans as users of information. One conclusion he (2014) draws from the multifaceted development and transformation of people and systems is, "In neoliberalism, one must create a market out of one's self. This requires self-positioning, which necessitates seeing one's self from the marketplace eyes of others, as a person within a market of competing goods (and persons being marketplace goods as well)" (p. 87). Neoliberalism, as an idea and as an influential way of being, will arise again in chapter 3.

One of the rather enduring programs of thought and action over the most recent years is that of social justice. There is a work that collects many approaches to social justice, and this work can provide evidence of the thought and action. Nicole Cooke and Miriam Sweeney (2017) edited the papers that address specific issues related to social justice. The first essay in the collection, by Kevin Rioux (2017), begins by stating, "Marginalization, discrimination, lack of economic opportunity, and unequal access to information resources are all among the fairness issues that continue to affect communities served by libraries and other information organizations" (p. 19). The list he offers is not exhaustive; issues of social justice can also include race and gender in particular. One of Rioux's contributions to an understanding of social justice is a figure that illustrates terms that are frequently associated with the core idea: critical/progressive lens, human rights, inclusion and diversity, ethics, community engagement and development, and policy and standards (pp. 34–35). Those concepts should not be forgotten and should be kept in mind as one contemplates how to achieve social justice through library and information agencies. As a means of realizing the goals through LIS curricula, Rioux (2017) asserts some specific assumptions:

> Assumption 1: All humans have an inherent worth and deserve information services that help address their needs. . . .
>
> Assumption 2: People perceive reality and information in different ways, and in different contexts. This needs to be acknowledged. . . .
>
> Assumption 3: There are many different types of information and knowledge, and these are societal resources. . . .
>
> Assumption 4: LIS theory, practice, research, and professional preparation are pursued with the ultimate goal of bringing positive change to service constituencies. . . .
>
> Assumption 5: The provision of information is an inherently powerful activity. Distributing information is, in itself, a political act. (pp. 39–41)

The assumptions provide a beginning for consideration of thinking and acting related to social justice.

Julie Ann Winkelstein (2017) uses her essay to articulate particular action aimed at library educators and librarians engaged in social justice. She (2017) says, "Libraries are intended to be regarded as safe and information rich spaces, yet the people who have the fewest alternatives for meeting their safety and information needs often do not experience public libraries as secure and may not even find access to the information they are seeking.

It is the responsibility of librarians to correct these systemic inequalities" (p. 139). The implied openness of, perhaps especially, public libraries is contingent upon the environment in which people live, the limitations of people's lives, and the wherewithal of people's experiences. Winkelstein (2017) further writes, "Feedback from students and other *communities* about how libraries are perceived can inform future librarians of what their public does not know about them" (p. 141; emphasis added). What community members are *not* aware of is related to the aforementioned implied openness. And, as Winkelstein emphasizes throughout the essay, the lack of awareness and the existing perceptions act as constraints on librarians' abilities to meet people's complete needs. She (2017) concludes that there are essential questions that need to be asked; these questions exist at the individual level (for example, "What social and economic barriers impact a library patron's ability to receive needed library services?" [p. 146]) and at the institutional level (for example, "How do we define and live out the core library values of intellectual freedom, diversity, and the public good?" [p. 147]).

In 2017 another collection of essays on "critical librarianship" was published with the objective of "increasing interest to practitioners" by pointing out that "critical librarianship seeks to bridge the gap between theory and practice in LIS" (Nicholson and Seale, 2017, pp. 1–2). The authors (2017) add, "It uses a reflexive lens to expose and challenge the ways that libraries and the profession 'consciously and unconsciously support systems of expression,' thereby pursuing a socially just, theoretically informed praxis" (p. 2). A substantial portion of the content of the collection explicitly seeks to form connections between theory and practice. There are also pieces that address education, especially the state of iSchools. Other essays look to explore how critical librarianship fits into the community of LIS.

In one essay in the collection Lua Gregory and Shana Higgins (2017) begin with a historical observation: "The proliferation of libraries and the inception of library science as a field of study and as a profession correspond with the rise of corporate capitalism in the United States" (p. 22). The last third of the nineteenth century saw an increase in the power and expanse of capitalism, with advances made in technology, transportation, and other areas, but also some oppression of laborers in these same areas (rail travel is but one example that signaled benefits for some but oppression for others). The authors note that "efficiency" was a governing ideology during this time, both in corporate business and in librarianship: "Parallels may be drawn between the incorporation of American business, the adoption of scientific management (organization, standardization, and management of resources) and the gospel of efficiency in the development of the library profession"

(Gregory and Higgins, 2017, p. 25). Gregory and Higgins (2017) mention Justin Winsor, Melvil Dewey, and Frances B. Hawley as spokespersons for the gospel. The authors present this history so that readers can come to a more complete understanding of the present state of the profession. They (2017) write, "In the transition from the Gilded Age to Progressive Era, 'dialectical interactions' [borrowed from Paolo Freire] regarding labor and exploitation, efficiency, a corporate ideal, and educational tensions between practicality and theoretical concerns, are evident in the historical record of librarianship in the United States" (p. 31). Gregory and Higgins (2017) emphasize that the critical approach has the goal of transforming praxis, in part through resistance to the capitalist past (pp. 34–35).

Where will (should?) awareness of critical librarianship emerge from? Ian Beilin (2017), in another essay in the collection, suggests that the academic world needs to be a deliberate source for future discourse that can generate larger-scale understanding of the critical imperative. In a statement of the challenge and a potential solution, he (2017) says,

> But academia influences both the articulation and reception of critical librarianship in ways other than the purely intellectual. The social facts of the North American (and European) academy cannot be ignored: the dominance of middle-class values (and people of the upper middle class origins), the separation of especially tenure-track and tenured faculty from other workers in the institution through professional status markers, titles, privileges, etc., and the "lifestyle" of academia (traveling to conferences around the country and the world, the availability of research grants and other funds to support research, etc.). In academic librarianship especially, the academy's whiteness and eurocentrism are particular pronounced. (p. 198)

The news may not be quite so dire, but there are desiderata in the academic world, as Beilin (2017) adds: "While examples of library scholarship inspired by critical theory are numerous, it is not mainstream or widespread. In fact, there is both an unfamiliarity with and hesitancy towards theoretical work in LIS in general" (p. 199). Beilin's words strike at the heart of how and where future librarians are introduced to critical approaches to the profession. It is extremely difficult to disagree with his (2017) conclusion: "It is the responsibility of the privileged to work towards those who are excluded and marginalized; to learn, in short, how to build a community for struggle and resistance on the terms of the *oppressed*" (p. 207; emphasis in original).

More could be said about the contents of the collection of essays, but attention will shift now to a couple of articles that are cited in the collection and that enhance the present discussion. Ajit Pyati (2006) advocates for the inclusion of Critical Theory (capitals are used to designate the ways of thinking typified by the Frankfurt School). He (2006) writes, "critical theory is highly relevant to a critique of techno-capitalism and its association with information society ideology. Critical theory's interrogation of techno-capitalism is of growing importance, mainly because of the increased importance of culture, technology, media, information, knowledge, and ideology in more domains of social life" (p. 84). Pyati concentrates on the thinking and writing of Herbert Marcuse and says, "Marcuse's focus, for instance, on 'technical rationality' as a root of domination in *One-Dimensional Man* (1964) is a useful construct for understanding how discourses of information technology are being used to perpetuate modernist notions of information and capitalist logics of consumption" (pp. 84–85). Inherent in what Pyati says is that the critique of Critical Theory includes the commodification of some things that were not previously commodified, information to be included here. What is needed is an examination of assumptions that underlie the present state of capitalist information—including production, retrieval, and use. A question that resides in Pyati's work is the nature of the ideology underlying the "information age" or "information society." He (2006) concludes, "The form of this critical theory–informed technological activism is yet to be determined in the context of libraries; however, this type of activism would reflect a shift in orientation that envisions libraries as active agents in shaping technology for radical democratic ends and contesting ideologies of commoditization, privatization, and technological determinism" (p. 87).

Another cited work is that by Annie Downey (2016), which concentrates on information literacy (IL). Early on, she (2016) echoes a critical information tenet: "Critical information is not just the message itself, but also the context in which it is transmitted and understood" (p. 2). This tenet has special importance for information literacy because IL addresses the challenges facing novice information seekers and users. It is important to avoid reifying information as an end in itself; what informs people is situated and is sought by individuals with agency. Downey (2016) emphasizes that, "as educators in their own right, librarians should not pretend to be neutral and that they should also not hold to the false notion that libraries are neutral" (p. 161). The underlying thought is that libraries exist to provide accurate and honestly arrived at works; in a period of concern for post-truth, the thought is both valid and essential. This is not to say that libraries do not contain dissent, but critical IL is intended to give students the wherewithal to engage in the discourse that comprises information. Downey (2016) concludes with a quotation from Accardi, Drabinski, and Kumbier (2010): critical IL is "a library instruction praxis that promotes critical engagement with information sources, considers students collaborators in knowledge production practices (and creators in their own right), recognizes the affective dimensions of research, and (in some cases) has liberatory aims" (p. xiii). The authors, plus Downey, envision an evolution of IL in which the students are genuine participants.

Other contributions come close to the thesis of this book. For example, a collection of essays addresses the notion of the library as place. Gloria Leckie and John Buschman (2007) speak of libraries and the spaces they represent in the lives of people:

> We know that [libraries] acquire and house an ever-changing array of cultural resources for public use. We also know libraries are a type of social and cultural institution, fitting within a larger context of other institutions, agencies, and corporate interests, such as schools, governments, public services, businesses, and other socially created entities. Accordingly, a wide variety of people (both users and staff) visit libraries, bringing their individual values, beliefs, expectations, assumptions, daily practices, and cultural awareness. (p. 3)

These items describe what we may already know, but what do they mean for librarians and for communities? The realization raises questions about the public's apperception of libraries, the tangible elements of use of libraries, and the reasons why people are drawn to the institutions. Leckie and Buschman (2007) suggest that there are characteristics that typify "primary places." First, in popular parlance at this time, spaces such as libraries (and other places) are referred to as "third spaces," to be distinguished from home and work. Third spaces may still be primary (rather than secondary or tertiary) if one follows the authors (2007): "Primary places are affected by three realms, or forces, including nature, social relations, and meaning. When these three realms are combined in particular ways, 'place' thus becomes a force in itself, altering the flow of interactions (whether of people, institutions, or cultural processes) within it" (p. 10). If one accepts their extension, it is possible to view libraries as primary places.

Leckie and Buschman do not stop with that explication of libraries as vital spaces. They quote Stephen Carr and colleagues (1992) and their description of public space:

> Public space is the stage upon which the drama of communal life unfolds. The streets, squares and parks of a city give form to the ebb and flow of human exchange. These dynamic spaces are an essential counterpart of the more settled places and routines of work and home life, providing the channels for movement, the nodes of communication and the common grounds for play

and relaxation. There are pressing needs that the public space can help people to satisfy, significant human rights that it can be shaped to define and protect and special cultural meanings that it can best convey. (p. 3)

The key to the description may be the idea of libraries being a counterpart to home and work (third space). Thus, libraries enable different and necessary activities, including communicative activities. This counterpart is, according to the authors (and accepted by Leckie and Buschman), vital to life in this world. In short, the third space is needed. Leckie and Buschman (2007) set the tone for the essays included in the collection.

Only one additional essay will be discussed here; Paulette Rothbauer (2007) writes about the community of lesbian, gay, bisexual, and queer (LGBQ) patrons. She opens by saying, "Library uses can also be analyzed within a framework of spatial practices informed by ideas from recent geographies of sexuality, identity, and place" (p. 101). Rothbauer cites Gill Valentine (2001), who says, "Space was conceptualized as an objective physical surface with specific fixed characteristics upon which social identities and categories were mapped out. Space was, in effect, understood as the container of social relations and events. Likewise, social identities and categories were also taken for granted as 'fixed' and mutually exclusive" (p. 3). In short, the community is a dynamic one, and considerations of things like space are emergent issues. By emergent I mean that communities, such as LGBQ patrons, not only have needs and desires that are *different* from what has been established but have needs and desires that are themselves evolving. The importance of space is explicitly recognized and stated by Rothbauer (2007): "Space is understood to play an active role in the constitution and reproduction of social identities; and social identities, meanings and relations are recognized and producing materials and symbolic or metaphorical spaces" (pp. 101–2). An essential component of the material and symbolic space is safety for an oppressed group. This realization refers both to the physical space of the library *and* the symbolic space. Included here are the informational materials that the community needs and wants. Libraries, when effectively serving the community, have a variety, and an amount, of materials of interest to LGBQ patrons.

Related to the last stated point, Rothbauer (2007) offers, "It is precisely through the traditional mode of service to LGBQ patrons—namely through access to texts—that libraries can contribute to the creation of queer spaces" (p. 111). This moves beyond safety to access; collection development should acknowledge the legitimacy of the community's needs and should respond by meeting those needs. One way to accomplish this is actually a means that is employed by librarians as a matter of course—seek advice from members of the community to assist in identifying and meeting needs. In terms of the level of success in meeting the community's needs, Rothbauer writes,

> The readers in my study found the LGBTQ collections to which they had access to be inadequate, and yet such texts supported the creation of social and ideological spaces that allowed that to claim spaces within their communities—communities within which libraries are situated as members by virtue of their provision of textual representations of lesbian, queer, bisexual, gay, and trans experience. This spatial frame privileges the meaning of the library in the lives of its users, rather than assigning meaning based solely on the limitations of its collections. (p. 112)

Michael Harris (1986) offers a (self-avowedly) Marxist-leaning diagnosis of the state of library services in the United States and, perhaps more importantly, a proposed theory to address library services. He (1986) critiques contemporary research into library science, saying that the governing "pluralist" perspective "has rendered many troubling questions in librarianship 'unproblematic' and offering an alternative 'paradigm candidate'" will be the gist of his contribution (p. 217). To get right to his (1986) point, he sets forth a proposal for new theoretical modeling:

Propositions

1. Libraries are essentially collections of books (and periodicals).
2. Libraries will become something other than collections of books when, and only when, the creators and producers decide to package high culture in some form different from the printed book.
3. Any attempt to redefine the mission of the library to emphasize mass taste cultures will be vigorously resisted by high culture creating and producing institutions.
4. Any attempt to reduce library consumption of the symbolic products of the high culture producing institutions through cooperation, or use of non-print formats, will be vigorously resisted.
5. High culture creators and producers expect libraries to consume their symbolic product without consideration of whether that symbolic product will ever be used.
6. High culture creators and producers consider librarians to be incapable of creating, producing, or legitimating high culture, and any attempt on the part of librarians to participate in the creation and production of culture will be vigorously resisted.

7. High culture creators and producers are opposed to censorship, but uniformly agree that library collections can be built in a uniform and neutral manner by simply attending to the clearly demarcated body of printed works endorsed by the creators and producers of high culture.
8. The power to define the canon—the Book—is symmetrically distributed among those who create and produce high culture.
9. Librarians are directly linked to, and dependent upon, the creators and producers of high culture. (pp. 242–43)

There are several other points to his proposal, but the aforementioned address some of the major points of his theoretical proposal. Harris (1986) admits that he constructs his theory on a broad reading of social science research. His propositions should be taken seriously but, in light of what has been presented earlier, there are some serious questions relating to what *is* and what *has been*; his suggestion relates more to what he sees *will be*.

Harris and colleagues (Stan Hannah and Pamela Harris) (1998) elaborate on what they see as the political state in which libraries exist: "We need to note that it appears that the state's role is to reproduce capitalism, and in the United States this has meant that the state must simultaneously play two contradictory roles, that of accumulation and that of legitimation" (pp. 55–56). They further state, "What is needed is a vision that will transcend the fatalistic pessimism and wistful optimism so prevalent in our thinking on the role of the library in the information society" (p. 71). Without necessarily agreeing with the first of their statements, the latter forms a guide for what is to come in future chapters.

I would be remiss if I did not mention at least some of the thought of John Buschman. Perhaps his best-known work is his book *Dismantling the Public Sphere* (2003). It is a rich critique of the state in which libraries operate . . . too rich to summarize adequately here (readers should turn to the book for his complete and complex argument). It must be noted that his thesis and the gist of the one presented in this work are sympatico in many ways. He (2003) writes, for example, "our field has been called upon to play a 'crucial' role in bringing the information society and the 'new' economy about, but without the public funding support for that expanded (and essentially economic) mission" (p. 169). He (2003) is particularly critical of the "new public philosophy": "The new public philosophy trends and practices in librarianship represent not merely another variation on the corruption of the communicative processes that make the democratic sphere but also its *dismantling* in the ways it has been enacted and embodied in our field" (p. 170; emphasis in original). Buschman (2005) invokes political philosopher Sheldon Wolin

(1981) in his critique, saying that in the new public philosophy, "economics now dominates public discourse. [It] becomes the paradigm of what public reason should be [and] prescribes the form that 'problems' have to be given before they can be acted upon" (p. 23). Buschman (2005) elaborates on what a move to the new public philosophy means: "This new public philosophy has a logic all its own, and it has redefined the circumstances under which libraries . . . operate. Under a still-developing public philosophy that puts economic purposes ahead of the common good, public (that is, tax) monies available to public, cultural institutions has substantially dried up" (p. 5). In more recent years there have been some successes when it comes to tax referenda, but the underfunding predicament certainly has not disappeared.

Buschman draws heavily from the philosophy of Jürgen Habermas, more about whom will be said in chapter 2. The public sphere has been problematized in many ways, not the least of which is economically. That is a trend that cries for response and refutation. A genuine and open sphere is called for. Perhaps Buschman's (2003) most pertinent (to my purposes) statement is, "Our basic professional credo is to include the excluded from the discourses organized in our resources. And . . . , the existence of those resources, preserved and organized over time (as libraries do), tends to connect separate discourses and allow for a cross checking of validity claims both currently and in the future" (p. 178). Perhaps almost as important is his (2003) conclusion that, "if Karl Marx told us that economic power was an important factor in our understanding of society, Max Weber told us that ideas are as well. Our ideas—of becoming professional knowledge managers and information entrepreneurs—should not be so limited, so economically driven. Such visions pale in comparison to the deeper, more sustainable and democratic purposes of librarianship" (p. 181).

Concluding Words

A few thoughts can conclude this chapter. There are some people who believe that libraries are either moribund or that they have to revise their purposes radically in order to survive. Such thinking ignores the reality that libraries of all types have been evolving rapidly in the "information age." Libraries provide one thing that many people do want—reading matter (of the useful or the recreational varieties). Libraries of all types provide access to a world of information in the forms of data and "texts." Libraries provide professional expertise that, for example, bookstores cannot and do not provide. These services include advice for readers as well as assistance with the most technical and esoteric information. Libraries offer programming for all members of their communities, from reading clubs for children to discussion forums for community members. In short, libraries are part and parcel of their communities and are *of* their communities. As I (2017) have written, "The rhetoric on the death of libraries is empty and easily refutable. What is most needed for the future of the profession is a rejection of corporatization [and the same goes for education]. . . . And critical thought about the directions of services and access—with openness to communities at the fore" (p. 170). There is, without question, a political dimension to the present and future of libraries, and this realization prompts discussion of politics generally here. Serious thought and writing about conservatism and liberalism form the content of the next two chapters.

References

Accardi, M. T., Drabinski, E., and Kumbier, A. (Eds.). (2010). *Critical library instruction: Theories and methods.* Duluth, MN: Library Juice Press.

ACONDA Final Report. (1970). Subcommittee on social responsibilities report, p. 1.

American Library Association. (1925). *Second annual report of the Board of Education for Librarianship.* Chicago: ALA.

Asheim, L. (1953). Not censorship but selection. *Wilson Library Bulletin* 28(9), 63–67.

Bakhtin, M. M. (1986). *Speech genres and other late essays.* V. W. McGee (Trans.). Austin: University of Texas Press.

Beilin, I. (2017). Critical librarianship as an academic pursuit. In K. P. Nicholson and M. Seale (Eds.), *The politics of theory and the practice of critical librarianship* (pp. 195–210). Sacramento, CA: Library Juice Press.

Berman, Sanford. (1993 [1971]). *Prejudices and antipathies: A tract on the LC subject heads concerning people.* Jefferson, NC: McFarland and Company.

Berninghausen, D. K. (1953). The history of the ALA Intellectual Freedom Committee. *Wilson Library Bulletin* 27(10), 813–17.

Billey, A., Drabinski, E., and Roberto, K. R. (2014). What's gender got to do with it? A critique of RDA 9.7. *Cataloging & Classification Quarterly* 52(4), 412–21.

Blair, D. C. (2006). *Wittgenstein, language and information: "Back to the rough ground."* Berlin: Springer.

Bobinski, G. S. (1969). *Carnegie libraries: Their history and impact on American public library development.* Chicago: ALA.

Buckland, M. (2017). *Information and society.* Cambridge, MA: MIT Press.

Buckland, M. K. (1988). *Library services in theory and context.* Second edition. Oxford: Pergamon Press.

Budd, J. M. (2001). Instances of ideology in discursive practice: Implications for library and information science. *Library Quarterly* 71(4), 498–517.

Budd, J. M. (2006). Toward a practical and normative ethics for librarianship. *Library Quarterly* 76(3), 251–69.
Budd, J. M. (2011). Meaning, truth, and information: Prolegomena to a theory. *Journal of Documentation* 67(1), 56–74.
Budd, J. M. (2017). *Six issues facing libraries today: Critical perspectives*. Lanham, MD: Rowman & Littlefield.
Budd, J. M. (2018). *The changing academic library: Operations, culture, environments*. Chicago: ACRL.
Bukoff, R. N. (1995). Censorship and the American college library. *College & Research Libraries* 56(5), 395–407.
Burgess, J. T. F. (2019). Principles and concepts in information ethics. In J. T. F. Burgess and E. J. M. Knox (Eds.), *Foundations of information ethics* (pp. 1–16). Chicago: ALA.
Buschman, J. (2005). Libraries and the decline of public purposes. *Public Library Quarterly* 24(1), 1–12.
Buschman, J. E. (2003). *Dismantling the public sphere: Situating and sustaining librarianship in the age of the new public philosophy*. Westport, CT: Libraries Unlimited.
Butler, P. (1961 [1933]). *An introduction to library science*. Chicago: University of Chicago Press.
Carr, S., Francis, M., Rivlin, L., and Stone, A. (1992). *Public space*. Cambridge: Cambridge University Press.
Cassell, K. A. (1987). The women's rights struggle in librarianship: The task force on women. In M. L. Bundy and F. J. Stielow (Eds.), *Activism in American librarianship, 1962–1973* (pp. 21–29). New York: Greenwood Press.
Chaplin, J. (1872). *Life of Henry Dunster*. Boston: Osgood.
Cooke, N. A., and Sweeney, M. E. (Eds.). (2017). *Teaching for justice: Implementing social justice in the LIS classroom*. Sacramento, CA: Library Juice Press.
Dancy, J. (1993). *Moral reasons*. Oxford: Blackwell.
Darnton, R. (2014). *Censors at work: How states shaped literature*. New York: W. W. Norton.
Day, R. E. (2011). Death of the user: Reconceptualizing subjects, objects, and their relation. *Journal of the American Society for Information Science and Technology* 62(1), 78–88.
Day, R. E. (2014). *Indexing it all: The [subject] in the age of documentation, information, and data*. Cambridge, MA: MIT Press.
DeLapp, K. (2013). *Moral realism*. London: Bloomsbury.
Dexter, F. B. (1918). *Selections from the miscellaneous historical papers of fifty years*. New Haven: Tuttle, Morehouse and Taylor.
Ditzion, S. (1947). *Arsenals of a democratic culture: A social history of the American public library movement in New England and the middle states from 1850 to 1900*. Chicago: ALA.
Downey, A. (2016). *Critical information literacy: Foundations, inspiration, and ideas*. Sacramento, CA: Library Juice Press.

Drabinski, E. (2013). Queering the catalog: Queer theory and the politics of correction. *Library Quarterly: Information, Community, Policy* 83(2), 94–111.

Dresang, E. T. (2006). Intellectual freedom and libraries: Complexity and change in the twenty-first-century digital environment. *Library Quarterly* 76(2), 169–92.

Dunn, D. J. (1984). Pico and beyond: School library controversies. *Law Library Journal* 77(8), 435–64.

Epstein, R. A. (2003). *Skepticism and freedom: A modern case for classical liberalism.* Chicago: University of Chicago Press.

Ferguson, A. (1999). U.S. district court declares filters on all library computers unconstitutional. *School Library Journal* 45(1), 17.

Flexner, A. (1930). *Universities: American, English, German.* New York: Oxford University Press.

Francoeur, S. (2011). Prudence and controversy: The New York Public Response to post-war anti-communist pressures. *Library & Information History* 27(3), 140–60.

Franklin, B. (1964). *The autobiography of Benjamin Franklin.* Second edition. New Haven: Yale University Press.

Garrison, Dee. (2003). *Apostles of culture: The public library and American society, 1876–1920.* Madison: University of Wisconsin Press.

Gilman, D. C. (1898). *University problems in the United States.* New York: The Century Company.

Glick, A. (1998). Judge says web filters might violate First Amendment. *School Library Journal* 44(5), 22.

Goldhor, H. (1972). *An introduction to scientific research in librarianship.* Urbana: University of Illinois, Graduate School of Library Science.

Goldman, A. I. (2002). *Pathways to knowledge: Private and public.* Oxford: Oxford University Press.

Gregory, L., and Higgins, S. (2017). In resistance to a capitalist past: Emerging practices of critical librarianship. In K. P. Nicholson and M. Seale (Eds.), *The politics of theory and the practice of critical librarianship* (pp. 21–38). Sacramento, CA: Library Juice Press.

Hamlin, A. T. (1981). *The university library in the United States: Its origins and development.* Philadelphia: University of Pennsylvania Press.

Harding, T. S. (1971). *College literary societies: Their contribution to higher education in the United States, 1815–1876.* New York: Pageant Press.

Harris, M. H. (1986). State, class, and cultural reproduction: Toward a theory of library service in the United States. In W. Simonton (Ed.), *Advances in librarianship* (pp. 211–52). Orlando: Academic Press.

Harris, M. H., Hannah, S. A., and Harris, P. C. (1998). *Into the future: The foundations of library and information services in the post-industrial era.* Second edition. Greenwich, CT: Ablex.

Hauptman, R. (2002). *Ethics and librarianship.* Jefferson, NC: McFarland and Company.

Hernon, P., and McClure, C. R. (1986). Unobtrusive reference testing: The 55 percent rule. *Library Journal* 111(7), 37–40.

Hurt, C. D., and McGovern, J. (1991). Demographic analysis of the placement of the Boston Public Library in relation to the Irish population. *Public Libraries* 30(3), 145–49.

Husserl, E. (1962). *Ideas: General introduction to pure phenomenology.* New York: Collier.

Husserl, E. (1970). *The crisis of European sciences and transcendental phenomenology.* D. Carr (Trans.). Evanston, IL: Northwestern University Press.

James, W. (1903). The Ph.D. octopus. *Harvard Monthly* 36(1), 1–9.

Jensen, R. (2008). The (perceived) returns to education and the demand for schooling. *Quarterly Journal of Economics* 125(2), 86–98.

Josey, E. J. (1987). The civil rights movement and American librarianship: The opening round. In M. L. Bundy and F. J. Stielow (Eds.), *Activism in American librarianship, 1962–1973* (pp. 13–20). New York: Greenwood Press.

Knox, E. J. M. (2015). *Book banning in 21st-century America.* Lanham, MD: Rowman & Littlefield.

Kravitz, N. (2002). *Censorship and the school library media center.* Westport, CT: Libraries Unlimited.

Labaree, R. V. (1994). The regulation of hate speech on college campuses and the Library Bill of Rights. *Journal of Academic Librarianship* 19(6), 372–77.

Laugher, C. T. (1973). *Thomas Bray's grand design: Libraries of the Church of England in America, 1695–1785.* Chicago: ALA.

Learned, W. S. (1924). *The American public library and the diffusion of knowledge.* New York: Harcourt, Brace and Company.

Leckie, G. J., and Buschman, J. E. (2007). Space, place, and libraries: An introduction. In J. E. Buschman and G. J. Leckie (Eds.), *The library as place: History, community, and culture* (pp. 3–25). Westport, CT: Libraries Unlimited.

Lewin, K. (1947). Frontiers in group dynamics. II. Channels of group life, social planning and action research. *Human Relations* 1, 143–53.

Lewis, A. (Ed.). (2008). *Questioning library neutrality: Essays from Progressive Librarian.* Duluth, MN: Library Juice Press.

Lyotard, J.-F. (1991). *Phenomenology.* B. Beakley (Trans.). Albany, NY: SUNY Press.

Mediavilla, C. (1997). The war on books and ideas: The California Library Association and anti-communist censorship. *Library Trends* 46(2), 331–46.

Merleau-Ponty, M. (1962). *The phenomenology of perception.* C. Smith (Trans.). London: Routledge.

Nicholson, K. P., and Seale, M. (2017). Introduction. In K. P. Nicholson and M. Seale (Eds.), *The politics of theory and the practice of critical librarianship* (pp. 1–18). Sacramento, CA: Library Juice Press.

Noble, S. U. (2018). *Algorithms of oppression: How search engines reinforce racism.* New York: New York University Press.

Palmer, R. E. (1969). *Hermeneutics: Interpretation theory in Schliermacher, Dilthey, Heidegger, and Gadamer.* Evanston, IL: Northwestern University Press.

Peace, A. G. (1997). Academia, censorship, and the Internet. *Journal of Information Ethics* 6(2), 35–47.
Peperzak, A. T. (2004). *Elements of ethics.* Palo Alto, CA: Stanford University Press.
Pinker, S. (2014). *The village effect: How face-to-face contact can make us healthier, happier, and smarter.* New York: Spiegel and Grau.
Pyati, A. (2006). Critical theory and information studies: A Marcusean infusion. *Policy Futures in Education* 4(1), 83–89.
Raber, D. (2003). Librarians as organic intellectuals: A Gramscian approach to blind spots and tunnel vision. *Library Quarterly* 73(1), 33–53.
Raber, D. (2007). ACONDA and ANACONDA: Social change, social responsibility, and librarianship. *Library Trends* 55(3), 675–97.
Rawlinson, N. (1990). Give 'em what they want. *Library Journal* 115(10), 77–79.
Rawls, J. (2001). *Justice as fairness: A restatement.* E. Kelly (Ed.). Cambridge, MA: Belknap Press.
Richardson, J., Jr. (1982). *The spirit of inquiry: The Graduate Library School at Chicago, 1921–1951.* Chicago: ALA.
Richardson, J. V., Jr. (1992). *The gospel of scholarship: Pierce Butler and a critique of American librarianship.* Metuchen, NJ: Scarecrow Press.
Ricoeur, P. (1992). *Oneself as another.* K. Blamey (Trans.). Chicago: University of Chicago Press.
Rider, F. (1944). *The scholar and the future of the research library: A problem and its solution.* New York: Hadham Press.
Rioux, K. (2017). Toward a unified social justice stance for library and information science curricula. In N. A. Cooke and M. E. Sweeney (Eds.), *Teaching for justice: Implementing social justice in the LIS classroom* (pp. 19–50). Sacramento, CA: Library Juice Press.
Robbins, L. S. (1994). The Library of Congress and Federal Loyalty Programs, 1947–1956: No "communists or cocksuckers." *Library Quarterly* 64(4), 365–85.
Robbins, L. S. (1996). *Censorship and the American library: The American Library Association's response to threats to intellectual freedom, 1939–1969.* Westport, CT: Greenwood Press.
Robinson, C. (1989). Can we save the public's library? *Library Journal* 114(14), 147–52.
Robinson, O. (1876). Librarians and readers. *Library Journal* 1, 123–24.
Rosenzweig, M. (2008). Politics and anti-politics in librarianship. *Progressive Librarian No. 3*, 1–6.
Rothbauer, P. (2007). Locating the library as place among lesbian, gay, bisexual, and queer patrons. In J. E. Buschman and G. J. Leckie (Eds.), *The library and place: History, community, and culture* (pp. 101–15). Westport, CT: Libraries Unlimited.
Rudolph, F. (1962). *The American college and university: A history.* New York: Vintage Books.
Samek, T. (2001). *Intellectual freedom and social responsibility in American librarianship, 1967–1974.* Jefferson, NC: McFarland and Company.

Searle, J. (1984). *Minds, brains and science.* Cambridge, MA: Harvard University Press.
Shafer-Landau, R. (2003). *Moral realism: A defence.* Oxford: Clarendon Press.
Shera, J. H. (1949). *Foundations of the public library: The origins of the public library movement in New England, 1629–1855.* Chicago: University of Chicago Press.
Shera, J. H. (1976). *Introduction to library science: Basic elements of library service.* Littleton, CO: Libraries Unlimited.
Shiflett, O. L. (1981). *Origins of American academic librarianship.* Norwood, NJ: Ablex.
Shores, L. (1963). *Origins of the American college library, 1638–1800.* Hamden, CT: Shoe String Press.
Smith, G. H. (2013). *The system of liberty: Themes in the history of classical liberalism.* Cambridge: Cambridge University Press.
Sokolowski, R. (2000). *Introduction to phenomenology.* Cambridge: Cambridge University Press.
Steele, J. E. (2018). Censorship of library collections: An analysis using gatekeeping theory. *Collection Management 43*(4), 229–48.
Swan, J., and Peattie, N. (1989). *The freedom to lie: A debate about democracy.* Jefferson, NC: McFarland and Company.
US Department of the Interior, Bureau of Education. (1876). *Public libraries in the United States of America: Their history, condition, and management.* Washington, DC: Government Printing Office.
Valentine, G. (2001). *Social geographies: Space and society.* Harlow, England: Pearson Education/Prentice-Hall.
Van Slyke, A. A. (1995). *Free to all: Carnegie libraries & American culture, 1890–1920.* Chicago: University of Chicago Press.
Veblen, T. (1923). *The higher learning in America: A memorandum on the conduct of universities by business men.* New York: B. W. Huebsch.
White, C. M. (1976). *A historical introduction to library education: Problems and progress to 1951.* Metuchen, NJ: Scarecrow Press.
White, H. D. (2019). Patrick Wilson. *Knowledge Organization 46*(4), 279–307.
White, H. S. (Ed.). (1986). *Education for professional librarians.* White Plains, NY: Knowledge Industry Publications.
Whitehill, W. M. (1956). *Boston public library: A centennial history.* Cambridge, MA: Harvard University Press.
Wiegand, S. A., and Wiegand, W. A. (2007). *Books on trial: Red scare in the heartland.* Norman: University of Oklahoma Press.
Wiegand, W. A. (1989). *"An active instrument for propaganda": The American public library during World War I.* New York: Greenwood Press.
Wiegand, W. A. (1996). *Irrepressible reformer: A biography of Melvil Dewey.* Chicago: ALA Editions.
Wiegand, W. A. (2015). *Part of our lives: A people's history of the American public library.* Oxford: Oxford University Press.

Williams, P. (1988). *The American public library and the problem of purpose*. New York: Greenwood Press.

Williamson, C. C. (1971). *The Williamson reports of 1921 and 1923*. Metuchen, NJ: Scarecrow Press.

Wilson, P. (1968). *Two kinds of power: An essay on bibliographic control*. Berkeley: University of California Press.

Wilson, P. (1977). *Public knowledge, private ignorance: Toward a library and information policy*. Westport, CT: Greenwood Press.

Wilson, P. (1983). *Second-hand knowledge: An inquiry into cognitive authority*. Westport, CT: Greenwood Press.

Winkelstein, J. A. (2017). Social justice in action: Cultural humility, scripts, and the LIS classroom. In N. A. Cooke and M. E. Sweeney (Eds.), *Teaching for justice: Implementing social justice in the LIS classroom* (pp. 139–68). Sacramento, CA: Library Juice Press.

Wolin, S. (1981). The new public philosophy. *Democracy 1*(4), 23–36.

CHAPTER TWO

How Do We Talk to One Another?

Introduction

The thrust of this chapter is an examination of how we converse about difficult and contested issues. This may seem simple and straightforward, but it is not. Before we delve deeply into examples of these contested issues, it is necessary to take a careful look at language, speech, and the ways we employ both to express ourselves to each other. This examination of language and speech is vital and must embrace some substantial detail. Many questions will be asked and answered here before we can get into the conversations that are possible. These include matters of *how* we speak to one another, how we frame our speech and our arguments. The matters apply to all sides of a contest. We must begin here.

A reasonable place to start is with the philosophy of language, which can elucidate the background of discourse and conversation. Simon Blackburn (1984) presents a graphic representation of the elements of language in use: in it he connects speakers, language, and the world. The connections are informed by the theory of meaning, the theory of knowledge, and the theory of truth (p. 81). Speakers employ language to represent the world; the theories are component parts of communication. The figure illustrates how speak work in daily life. As Blackburn (1984) says, "The speaker uses language. With it he can put himself into various relations with the world. He can describe it, or ask questions about it, issue commands to change it, put himself under obligations to act in various ways. . . . The task of the philosopher is to obtain some stable conception about this triangle of speaker, language, and world" (p. 3).

An aside is appropriate here. According to Blackburn (1984), one of the obstacles to both the functioning of the triangle and the philosopher's interpretation of its use is the presence of a positivistic bent. He (1984) states that positivism is "the analysis of propositions about theoretical entities into ones about regularities of experience" (p. 152). Some may claim that positivism is dead and has no application in the social sciences; others maintain that it is alive and well in inquiry. Kincheloe and Tobin (2009) aver, "As these insidious modes of positivism creep into research practices, they work to promote a belief that what we perceive about the world in our unexamined first glance is simply 'what is.' . . . Knowledge is a far more slippery and complex concept than researchers traditionally assume" (p. 519). If these individuals are correct, the beginning stance in the social sciences is that human action is not direct from the inquiry of the natural sciences. Kincheloe and Tobin (2009) state, "A central dimension of our argument is that many of the tenets of positivism are so embedded within Western culture, academia, and the world of education in particular that they are often invisible to researchers and those who consume their research" (p. 513). What must be remembered is that human action, including communication, is volitional; it is a product of will. This observation is important and should be kept in mind throughout this chapter.

Blackburn (1984) is also a realist when it comes to language and meaning. He describes his position:

> To take a simple example, moral commitments are often thought of as not really beliefs, but as more like attitudes, emotions, or prescriptions: this contrast in turn may look very different if we think of beliefs in pragmatic or instrumental terms rather than in terms of correspondence with facts. . . . Quietism is currently expressed by denials that there is a "god's-eye view" or an "external" or "Archimedean" point from which we can discover whether some commitment is, as it were, describing the undraped figure of nature or imposing clothing. (p. 147)

Blackburn is not alone in asserting such claims. As Michael Polanyi and Harry Prosch (1975) state, "Intellectual assent to the reduction of the world to its atomic elements acting blindly in terms of equilibrations of forces, an assent that has gradually come to prevail since the birth of modern science, has made any sort of teleological view of the cosmos seem unscientific and woolgathering to us" (p. 162). They (1975) continue, "We might justifiably claim, therefore, that everything we know is *full* of meaning, is not absurd at all, although we can sometimes fail to grasp these meanings and fall into absurdities. . . . [M]eanings can be missed, since the emergence of life opens up the possibility of success but also, of course, the chance of failure" (p. 179).

The matter of truth can enter here. As Michael Devitt and Kim Sterelny (1999) say,

> What does a sentence represent? Think of an indicative sentence, the sort that is typically used in making an assertion (as opposed to asking a question, issuing a command, etc.). The sentence represents the situation that would *make it true*; it represents its *truth condition*. We cash this out as follows: the sentence is true is a certain situation in the world obtains and not true is the situation does not. So, the hypothesis is that this property of a sentence is the core of its meaning. . . . The hypothesis is in the spirit of the popular philosophical slogan, "The meaning of a sentence is its truth condition." (p. 20; emphasis in original)

When we explore truth in a little while, a number of theories will be presented, but (spoiler alert) the correspondence theory will, by and large, be the preferred one. This assertion can apply to the assessment of knowledge as well. Keith Lehrer (1990) provides a succinct and complete definition of what constitutes knowledge:

> [Analysis of Knowledge] S knows that p if and only if (i) it is true that p, (ii) S accepts that p, (iii) S is completely justified in accepting that p, and (iv) S is completely justified in accepting p in some way that does not depend on any false statements. (p. 18; emphasis in original)

The last component of that statement may be the most important; no false component can be a portion of what constitutes an analysis of truth. This component separates the statement from the more simplistic, "Truth is justified true belief." Even with all this said, knowledge is a contested phenomenon. There are disagreements about what constitutes knowledge and knowing something. Jean-François Lyotard (1984) offers what he claims to be a postmodern picture of knowledge:

> The nature of knowledge cannot survive unchanged within this context of general transformation. It can fit into the new channels, and become operational, only if learning is translated into quantities of information. We can predict that anything in the constituted body of knowledge that is not translatable in this way will be abandoned and that the direction of new research will be dictated by the possibility of its eventual results being translatable into computer language. (p. 4)

The reduction to information (and this is not to shortchange information) is a perversion of knowledge in its actual form. What we are left with is some set of claims that propose to be knowledge, which is not the same thing.

The foregoing anticipates the point of meaning, of semantics, which should be covered in a bit more detail. (For readers who wish to examine semantics in detail, they can turn to Kate Kearns's study [2011].) Years ago Alfred Tarski (1944) offered a definition: "*Semantics* is a discipline which, speaking loosely, *deals with certain relations between expressions of a language and the objects* (or 'states of affairs') *'referred to' by those expressions*" (p. 345; emphasis in original). Paul Elbourne (2011) distinguishes between two fundamentally distinct ideas regarding meaning: "The *referential theory of meaning* proposes the most direct mechanism: meanings of words simply are things in the world. . . . On the other side of the floor, we have the advocates of the *internalist theory of meaning*. They suggest that word meanings are most fruitfully thought of as ideas or concepts in our heads" (pp. 14–15; emphasis in original). By using common sense we can conclude that meaning cannot exist without both of these theories being true, at least to some extent. If something is not in the world, it is difficult to have meaning construed otherwise than the fact of the thing being in the world. On the other hand, it is possible to hold *and to share* meanings of abstract concepts in the mind. For example, a person can see a tree in nature and comprehend what the tree is, including some details, such as species. That same person can also hold memories of a particular tree that had a tire swing attached to it that the person would play on as a child. Even more abstract concepts, such as mathematics, can be held in the mind. As Elbourne (2011) says, "The difference between abstract and *concrete* objects is widely thought to be of fundamental philosophical significance" (p. 19; emphasis in original). The two are of significance, but both may be held to be meaningful to a reasonable person.

There is the matter of the meaning of sentences, as well as of words. Elbourne (2011) notes that "the internalist theory of meaning maintains that the meanings of sentences are internal mental structures, just as the meanings of words are. . . . Referentialists generally suppose that sentence meanings are abstract objects" (pp. 43–44). If words can have concrete meanings, then some sentences may also have concrete meanings. A simple declarative sentence, such as, "That is an oak tree," can have concrete meaning. It is also easy to imagine that some complex sentences are abstract and express beliefs, propositions, or other abstract concepts. The upshot from all of this discussion is that the meanings of words, sentences, and utterances can include concrete and/or objective elements. Elbourne (2011) notes Paul Grice's Cooperative Principle, which includes some communicative aspects:

A. The Maxim of Quantity
  i. Make your contribution as informative as is required.
  ii. Do not make your contribution more informative than is required.
B. The Maxim of Quality: Try to make your contribution one that is true
  i. Do not say what you believe to be false.
  ii. Do not say that for which you lack adequate evidence.
C. The Maxim of Relation
  i. Be relevant.
D. The Maxim of Manner: Be perspicuous
  i. Avoid obscurity.
  ii. Avoid ambiguity.
  iii. Be brief (avoid unnecessary prolixity).
  iv. Be orderly. (pp. 132–33)

The Cooperative Principle allows for interpretation and makes understanding in communicative situations possible. We will return to some of these maxims when we address the ethics of discourse.

Meanwhile (and by way of further introduction), there is the matter of what exactly is speech. A pioneer in this arena is J. L. Austin (1975). Among other things, he defined precisely what "performative" language is: "The name is derived, of course, from 'perform,' the usual verb with the noun 'action': it indicates that the issuing of the utterance is the performing of an action—it is not normally thought of as just saying something" (pp. 6–7). Austin (1979) provides a thoroughgoing definition of performative utterances:

> They will be perfectly straightforward utterances, with ordinary verbs in the first person singular present indicative, and yet we will see at once that they couldn't possibly be true or false. Furthermore, if a person makes an utterance of this sort we should say that he is *doing* something rather than merely *saying* something. This may sound a little odd. (p. 235; emphasis in original)

He (1975) continues, "In very many cases it is possible to perform an act of exactly the same kind *not* by uttering words, whether written or spoken, but in some other way" (p. 8; emphasis in original). For example, a raised fist in certain circumstances can carry performativity. Not all speech acts are performative; this designation is particular, but it does relate to many illocutionary statements. Illocution is another innovation by Austin to distinguish those speech acts that indicate what is *done* through speech. John Searle (1969) elaborates on illocutionary speech acts, especially assertoric statement. In terms of preparatory action, he (1969) claims, "1. S has evidence (reasons, etc.) for the truth of *p*. 2. It is not obvious to both S and H that H knows (does not need to be reminded of, etc.) *p*" (p. 66; emphasis in original). There is also a sincerity condition: "S believes *p*" (Searle, 1969, p. 66; emphasis in original). That is followed by an essential condition, "Counts as an undertaking to the effect that *p* represents an actual state of affairs" (Searle, 1969, p. 66; emphasis in original).

One of the things that Searle has consistently held is that speech and speech acts are social events; they depend not on a solipsistic mind speaking only to itself but a collective of persons engaged in some sort of collective action. For example, he (1979) writes, "literal meaning is dependent on context in the same way that other non-conventional forms of intentionality are dependent on context" (p. 135). Searle makes mention of intentionality in that passage; he would devote an entire book to the topic. Searle (1983) defines it thusly: "Intentionality is that property of many mental states and events by which they are directed at or about or of objects and states of affairs in the world. If, for example, I have a belief, it must be a belief that such and such is the case" (p. 1). He (1983) elaborates, "Intentional states represent objects and states of affairs in the same sense of 'represent' that speech acts represent objects and states of affairs (even though . . . speech acts have a derived form of Intentionality and thus represent in a different manner from Intentional states, which have an intrinsic form of Intentionality" (pp. 4–5). He (1983) emphasizes, "Language is derived from Intentionality and not conversely. . . . The distinction between propositional content and illocutionary force, a distinction familiar within the theory of speech acts, carries over to Intentional states" (p. 5).

In other words, according to Searle, beliefs (for example) precede speech. If one believes that liberty is the principal hallmark of politics, one then develops propositional speech acts to express that belief. (Note that this example is taken from the theme of this book—political speech by people from the conservative and liberal sides.) The example draws directly from Searle's (1983) assertion "that for a speaker to mean something for an utterance is for him to have a certain set of intentions directed at an actual or possible audience: for a speaker to mean something by an utterance is for him to make that utterance with the intention of producing certain effects on his audience" (p. 161). The place of the audience is extremely important; people generally speak *to* someone. This is the thrust of the present chapter on ways people can converse with one another. It is also important for our comprehension of the matter that we grasp Searle's (1983) directions of causality. In our visual perception there is a "world-to-mind" causal relationship: features of an object *cause* our experience. In our intentional action, or experience of acting, there is a "mind-to-world" fit: experience *causes* the actions we take (see p. 91). Therefore, there is a complex, and ordered, causal fit in our beliefs and our actions. The perceptual experience of liberty comes before our intentional actions to bring about liberty.

Other commentators have similar opinions to Searle, although they may express their views uniquely. One is Patrick de Gramont (1990), who says, "our understanding of how we represent our reality need no longer depend upon theories that are limited to being metaphors of the mind which presume what they should explain" (p. 45). That is, he is not in favor of the philosophical stance regarding the language of thought. There is a concreteness of perception that is related to the world-to-mind causal fit. De Gramont (1990) does limit the efficacy of language and speech in a way that privileges speech over nonverbal actions: "Words may conform to standard meanings that a community of speakers will understand, but they do so at the expense of the lived specificity of nonverbal understanding" (p. 47). There can be expressions (nonverbal) of puzzlement, agreement, or anger, for instance, that do communicate clearly from one person to another. De Gramont (1990) also stresses the contextuality of language, upon which communication depends. "What this means . . . is that in referring to things, we are completely dependent upon a coordinate system of terms and predicates that can only tell us how things are defined within a language system" (p. 57). He (1990) employs an example from physics to make his point: "It is as meaningless to question the absolute reference of a word as it is to question absolute position and velocity in physics" (p. 57). There is uncertainty when it comes to communication. Sometimes that uncertainty can be anticipated (perhaps more frequently in formal communication) and corrected for, but sometimes it cannot be anticipated (perhaps more frequently in informal speech). This uncertainty must be recognized and must be seen to obtain in speech acts.

A similar viewpoint on uncertainty is expressed by François Recanati (2012), who states, "Singularism holds that our thought is about individual objects as much as it is about properties. Objects are given to us directly, in experience, and we do not necessarily think of them as bearers of such and such properties" (p. 4). The challenge for every individual is to come to the realization that objects do have properties, but that objects may have multiple properties. What Recanati avers, though, is that "there are also *singular thoughts*; thoughts that are directly about individual objects, and whose content is a singular proposition—a proposition involving individual objects as well as properties" (p. 5; emphasis in original). Recanati (2012) then questions such a stance, which has been held by luminaries that include Bertrand Russell, and maintains that our presentation (in the mind and through expression) can actually be descriptive and nondescriptive. That is, there is a possibility for uncertainty.

The introduction can conclude with a turn back in time for the moment. Over a half century ago, Ferdinand de Saussure (1966) wrote the *Course in General Linguistics*, in which he proposed a new science of semiology. It must be noted that the study of signs predates Saussure; Charles Sanders Peirce examined the place of semiotics in the larger study of language. Saussure, though, envisioned semiology as superordinate to linguistics. For instance, he (1966) wrote, "Contrary to all appearances, language never exists apart from the social fact, for it is a semiological phenomenon. Its social nature is one of its inner characteristics. Its complete definition confronts us with two inseparable entities" (p. 77). He (1966) suggests a graphic presentation: in it, language is connected to, and informs, a community of speakers. One of the features of Saussure's semiology is that there is a complex relation among language (the global concept of linguistic communication), languages (the natural iterations of language, such as English, French, Latin, etc.), and speech (the social exchanges that employ languages), under the larger idea of *signs*. The first three elements are discussed by David Holdcroft (1991), who asks, "How, then are language (*langue*) and speech (*parole*) related to each other, and both to natural language (*langage*)?" (p. 20; emphasis in original). By way of an answer he offers a comparison of features:

Langue	*Parole*
Social	Individual
Essential	Contingent
No active individual role	Active role
Not designed	Designed
Conventional	Not conventional
Furnishes a homogeneous subject matter for a branch of social psychology	Furnishes a heterogeneous subject matter studied by different disciplines (pp. 20–21)

Holdcroft (1991) adds, "The domain of *parole*, everything to do with *langage* that remains when *langue* has been subtracted, is positively vast" (p. 31; emphasis in original).

Given Holdcroft's commentary, Saussure (1966) elaborates on semiology: "I propose to retain the word *sign* [*signe*] to designate the *signified* [*signifié*] and *signifier* [*significant*]; the last two terms have the advantage of indicating the opposition that separates them from each other and from the whole of which they are parts" (p. 67; emphasis in original). Roy Harris (1987) explicates the variables in Saussure's conception: the *signified* equals the concept intended by the communication; the *signifier* equals a sound pattern (usually through speech but, conceivably, via writing as well); the *sign* is *signifier* plus the *signified* (p. 58). For Saussure, these are technical terms that form the foundation of semiology. Roland Barthes (1967) also helps us to grasps the complexity: "Any speech, as soon as it is grasped as a process of communication, is *already* part of the language" (p. 16; emphasis in original). That is, the spoken word becomes a component of language by means of *being* spoken. The articulation of a concept or idea is part of language by virtue of the intention of being communicative. All of this commentary on semiology predates Searle, but Searle encapsulates the purposiveness of speech and languages (as well as *language* writ large). It may even be said that all of this portion of the discussion contributes to meaning. Harris (1987) sums up,

> Even if speech were a separate natural (i.e. physiological) endowment, it could not be exercised unless society provided a public instrument (*la langue*) for its exercise. The particular for this instrument takes will vary from one society to another: and here the distinction between *langage* and *langue* ties in with the Sausurrean doctrine of arbitrariness of the linguistic sign. (p. 16; emphasis in original)

The variability of social practices and usages contributes, as Holdcroft (1991) points out, to the arbitrariness of the sign. There is not a universal fixity to speech; therefore, while there is substantial regularity, there is no universal fixity to signs. Pierre Guiraud (1975) helps us comprehend this phenomenon: "A sign is a stimulus—that is, a perceptible substance—the mental image of which is associated in our minds with that of another stimulus. The function of the former stimulus is to evoke the latter with a view to communication" (p. 22).

Saussure's semiology came to be referred to as "structural" linguistics (again, a difference from the linguistics of other types and even much of the linguistics that was contemporary with him). Structuralism spread to other fields, such as anthropology, and was known by a pattern or set of patterns that underlay a seemingly diverse surface. In other words, there is a structure to linguistics, anthropology, sociology, and even philosophy. As we will see, there has been a reaction to structuralism. As Terence Hawkes (1977) explains, structuralism is a realization of the relationships, primarily between the observer and the observed; *that* is the order that is apparent. We construct, and perceive, the relationships among things rather than there being things in themselves (p. 22).

Jürgen Habermas and Communicative Action

The foregoing discussion of language, meaning, signs, etc. signals one particular aspect of communication: it is active. That is to say, communication requires some volitionary action on the parts of both speaker/writer and hearer/reader. (Note that the responsibilities for action exist at both ends of the communicative process.) The active participation, then, is social; it is not the independent acts of individuals. It is a collaborative process that relies upon reasoned speech and reasoned listening. Also, the process is iterative; it does not *belong* solely to one participant or another. All of these elements of action mean that the act of communication is complex; it is not the simple exchange of, say, greetings between two people. This complexity is what will be explored and defined within this section. For there to be a conversation between people who do not necessarily agree on political matters, understanding the complexity is essential.

Habermas has focused a considerable amount of his attention on what he calls communicative action and has examined what is needed for effective action. By way of introduction, he (1990) states, "I speak of *communicative* action when actors are prepared to harmonize their plans of action through internal means, committing themselves to pursuing their goals only on the condition of an agreement—one that already exists or one to be negotiated—about definitions of the situation and prospective outcomes" (p. 134; emphasis in original). The concept of an agreement is essentially important to communicative action; the end result of the action depends upon the agreement about key points. Habermas (1998a) emphasizes the importance of speech and speech acts, as well as language, as useful tools for action:

> I would like to defend the thesis that not only language but speech too—that is, the employment of sentences in utterances—is accessible to formal analysis. Like the elementary units of language (sentences), the elementary units of speech (utterances) can be analyzed from the methodological stance of a reconstructive science. (p. 26)

The "reconstructive sciences" require some explication, which Maeve Cooke (1994) provides:

> The reconstructive sciences are empirical sciences, to the extent that the status of their reconstructions of general structures and universal conditions is *hypothetical* and these hypotheses must be subjected to the usual methods of testing. This means, for instance, that Habermas's reconstructions of the universal presuppositions of communication in modern societies must be open

to checking against speakers' intuitions, scattered across as broad a sociological spectrum as possible. (p. 2; emphasis in original)

Cooke (1994) adds, "The theory of communicative action relies in particular—although by no means exclusively—on a reconstructive theory that seeks to identify the universal presuppositions of everyday communication in modern societies" (p. 3). His science pervades the entirety of the examination of communicative action.

Habermas's theory of communicative action is grounded in the reason that the communicative participants should possess and exercise. By stressing the active component, he renders necessary reason and rationality. If there is to be a resulting knowledge from communication, there has to be a process based in reason. He (1984) says, "The close relation between knowledge and rationality suggests that the rationality of an expression depends on the reliability of the knowledge embedded in it" (p. 8). His conception of knowledge is very different from that of Lyotard, who sees knowledge as coopted by external and deleterious forces. For Habermas, knowledge has to be the product of the communicative process and must be fallible at the outset. It is the reason and rationality that are essential components of communicative action as part of the reconstructive science that relates the claims to the objective world and must be open to objective judgment (see Habermas, 1984, p. 9). Communication includes propositional logic that should be related to the broad idea of rationality. Argumentation is a central tool of rational communication; participants reach consensus by means of reasoned argumentation. It should be pointed out that, according to William Outhwaite (1994), there is a warning from Habermas that maintains that argumentation is *not the same* as communicative action, that the former is a specific form of communication (p. 112). That said, argumentation is something that Habermas addresses specifically, so it cannot be ignored.

Habermas (1984) also states, "Well-grounded assertions and efficient actions are certainly a sign of rationality; we do characterize as rational speaking and acting subjects who, as far as it lies within their power, avoid errors in regard to facts and means-ends relations" (p. 15). These characteristics fit with the reasoned argumentation that he advocates. These are rigorous strictures that may not always exist in the course of communication among individuals. What they are constitute the necessity for reasoned outcomes. These are somewhat idealistic stances, which he continues with the claim,

> In contexts of communicative action, we call someone rational not only if he is able to put forward an assertion and, when criticized, to provide grounds for

it by pointing to appropriate evidence, but also if he is following an established norm and is able, when criticized, to justify his action by explicating the given situation in the light of legitimate expectations. (p. 15)

The assertoric element is a specific component of argumentation and of speech acts generally. While he speaks of the matter of criticism, he adds that there must be evidence to support the speaker's position. What is missing is the reasoned response of altering that position if the evidence (which might be presented by the correspondent) necessitates a change of mind. When there is critique, there must be the occurrence of deference to evidence, the ultimate arbiter.

Habermas (1984) does concede that anyone who is self-deceptive does not behave rationally. That lack of rationality could be fatal to reasoned communicative action, but, according to Habermas, the irrationality can be overcome if one is willing to seek rationality in the face of the self-deception. That is, deception need not be fatal or permanent if a speaker is fully willing to seek reasons for beliefs and, eventually, for speech. For the process to succeed there must be an open-mindedness on the part of the speaker. There has to be a willingness to act rationally, to exercise reason, and to seek evidence that can be weighed carefully (see p. 21). The act of argumentation is where the reason and rationality play out in a complex set of forms, expressions, and claims (see Habermas, 1984, p. 23, for a graphic that illustrates such a set). The set ranges from the theoretical to the practical to the explicative. It is a concise illustration of the interworkings of the cognitive, the moral, the evaluative, and the expressive. All of those elements are necessary for communicative action to be realized. And they must be occurrent in all of the participants so that argumentation and critique take place.

The processes are complex, and Habermas readily recognizes the complexity. He (1994) writes, "The meaning of the question 'What should I do?' undergoes a further transformation as soon as my actions affect the interests of others and lead to conflicts that should be regulated by an impartial manner, that is, from the moral point of view" (p. 5). He (1984) takes the question further:

> Thus, the question "What should I do?" takes on a pragmatic, an ethical, or a moral meaning depending on how the problem is conceived. In each case it is a matter of justifying choices among alternative available courses of action. But pragmatic tasks call for a different *kind of action*, and the corresponding question, a different *kind of answer*, from ethical and moral ones. (p. 8)

He (1998) graphically presents the pragmatic structure to which he refers:

Table 2.1.

Mode of communication	Type of speech act	Theme	Thematic validity claim
Cognitive	Constatives	Propositional content	Truth
Interactive	Regulatives	Interpersonal relation	Rightness, appropriateness
Expressive	Avowals	Speaker's intention (p. 81)	Truthfulness

The social dynamic of communication is apparent in the table. Habermas (1984) enhances that dynamic: "For the interpreter it is not a question of hermeneutic *charity* but a methodological precept that he proceed from the presumptive rationality of the questionable expression in order, if necessary, to assure himself step by step of its irrationality" (p. 55). This is not the place to delve deeply into hermeneutics, but a definition here is useful for the articulation of Habermas. As Richard Palmer (1969), who offers what may be the most complete and thorough historical and contemporary study of the topic, writes, "Hermeneutics is the process of deciphering which goes from manifest content and meaning to latent or hidden meaning. The object of interpretation, i.e., the text in the very broadest sense, may be the symbols in a dream or even the myths and symbols of society or literature" (p. 43). If there has to be simplified idea of hermeneutics, it is the process of interpretation. These writings confirm the social sense of communication, especially as the act of interpreting. Stephen White (1988) elaborates on the idea of the social:

> Habermas's conception of communicative action, on the other hand, implies a structure of *intersubjectivity* from which one can derive a mutual "speech-act-immanent *obligation to provide justification* (emphasis in original)" for the different sorts of claims which are continually raised in understanding-oriented action. This obligation is one which every actor has "implicitly recognized," *simply by virtue of having engaged in communicative action*. (p. 51; emphasis added)

The very concept of intersubjectivity runs completely through Habermas's thought (on modernity, politics, and other issues as well). The very idea of communicative *action* affirms that intersubjectivity. People communicate with one another to certain purposes, which include assertoric statements, inquiries, persuasion, etc. Thomas McCarthy (1979) suggests, "Habermas's entire project . . . rests on the possibility of providing an account of communication that is both theoretical and normative, that goes beyond a pure hermeneutics without being reducible to a strictly empirical-analytic science" (p. 272). The normative element is what we are focusing on at this time (a volume could be written on the theoretical side, but the point of libraries being the locus for practical, normative discourse is the cause of the moment). How do people employ reason in speaking to one another? Habermas (1984) offers a partial answer:

> The concept of *communicative action* refers to the interaction of at least two subjects capable of speech and action who establish interpersonal relations (whether by verbal or by extra-verbal means). The actors seek to reach an understanding about the action situation and their plans of action in order to coordinate their actions by way of agreement. The central concept of *interpretation* refers in the first instance to negotiating definitions of the situation which admit of consensus. (p. 86; emphasis in original)

While political speech presents a unique challenge, the communicative-action program has greater potential than any theoretical-practical idea that has been offered. That potential may be criticized by some, but the practical-moral elements of the program can be employed both to understand speech and to structure speech acts so as to realize a joint understanding among individuals.

Habermas (1994) himself explains his program and the efficacy of the practice of political speech (note that political speech is not the only type, but it has always been important, and may never have been as important as it is at this time). He (1984) says, "Pragmatic discourses point to the necessity of compromise as soon as one's own interests have to be brought into harmony with those of others. Ethical-political discourses have as their goal the clarification of a collective identity that must have room for the pursuit of diverse individual life projects" (p. 16). The emphasis on compromise must be remembered. If there is to be success in civil discourse surrounding politics, there will have to be compromise, as we will soon see. And the ethical component is essential. J. Donald Moon (1995) clarifies what is meant by this ethical political communication:

> Habermas has presented one of the most powerful accounts of a discourse-based morality; it is grounded in an understanding of practical reason which explains how the validity of norms can be tested, thereby demonstrating their cognitive character. According to Habermas, valid norms can be freely accepted by all

of the individuals who are affected by them. Thus, a society whose institutions and practices were governed by valid norms would instantiate the ideal of a moral community. (p. 143)

The sort of moral community that this book advocates relies on the ethical and moral communicative activities that Habermas advocates.

There is one additional point to be introduced in this section (and to which we will return), and that is the idea and reality of the lifeworld. *Lifeworld* is a complex concept that refers, in part, to the construction of reality each person makes on the basis of the circumstances, events, and understandings of her or his life. For Habermas, lifeworld includes the environment that includes competences, practices, and attitudes that are present to one's consciousness and actions. He (1990) writes,

> The actor stands face to face with the situationally relevant segment of the lifeworld that impinges on him as a problem, a problem he must resolve through his own efforts. But in another sense, the actor is carried or supported from behind, as it were, by a lifeworld that not only forms the *context* for the process of reaching understanding but also furnishes *resources* for it. The shared lifeworld offers a storehouse of unquestioned cultural givens from which those participating in communication draw agreed-upon patterns of interpretation for use in their interpretive efforts. (p. 135; emphasis in original)

It becomes starkly evident that lifeworld is not merely individual; it is shared insofar as participants are able to share experiences and thoughts. This is of vital concern and will feature prominently in the next chapter.

Discourse Analysis and Discursive Practice

"Discourse" is the formal term we will apply to the political conversations that can take place, particularly in libraries. It is a complicated phenomenon, and it carries a complex set of concepts and practices. Before getting into some of the details of discourse analysis, a prefatory array of remarks can be shared from work I (2006) have done:

> *Version 1.* I want you to believe me. For you to believe me, I have to be credible to you. To be credible to you, I must speak in lexical terms that are familiar to you; I have to be understood. The lexical comprehension is one part of understanding; I also have to communicate in ways that fit your knowledge base, that will have a context within your mind. Understanding is one path to belief; it is necessary, but it is not sufficient. Your belief in what I say is also dependent upon your acceptance of what I say. (p. 65; emphasis in original)

These premises cover a considerable amount of the concerns that typify discourse and discourse analysis. But they do not cover everything:

> *Version 2.* I want you to believe me. I still have to be credible to you. In order to accomplish this credibility I will call upon traditions, customs, sources, powerful institutions, and other necessary social relations. I will ensure that you believe me by making it impossible for you to disbelieve me. What I say will build upon a substantial accumulation of discourse that has been established as authoritative. You believe me because you believe that set of discursive practices. The practices are not a continuous line from the past, although they have roots in the past. Their history has been disjointed, but it has managed to gain acceptance over, and through, time. All of your affiliations influence your belief structure—your education, your political party, your geographic location, your religious views, your occupation, your family, your friends, and your economic status. (Budd, 2006, p. 66; emphasis in original)

What precedes is rife with difficult statuses, ideas, and practices. We can now turn to what the commentators on discourse analysis have to say.

While discourse analysis carries complications, the first challenge we face is defining discourse itself. David Howarth (2000) presents a beginning of a definition:

> Discourse theory begins with the assumption that all objects and actions are meaningful, and that their meaning is a product of historically specific systems of rules. It thus inquires into the way in which social practices construct and contest the discourses that constitute social reality. These practices are possible because systems of meaning are contingent and can never completely exhaust a social field of meaning. (p. 8)

The realm of meaning has been discussed earlier, but discourse is a carrier of meaning. That realization is made problematic by the contesting of what may be said and/or written, first of all. Disagreement is common in discursive practice *because* meaning can be contingent and interpretations can be inexhaustible. Given such challenges, how is communication possible? The answer has already been hinted at by the nature of meaning and its existence in its inherent state plus the sharing that can take place. The sharing is addressed by Michael Stubbs (1983), who says that discourse analysis "refers to attempts to study the organization of language above the sentence or above the clause, and therefore to study larger linguistic units, such as conversational exchanges or written texts. It follows that discourse analysis is also concerned with language in use in social contexts, and in particular with interaction or dialogue between speakers" (p. 1). He (1983) continues,

"It follows also that language and situation are inseparable. There is no deterministic relationship, of course, except in highly ritualized situations" (p. 1). Howarth (2000) adds, in concert with Stubbs, "discourse theory stands against those positivistic, behaviouralist [sic] and structuralist accounts of social life that concentrate simply on observable facts and actions, or which disregard everyday social meanings in favour of unconscious structural laws" (p. 11).

At this point what constitutes "discourse" should be explored. There are some commentators who address this very matter. Tim Dant (1991), for instance, states, "As an object, discourse is available on two levels. Firstly, to a participant . . . for whom the object has a reality that can be described and understood. Secondly, to an analyst . . . for whom the object has structural features that enable it to be understood in relation to other, similar structural forms" (p. 99). The divide exists, according to Dant, between those engaged in the discourse and those who examine it according to structures. This definition exists from the point of view of those who use discourse for certain purposes that can be analyzed. The actuality of discourse remains to be described, so Sara Mills (1997) presents one: "This, a discourse is not a disembodied collection of statements, but groupings of utterances or sentences, statements which are enacted within a social context, which are determined by that social context and which contribute to the way that social context continues its existence" (p. 11). The social component arises again, and its essential character is made prominent. Gillian Brown and George Yule (1983) call discourse "transactional language, which is primarily 'message-oriented.'" They (1983) write, "In primarily transactional language we assume that what the speaker (or writer) has primarily in mind is the efficient transference of information" (p. 2). Conversations best typify this description, but, it should be noted, the structure allows for serious and extended conversation, as well as brief, "signal"-oriented conversation of the type that may be exemplified by the exchange, A: "Where is Jane?" B: "She's at the grocery store." Much longer and more detailed conversations may be analyzed as well.

The "what" of discourse opens the door to the "how." James Paul Gee (1999) attempts to bring the two together in a rudimentary way (that still has importance for understanding). He (1999) puts the two together in a superficial way:

1. *The meaning and value of aspects of the material world*
2. *Activities*
3. *Identities and relationships*

4. *Politics (the distribution of social goods)*
5. *Connections*
6. *Semiotics (what and how different symbol systems and different forms of knowledge "count").* (p. 12)

Gee (1999) makes the point that the analysis of discursive practice is marked by multiple grammars:

> Each social language has its own distinctive grammar. However, two different sorts of grammars are important to social languages, only one of which we ever think to study formally in school. One grammar is the traditional set of units like nouns, verbs, inflections, phrases and clauses. These are real enough, though quite inadequately described in traditional school grammars. Let's call this "grammar one."
>
> The other—less studied but more important—grammar is the "rules" by which grammatical units like nouns and verbs, phrases and clauses, are used to create *patterns* which signal or "index" characteristic *whos-doing-whats-within-Discourse*. That is, we speakers and writers design our oral or written utterances to have patterns in them in virtue of which interpreters can attribute situated identities and specific activities to us and our utterances. We will call this "grammar two." (p. 29, emphasis in original)

The difference that Gee speaks of is also socially oriented. The kind of communication that exists between a communicator and interpreter is vitally important and is directly related to the object of the present chapter. There must be a clear and complex "grammar" that enables speakers/writers and hearers/readers to comprehend the discursive practice.

There are just a few more remarks that are pertinent to Version 1 of discourse analysis. They tend to affirm the social component of the conversational role that people have in talking about politics. John Gumperz (1982) makes a vital point that must be remembered relating to the informational aspect of discourse: "While all information on language ultimately derives from speech, the assumption is that the raw information collected in situ must first be sifted and recorded in more general form before it can be utilized in the linguist's generalizations" (p. 11). That is, we must examine, as Gumperz puts it, the strategic use of language through speech in use. The uses are many and varied, and the present section details many of those uses. Gumperz (1982) also affirms that analytical character of the study of discourse: "In determining what is meant at any one point in a conversation, we rely on schemata or interpretive frames based on our experience with similar situations as well as on grammatical and lexical knowledge" (p. 21).

More than understanding of language as such is needed to examine discursive practices; as we have seen, there are regularities of discourse and conversation that must be taken into account.

When it comes to a critical approach to discourse analysis, the thought of Norman Fairclough (2010) is necessary for our current program:

> I would highlight three themes of the paper as particularly significant for later work. First, the claim that ideologies are primarily located in the "unsaid" (implicit propositions). . . . The second theme is that norms of interaction involving aspects of the interpersonal meaning and forms (e.g., turn-taking systems) may be ideological, in addition to the more widely discussed case of ideational meanings and forms—the "content" of texts. The third theme is the theorisation [sic] of power as in part "ideological/discoursal," the power to shape orders of discourse, to order discursive practices in dominance. Even causal conversation has its conditions of possibility within relations of ideological/discoursal power. (p. 27)

Fairclough (2010) adds the matter of textual discourse as well. Texts are definitely verbal and are, in many instances, akin to speech in terms of communicative action. "I am claiming language use to be imbricated in social relations and processes which systematically determine variations in its properties, including the linguistic forms which appear in texts. One aspect of this imbrication in the social which is inherent to the notion of discourse is that language is a materials form of ideology, and language is invested by ideology" (Fairclough, 2010, p. 59).

As an aside (and apropos of the preceding comments), it is necessary at this time to reiterate some of the points already mentioned related to ideology. Howarth (2000) reminds us that "sciences and ideologies may coexist in the same discursive formation, and sciences themselves may have an ideological expression without necessarily compromising their claims to scientificity. In sum, ideologies are a particular sort of discursive practice, coexisting with other practices in a society" (p. 60). The words of John Thompson (1984) are also important: "The analysis of ideology is fundamentally concerned with *language*, for language is the principal medium of the meaning (signification) which serves to sustain relations of domination" (p. 131). The key point Thompson makes here is related to the relations of domination. This is one purpose of discourse, and it can be employed to gain a purchase over what is said, what is heard, and what actions ensue. One may think, initially, of recordings of the speeches of Hitler, and the influence he carried. Of course, as has been mentioned earlier, persuasion is only one of the manifestations of ideology. The expression of ideas themselves also counts as ideology, and it is this meaning that will be part of the conversational examples that will come later.

That said (and with regard to what will be analyzed here), ideology carries power that works against mutual understanding and agreement. As an illocutionary act, it must be acknowledged for what it can be (and do). Slavoj Žižek (1989) presents what influence ideology can carry:

> This is probably the fundamental dimension of "ideology": ideology is not simply a "false consciousness," an illusory representation of reality, it is rather this reality itself which is already to be conceived as "ideological"—"*ideological" is a social reality whose very existence implies the non-knowledge of its participants to its essence*—that is, the social effectivity, the very reproduction of which implies that the individuals "do not know that they are doing." "*Ideological" is not the "false consciousness" of a (social) being but this being itself in so far as it is supported by "false consciousness."* Thus we have finally reached the dimension of the symptom, because one of its possible definitions would also be "a formation whose very consistency implies a certain non-knowledge on the part of the subject": the subject can "enjoy the symptom" only in so far as its logic escapes him—the measure of the success of its interpretation is precisely its dissolution. (p. 21; emphasis in original)

An example of the influence of ideological language fits here. Eric Kelderman (2021) reports that, in the state of Iowa, there are efforts to remove tenure at the state's three universities: "Iowa's Republican-controlled legislature is considering a bill to eliminate tenure at those three public universities. The bill is nothing new; similar versions have been introduced for several years running, never to advance further than that. But this year, the bill passed a full-committee vote for the first time" (p. 7). Kelderman (2021) points out that all voices, regardless of political party or ideology, are protected by the academic freedom that comes with tenure. Kelderman (2021) concludes, "Even if the effort to end tenure dies this year, it is likely to reemerge in coming years. There are also several other bills aimed at scrutinizing political activity and academic content at the public universities. One would require the Board of Regents to survey employees' political beliefs" (p. 7). What if the bill were to pass, and what if the political power were to shift at some future time? Would the present party be dismayed that the tables might turn? The ideological strictures of teaching, for example, political science or economics would carry very serious ramifications for knowledge (see the quotation earlier by Lyotard).

The example, reported by Kelderman, illustrates the politicization of knowledge through ideology. This stance is validated by Diane Macdonell (1986), who says,

> There is a range of scientists and disciplines which are said to give some kind of knowledge . . . , but they are clearly not all the same. Where they conflict, epistemology can be called in to adjudicate between them, accrediting some and discrediting others. Above all, epistemology functions within bourgeois ideology to impose, even on the material sciences, an appearance of neutrality and truth. In this way, their power or lack of it seems guaranteed, whether by reason or by the way things are; and awkward questions about how the development of knowledges is socially controlled, how knowledges are used, what interests they serve, can all be conveniently forgotten. (p. 60)

What is at stake, then, is power, and power can be related to discourse according to Version 2.

A major feature of the second version is the expression and/or employment of power. Discursive practices can entail the relation of power of one party over another. Do note that these expressions of power are not merely distinctions of difference, of disagreement. This can signal that the words used in the practices are not neutral, that they carry formations of dominance or ascendency. Pierre Bourdieu (1991) points out that this use of language, which can be accredited by some "body," can be authoritative; in short it can be "performative" (pp. 69–70). Fairclough (1989) is of the opinion, "Power at these levels includes the capacity to control orders of discourse; one aspect of such control is ideological—ensuring that orders of discourse are ideologically harmonized internally or (at the societal level) with each other" (p. 30). The power, the authority may also be manifest as censorship—the withholding or distortion of information. "This structural censorship is exercised through the medium of the sanctions of the field, functioning as a market on which the prices of different kinds of expression are formed . . . and it condemns the occupants of dominated positions either to silence or to shocking outspokenness" (Bourdieu, 1991, p. 138). We must be aware that such censorship can certainly be political, but it is not limited to any political party. What is common to all sorts of censorship is a deleterious effect on liberty, something that serious conservatives and serious liberals believe deeply in.

One person, among those who can be associated with Version 2 must be examined—Michel Foucault. In one of his major works he (1972) asks a pointed question: "The description of the events of discourse poses a quite different question: how is it that one particular statement appeared rather than another?" (p. 27). In other words, why is it that one thing that is said comes to the fore, instead of another thing that is said? Foucault tends to express this question and seek answers in historical contexts primarily but not exclusively. He (1972) articulates a difference between his archaeological approach and traditional history by saying, "The analysis of the discursive field is oriented in a quite different way; we must grasp the statement in the exact specificity of it occurrence; determine its condition of existence, fix at least its limits, establish its correlations with other statements that may be connected with it, and show what other forms of statements it excludes" (p. 28). "Exclusion" is extremely important. When there is a dominant force of discursive practice, voices may be silenced. That in itself might have an impact on liberty, but that effect can be exacerbated by the disallowing of the alternative statements to arise to the point where it can be heard or read. Again, censorship becomes a possibility.

Foucault's idea of discourse analysis carries a unique feature. The dominant discursive practices not only identify and reflect the statements that are made, they contribute to the constitution of social action. The dominant practices not only make statements that are heard and read, they can exclude contesting messages and communicative action. As Howarth (2000) makes clear, discourses consist of four basic elements. These are "the *objects* about which statements are made, the *places of speaking* from which statements are enunciated, the *concepts* involved in the formulation of discourse, and the *themes* and *theories* they develop" (p. 52; emphasis in original). This description details the essential elements that comprise the components of discursive practice. The last of the four may be the most important; in particular, theorization is a key element of dominant discourse.

How do the practices of the dominant forces develop and exercise such dominance? Foucault (1972) offers one set of practices and loci where practices develop and are carried out:

> [Practice] is both reinforced and accompanied by whole strata of practices such as pedagogy—naturally—the book-system, publishing, libraries, such as learned societies in the past, and laboratories today. But it is probably even more profoundly accompanied by the manner in which knowledge is employed in a society, the way in which it is exploited, divided and, in some way, attributed. (p. 219)

Foucault's warning is echoed by Bourdieu (1988), who speaks specifically about the nature and practice of scientific communication:

> The risks of misunderstanding in the transmission of scientific discourse on the social world depend, in a very general way, on the fact that the reader tends to make the utterances of the language of construction function as they would function in ordinary usage.... Scientific discourse demands a scientific reading, capable of reproducing the operations of which it is itself the product. (p. 21)

Foucault (1970) brings home the problem of scientific discourse: "Historians want to write histories of biology in the eighteenth century; but they do not realize that biology did not exist then, and that the pattern of knowledge that has been familiar to us for a hundred and fifty years is not valid for a previous period" (p. 127). Dominant discursive forces may employ systemic dominant structures as a means to keep meaning away from those who do not share technical vocabularies or the social systems that control language and communication. Again, this is not necessarily the purview of one political party. There is a tendency for a group, when it is in a state of domination, to attempt to control discourse and discursive practice. As Howarth (2000) notes, "discourse theorists are concerned to produce *accounts* of actual discourses. Clearly, the truth claims of these accounts have to be evaluated and it is in this regard that the problem of truth and falsity is pertinent" (pp. 113–14).

The objects of discourse are a starting place for many analyses. Foucault (1972) expresses this himself:

> "Words and things" [it should be noted that the French title of Foucault's *The Order of Things* is actually *Les mot et les choses*] is the entirely serious title of a problem: it is the ironic title of a work that modifies its own form, displaces its own data, and reveals, at the end of the day, a quite different task. A task that consists of not—of no longer—treating discourses as groups of signs (signifying elements referring to contents or representations) but as practices that systematically form the objects of which they speak. (p. 49)

My (2006) own conclusion to the matter is that "speech, therefore, embodies epistemological, rhetorical, communicative, obfuscatory, political, cultural, and other intentions" (p. 75). Foucault (1977) sums up the nature of the challenge most effectively, and with reference to the purpose of the present book: "The imaginary is not formed in opposition to reality as its denial or compensation: it grows among signs, from book to book, in the interstice of repetitions and commentaries; it is born and takes shape in the interval between books. It is a phenomenon of the library" (p. 91).

Truth and Truth Claims

More than a decade ago I (2011) wrote, "Harvard Law Professor Cass Sunstein's (2009) recent book, *On Rumors*, should be read carefully by everyone who is interested in information studies in any way. The book's importance lies, not in the narrowness of the phenomena of rumors, but in Sunstein's expansion of what rumors are and how they manifest themselves" (p. 56). Sunstein (2009) himself says, "Far from being the best test of truth, the marketplace can ensure that many people accept falsehoods, or that they take mere fragments of lives, or small events, as representative of some alarming whole" (p. 10). These remarks set the tone for the present section of the chapter. Truth is essential to discourse, as individuals seek—separately or collectively—what is right and correct and what is a key to the conversations that take place. The goal of discourse, to which the library is an integral part, is absolutely necessary to honest and forthright conversation. That said, there has been a lot of thought and writing devoted to truth and what comprises it. It is, then, incumbent upon me in this examination to review the ideas related to what truth is and how it can become part of our lives.

In the popular mind, truth seems to be a simple and straightforward thing; what is not a lie or a deception is true. As we saw with the discussion on meaning (especially Alfred Tarski), truth is more complicated than that. This is why philosophers have been pondering the nature of truth for millennia. A review of some of these notions is necessary for us to progress toward discursive truth, which can be elusive (and that may appear to be counterintuitive to most people). To many, truth refers to the way things are, and the statement of what is true relates directly to the way things are. A common example is: the statement "snow is white" is true because snow is white. When one looks at falling snow one sees a white substance coming down from the sky. That popular viewpoint carries semantic power; it means something to a hearer or reader of the statement. This kind of statement provides a beginning for us to give serious consideration to truth and what it is.

To bring home the reality that truth is not simple we can turn to Burgess and Burgess (2011): "Inquiry, it is said, aims at the truth. Yet it's doubtful there is any such thing as *the* truth. So it might be better to say that inquiry aims at truths, and better still to say that different inquiries from archaeology to zoology aim at different truths from archaeological to zoological" (p. 1). They use the example of the sciences, where foci of attention from one discipline to another may be somewhat narrow and may be, at times, incongruent from one science to another. Nonetheless, it may be that we cannot set our sights on *one* single truth. For example, scientific knowledge is different from religious belief. If I am a Christian I may hold some different to be true that is different from an adherent of Judaism (or even from other Christian sects). When we speak of science, though, we should apply a particular set of criteria that is peculiar to the given scientific discipline. The danger an alligator presents to a swimmer will seldom present disagreements among discussants. If everything were that straightforward, there may not be much need for this section of the present book. But we do need to explore truth in detail.

There is one disclaimer that needs to preface discussion. In no way does what follows advocate "relativism." Relativism is defined, according to Frederick Schmitt (1995), as, "At least some truth-values are relative truth-values—truth-values relative to a person, culture, system of beliefs, cognitive framework, intellectual perspective, or conceptual scheme" (p. 60). This stance may be typified by a response such as, "That is your opinion; I believe the opposite." Michael Lynch (2005) postulates a particular viewpoint on relativism: "According to postmodern relativism, a belief is true just when it passes for true or when it is *justified relative to the standards accepted within the culture or community—the systems that account for how statements are created, distributed, and regulated*" (p. 38; emphasis in original). Schmitt (1995) elaborates on his position:

> The central point of contention in the theory of truth is whether truth involves a relation to thinkers. All theories agree that in *some* sense truth *does* involve such a relation. On the correspondence theory, for example, truth involves a relation between the bearer of truth-values (usually, a sentence, statement, or proposition) and the world (or facts, or objects and their properties), and this relation in turn entails a relation to thinkers. (p. 229; emphasis in original)

We will return to the correspondence theory, and others, momentarily, but the takeaway from Schmitt is that all claims to truth emanate from an individual's mind. What is important is the set of tools used by the individual to arrive at a truth claim. So while what Schmitt says is technically correct, it is too subtle to be useful to our purposes here.

At this point it is necessary to take a step back and to examine the predominant theories of truth as they relate to objectivity. Chase Wrenn (2015) elaborates on three such theoretical families:

> On one side is *realism*, the view that there are some claims whose truth does not depend on their being believed by anyone or even the possibility of anyone's knowing them. On another side is *relativism*, the view that the truth is always a matter of opinion, in the sense that the truth of any claim always depends on who believes it. The third contender is *anti-realism*, the view that

part of what makes a claim true is the fact that we can know it, and so claims we cannot know to be true or false cannot be true or false. Each view presents a different picture of how the world is, and each has its own advantages and disadvantages. (pp. 11–12; emphasis in original)

It should be noted that these are not the only views of truth; they are the ones that have something to do with objectivity. For example, pragmatists emphasize the utility of beliefs; what *works* or has the desired utilitarian results is true. William James (1909) is one prominent advocate from the past; Richard Rorty (1979) is a more contemporary adherent. We will not address this aspect of pragmatism because it has little to do with objectivity. Also, we will not spend time with the coherence theory of truth. This states, "<p> is true just in case <p> belongs to a coherent set of propositions" (Schmitt, 1995, p. 104). Consistency is the hallmark of this theory. While Wrenn says each of the views he addresses has advantages and disadvantages, the advantages of some outweigh those of others. I stated earlier that I adhere to the correspondence theory, and that will have to be defended.

Why truth? Any communicative action depends on reliable information, exchanged between and among the parties involved. Reliability is a matter of honesty, shared freely in the interests of inclusion of discussants under the auspices of truth. Where there is evidence, that should be a necessary component of the communication. When people converse, engage in discursive practice, they are (as we will see) obliged to be forthright and forthcoming with truthful information. Fred Dretske (1981) addresses this matter, "What information a signal carries is what it is capable of 'telling' us, telling us *truly*, about another state of affairs. . . . If everything I say to you is false, then I have given you no information" (p. 44; emphasis in original). Dretske adds "truth" deliberately; information is that which shapes or forms to something (in this case, to what is said). If there is no information exchanged there is no genuine communication, unless the hearer recognizes what is said as something untrue. Otherwise, there is either a mistake, a false belief, or deceit. People can certainly be mistaken; no one is perfectly informed. People may be deluded into believing something that is not true. When people deceive, though, there is an intentional act aimed at achieving a specific result. Misinformation and disinformation (something Dretske also addresses) are also forms of deceit. We can return now to what truth is and how it may be manifest in communication.

Previously in this chapter there was a substantive explication of meaning, what it is and what it can accomplish. Now it seems appropriate to address how meaning relates to truth, and how the structure of statements, utterances, and sentences contribute to truth. Chase Wrenn (2015) goes so far as to say,

> We can define truth in the following way:
> (a) It is atomic, and the object the singular term designates satisfices the general term, or
> (b) it is universal, and everything satisfices the general term, or
> (c) it is existential, and something satisfices the general term, or
> (d) it is a negation, and the sentence negated is false, or
> (e) it is a conjunction, and both the sentences conjoined are true, or
> (f) it is a disjunction, and either of the sentences composing it is true, or
> (g) it is a conditional, and if the sentence after "if" is true, then so is the sentence after "then." (p. 83)

This is an exhaustive list, and it covers many contingencies. The possibilities may not be endless, but this may be the most complete definition related to meaning that exists. The list includes the universal as well as the singular, the positive as well as the negative. Examples could be provided for each of the items on the list, but this is not the place to expand upon them in depth. Suffice it to say, the list is inclusive and demonstrates the principal possibilities for the determination of whether an utterance is true.

One of the most readable treatments of truth is the work of Michael Lynch (2005); it is intended to be accessible to any serious reader. Early on, he sets out determinants of truth in straightforward terms:

> So here are our truisms about truth:
>
> Truth is objective.
>
> Truth is good.
>
> Truth is a worthy goal of inquiry.
>
> Truth is worth caring about for its own sake.
>
> This is what I meant by saying that truth matters. (p. 19)

When Lynch makes the claim that truth is objective, he does not mean (and he is careful to point out) that utterances do not carry necessary certitude. That is, just because a person makes a statement or a claim that person's opinion or belief is inviolable. "Certainty is the privilege of the fanatic. The most dangerous man is he who is certain, absolutely sure, that his way is the right way" (Lynch, 2005, p. 29). This claim is especially pertinent to the content of the present chapter. Truth, while objective, is a goal that one strives for through examination and evidence (about which more will be said later). Lynch (2005) further says, "It is a confusion to think that a belief in objective truth necessarily implies a lack of respect for other ways of life and other types of beliefs. The cause of intolerance is not objectivity but dogmatism. It stems from a sense that one can't be wrong" (p. 33). By extension, the belief in truth as objective is a position of tolerance, a stance that is open to possibilities that puts one on the trail of truth.

Lynch (2005) places particular value on integrity, especially intellectual integrity: "*Intellectual* integrity is an aspect or part of integrity proper. It requires being willing to stand up for your best judgment of the truth, by being willing to act in accordance with that judgment when the need arises" (p. 131; emphasis in original). In other words, integrity requires commitment, commitment to the truth as he has defined it. Intellectual integrity also requires, simultaneously, tenacity and tolerance. The person embodying this integrity will be able to discern when others are adhering to beliefs that carry relativism, are boastful lies, or are mistaken in their set of beliefs (and conclusions based on those mistaken beliefs). Lynch (2005) adds some requirements: "A person with intellectual integrity is someone who is willing to *pursue* the truth. . . . [A] person of intellectual integrity stands for what she thinks is true *precisely because she thinks it is true*. . . . [I]ntellectual integrity also requires being *open* to the truth just because it is the truth" (pp. 132–33). These characteristics are not those of a zealot but are those of someone seriously driven to find the truth and to assess it accordingly.

What about truth and politics? Tim Heysse (2020) addresses this question: "Commitment to democracy in various senses entails commitment to the truth of political-normative and substantial statements" (p. 66). He (2020) maintains that democracy fosters true beliefs or, at the very least, the avoidance of false beliefs; this, he says, is an argument for desiring a democratic society (p. 56). He (2020) also claims that, recently, an epistemic rehabilitation of democracy (ERD) has taken place. What does this mean?

Three propositions summarize ERD:

1. As a system of political *rule*, democracy institutionalizes a principle of self-legislation entailing immanentism . . . ; only reasons acceptable to the citizenry are admissible in democratic decision-making and no one else's acceptance is required. . . .
2. The principle of self-legislation has certain formal properties. . . . But what lends self-legislation authority is that it is *true*. . . .

3. There is an epistemic argument in favour [sic] of democracy: democracy increases the probability that decisions that are the outcomes of democratic procedures are correct. (p. 61; emphasis in original)

The third proposition may be the most important; if there is a relationship to truth, there is not only a desirability for democracy but an imperative to bring it about. Politics, truth, and democracy *can* go hand in hand.

When we return to realist theories of truth there is a frequent qualification regarding justification. William Alston (1996) refers to "the extent to which a belief is *justified warranted, rational, well grounded*, or the like. To cut corners I will use the word JUSTIFIED to range over any positive epistemic status that is taken by some thinker to constitute truth" (p. 190; emphasis in original). While not every theorist shares Alston's view (for example, Simon Blackburn [2005] claims that justification is a political achievement meant to ensure that a belief is followed [see p. 166]), justification or warrant is a necessary component of a realist theory of truth. Correspondence theories include justification in one or another form so as to ground the theory in the world as it is. I mention earlier that I tend to follow correspondence as the soundest basis for true beliefs. Alvin Goldman (2002) offers an approach to justification: "Another possible approach to the theory of justification . . . is what I shall call *deontological evidentialism*. Deontological evidentialism, as I conceive of it, says simply that an agent should assign a degree of belief to a proposition in proportion to the weight of evidence she possesses" (p. 55). Goldman (2002) devotes a great amount of space to what constitutes evidence, and it includes, but is not limited to, physical evidence. Testimony from experts is among the kinds of justification he mentions. His reasoning for testimony is extensive (see Goldman, 2002, pp. 139–63).

A bit more can (and should) be said about correspondence theory before we move on. Schmitt (1995) presents the most straightforward interpretation: "A proposition is true just in case it corresponds to facts in the world" (p. 145). "Facts in the world" is a sweeping criterion. It refers to physical facts, of course, such as the age of the universe, biological data, etc. It also refers to social facts, such as who happens to be the current president of the United States. There are beliefs, discussed earlier, that do not fall within the purview of correspondence theory, such as religious beliefs, but other beliefs tend to be included under the theory. Richard Kirkham (1992) states a more elaborate version of the theory: "Correspondence as correlation and correspondence as congruence. The first of these, put very simply, says that every truth bearer is correlated to a state of affairs" (p. 119). He goes on:

> What the correspondence-as-correlation theory does *not* claim is that the truth bearers mirrors, pictures, or is in any way isomorphic with the state of affairs to which it is correlated. A truth bearer *as a whole* is correlated to a state of affairs *as a whole*. On the other hand, correspondence as congruence *does* claim that there is a structural isomorphism between truth bearers and the facts to which they correspond when the truth bearer is true. (p. 119; emphasis in original)

It is evident that correspondence as congruence is a much more stringent theory than its counterpart, so stringent that it is difficult to adhere to without opening oneself to criticism. While Bertrand Russell believed in congruence, others, such as J. L. Austin, declined to believe that correspondence mirrors the world as it is. It is not only much easier to believe in correspondence as correlation; it is more realistic to so believe.

Personally, I choose to agree with Garth Hallett (1988):

> I believe . . . that truth-as-correspondence . . . merits general acceptance, both as an account of usage and as a norm. . . . I believe, furthermore, that such correspondence typically embodies important values, that these values explain the traditional prestige of truth, and that the everyday concept of truth does indeed reveal a norm we should follow in every type of discourse, and specifically in theoretical discussion—for instance, here, in the discussion of truth itself. The uses of words not only do, as a matter of fact, repeatedly conform to their established uses, but they should consistently do so, in every area of inquiry. (p. 109)

There are just a couple of points that remain to be made with respect to truth and information. One is made by Labaree and Scimeca (2008), who warn, "The concept of truth remains largely undefined in the field of library and information science. As a consequence, analysis is predominantly considered only with a certain context related to interpreting truthfulness in practice, understanding truth as it is applied to existing philosophical theories or implied in philosophical discussions about knowledge creation, knowledge organization, and ideas about reality" (pp. 48–49). I (2011) have attempted to address the theoretical desideratum by stating a definition and a statement of theory:

> **Definition:** *Information* is meaningful communicative action that aims at truth claims and conditions.
>
> **Statement of Theory:** *Information* is comprised of those communicative actions (and *only* those communicative actions) that can be evaluated by a population—defined as the intended or potential bearers of the communica-

tion—as meaningful. Meaning is not limited to pure semantics, but includes context and history with evaluation. Further, information is true in that there is warrant for the communicative action, that this action includes no deliberate deception or omission, has inherent evaluative components, provides evidentiary justification, and is fundamental to ethics. (p. 70)

The adherence to the correspondence theory in discourse carries, as well, an ethical imperative. In fact, discourse itself carries an ethical imperative. That is what we will cover next.

Habermas and Discourse Ethics

Before delving into Habermas and his thinking about discourse ethics a bit of a beginning is needed. As we have just seen, truth carries a moral aspect, as well as being normative with respect to language and beliefs. It is also evident from the extensive discussion of discourse that it, too, carries a moral aspect. What will follow is *how* the moral and ethical elements of communication can manifest themselves. One concern is that communication and conversation be genuinely dialogic. That is, individuals do not engage in monologues because monologic communication tends to have a lack of listening. It is necessary to speak—that much is clear. It is also necessary to listen (hearken back to Goldman and the importance of testimony to justify beliefs). One of the people who not only urges dialogue but who sets forth both the necessity and the plan for dialogue is Mikhail Bakhtin. He writes (under the pseudonym Vološinov),

> *Word* is a *two-sided act*. It is determined equally by *whose* word it is and *for whom* it is meant. As word, it is precisely the *product of* the reciprocal relationship between speaker and listener, addresser and addressee. Each and every word expresses the "one" in relation to the "other." I give myself verbal shape from another's point of view, ultimately, from the point of view of the community to which I belong. A word is a bridge thrown between myself and another. If one end of the bridge depends on me, then the other depends on my addressee. A word is territory shared by both addresser and addressee, by the speaker and his interlocutor. (p. 86; emphasis in original)

In discussing this manner of thinking I (2001) wrote, "Bakhtin's definition is not intended to suggest that all communication is dialogic; only when the relationship between I and other is acknowledged and explicit can communication be genuinely dialogic" (p. 259). That relation between I and other is emblematic of one that will feature prominently in the next chapter—phenomenology. Much more will be said about this later.

Before turning to Habermas and his technical ideas about discourse ethics, some rather generic thoughts can be shared as a prelude. These thoughts can set the stage for a much more detailed look at discourse ethics.

1. Active participants in discursive practices/conversations are able to speak freely and openly, provided that no one individual dominates the conversation.
2. Active participants warrant the attention of the other participants; their speech should be listened and attended to.
3. The speech that takes place should be grounded in evidence that lends credence to what is said.
4. The evidence should follow the guidelines discussed earlier and can include empirical data, experience, and/or testimony by knowledgeable experts.
5. The exchanges that take place should be open and any discussion should be respectful and be based precisely on what has been said.

This list is by no means exhaustive, but it is intended to provide a basis for an ethical exchange of viewpoints and ideas. According to Habermas (1990),

> Discourse ethics . . . stands or falls with two assumptions: (a) that normative claims to validity have cognitive meaning and can be treated *like* claims to truth and (b) that the justification of norms and commands requires that a real discourse be carried out and thus cannot occur in a strictly monological form, i.e., in the form of a hypothetical process of argumentation occurring in the individual mind. (p. 68; emphasis in original)

(This hearkens back to Bakhtin.)

For Habermas, the meaning of discourse ethics is held to be a hallmark of argument. He (1994) says as much when he writes, "Anyone who seriously engages in argumentation must presuppose that the context of discussion guarantees in principle freedom of access, equal right to participate, truthfulness on the part of participants, absence of coercion in adopting positions, and so on" (p. 31). Some of these characteristics are systemic; they address the structure of conversation and the way it takes place. Some of them place an onus on the participants and make demands on people (such as truthfulness). By covering both, Habermas sets the tone for argumentation that is orderly and is intended to have moral results. He (1994) goes on to say,

> Every justified truth claim advocated by someone must be capable of being defended with reasons against the objections of possible opponents and must ultimately be able to command the rationally motivated agreement of the community of interpreters as a whole. Here an appeal to some *particular community of interpreters will not suffice*. (p. 53; emphasis added)

Reason and rationality must be components of this kind of argumentation. The last sentence of the quotation may be especially pertinent today; the argument has to be addressed to all, not solely to one group that may have an inherent bias or an avoidance of reason.

Habermas's position is affirmed by Seyla Benhabib (2002); she suggests, "The discourse model of ethics formulates the most *general principles* and *moral intuitions* behind the validity claims of a deliberative model of democracy" (p. 106; emphasis in original). Benhabib (2002) continues to emphasize the benefits to democracy of this approach to ethical communicative action. She says that all who adopt the norms "have an equal say in its validation if democratic legitimacy is to be attained. For discourse ethics, territorial boundaries and state borders are not coterminous with those of the moral community. Discursive communities can emerge *whenever* and *wherever* human beings can affect one another's actions and well-being, interests or identity" (p. 147; emphasis in original). If democracy is valued by citizens and communities, there should be an underlying structure that can allow for agreement and actions related to the agreement. It can also make possible just how agreement can be reached, through the necessities that Habermas outlines.

Discursive action signals power relations, with an aim of sharing influence and opinion, sharing rational arguments, and deliberating openly and freely. According to Benhabib (2002), there must be a set of principles that are adhered to so that the ultimate ends of discourse ethics can be achieved. She elaborates at some length:

> *Egalitarian reciprocity.* Members of cultural, religious, linguistic, and other minorities must not, by virtue of their membership status, be entitled to lesser degrees of civil, political, economic, and cultural rights than are members of the majority.
>
> *Voluntary self-ascription.* An individual must not be automatically assigned to a cultural, religious, or linguistic group by virtue of his or her birth. An individual's group membership must permit the most extensive form of self-ascription and self-identification; the state should not simply grant the right to define and control membership to the group at the expense of the individual. . . .

> *Freedom of exit and association.* The freedom of the individual to exit the ascriptive group must be unrestricted, although exit may be accompanied by the loss of certain formal and informal privileges. (pp. 148–49; emphasis in original)

The three items stated here are extremely important to the lives of individuals and to the efficacy of groups. For example, a person may decide to change political affiliation; that carries some freedoms, as well as some strictures. No one should be denied the ability to alter affiliation and exit and/or enter another group.

Benhabib's suggestions are practical and can affect anyone who would be engaged in ethical discursive practice. She addresses what individuals *should* be able to do as they engage in the conversations in which communities participate. This practical aspect is extremely important because it is a recipe for action. The kinds of conversations that take place in democratic societies are vital to the operation of political life. She includes minorities that can gain access to the practices that society as a whole seeks to accomplish. These factors must be emphasized because the idea of discourse and communicative practice is a realistic one. It seeks to tackle how individuals can function in political life. This is mentioned because some conceptions of discourse ethics are more idealistic than realistic. The idealistic is no less important, but it must be seen as one articulation of discourse ethics and, if one desires, can be seen as one means that can be employed in political life.

Habermas's components of discourse ethics may be seen as falling into the idealistic category. For example, he designates a universal principle of ethical conversation: "(U) *All* affected can accept the consequences and the side effects its *general* observance can be anticipated to have for the satisfaction of *everyone's* interests (and these consequences are preferred to those of known alternative possibilities for regulation)" (p. 65; emphasis in original). In a later work, Habermas (1998b) restated the universalization principle: "(U) A norm is valid when the foreseeable consequences and side effects of its general observance for the interests and value-orientations of *each individual* could be *jointly* accepted by *all* concerned without coercion" (p. 42; emphasis in original). The addition of the absence of coercion is vital; if there is to be freedom (for example, of exit or participation of the communicative action) there must be no coercion to participate or to leave.

Habermas (1990) follows up the universalization principle with the discourse ethics principle:

(D) Only those norms can claim to be valid that meet (or could meet) with the approval of all affected in their capacity *as participants in a practical discourse*. (p. 66; emphasis in original)

He (1998b) adjusts this to read, "(D) Only those norms can claim validity that could meet with the acceptance of all concerned in practical discourse" (p. 41). There is little difference in the meaning of the two expressions, but the first (1990) appears to be more complete and inclusive, even if more verbose. In the latter (1998b) expression Habermas emphasizes "acceptance" instead of "approval." That slight revision is not trivial; if "approval" were replaced in the first expression with "acceptance" the meaning of the principle would not simply be preserved but enhanced.

The two principles are essential to the kinds of conversations that can take place in the political sphere. The essential character rests on the participants' willingness to commit to the ethical practice of conversation. This means that the participants have to be committed to listening and assessing what others say. Given that requirement, possibilities open up and there are potentialities for compromise and understanding, as we will see in the next chapter. The outcome that is desired is not necessarily changing the minds of others but comprehending precisely why they hold the views they do and the *reasons* for the beliefs (and actions based on the beliefs). Habermas (1994) speaks to the essential matter by articulating the connection between the possibilities and the nature of the self and the commitments that follow from the essential principles:

The roles of agent and participation in discourse overlap in such processes of self-clarification. Someone who wishes to attain clarity about his life as a whole—to justify important value decisions and to gain assurance concerning his identity—cannot allow himself to be represented by someone else in ethical-existential discourse, whether in his capacity as the one involved or *as the one who must weigh competing claims*. (p. 11; emphasis added)

Discourse ethics, according to Habermas (1990), requires at least two people interacting in communicative action; moreover, ethical success requires that each participant recognizes one another as someone capable of assuming responsibility for their actions. What is needed is a mutual understanding of such a capability and a mutual respect that each participant will follow the requirements of discourse ethics. Nothing less will lead to an understanding, much less an agreement. Habermas (1994) expresses an even more strict observance:

My programmatic justification of discourse ethics requires *all* of the following:

1. A definition of a universalization principle that functions as a rule for argumentation
2. The identification of pragmatic presuppositions of argumentation that are inescapable and have a normative content
3. The explicit statement of that normative content (e.g., in the form of discourse rules)
4. Proof that a relation of material implication holds between steps (3) and (1) in connection with the idea of the justification of norms

Step (2) in the analysis, for which the search for performative contradictions provides a guide, relies upon a maieutic method that serves

2a. to make the skeptic who presents an objection aware of presuppositions he knows intuitively,
2b. to cast this pretheoretical knowledge in an explicit form that will enable the skeptic to recognize his intuitions in this description,
2c. to corroborate, through counterexamples, the proponent's assertion that there are no alternatives to the presuppositions he has made explicit. (pp. 96–97; emphasis added)

Not all agree with Habermas, his universalization principle, and his rules. Matthew Weinshall (2003) speaks for many when he says that *only* those who have been accepted and will participate will be included in conversations. If only the "competent" individuals are included, there is likely to be bias (p. 28). Habermas admits as much and states this fact repeatedly. Weinshall (2003) also criticizes the structure by saying that only those who are able to engage in instrumental rationality can participate (p. 32). These criticisms are stated by others as well. Again, Habermas admits the rationality requirement and recognizes that some will be disqualified. However, he also adds that intelligent and aware persons are ideally able to embody these characteristics and to participate according to principles and rules. The goal is to *state* the principles and rules so that discourse ethics can be achieved. This is his anticipation of the rules. Without his universalization principles and the dictates governing participation, though, there is little hope for realizing discourse ethics. For that reason, discourse ethics can be a goal that is worth aiming for. The foregoing discussion of discourse ethics summarizes Habermas's position, and it also sets the tone for what is to come.

Discussion

This chapter has sought to detail just what constitutes discourse and discursive practice. The complexities of communicative action are clearer now, as are the theories of discourse that define how people converse, semantically and semiotically. In particular, how we make meaning is explored. The chapter has drawn heavily from Habermas and his particular ideas concerning communication and discourse ethics. All of this is pertinent to what will follow in the next chapter, which will address the conversations that can occur in libraries. In a very real sense, the present chapter is a prelude to the ways libraries and librarians can facilitate conversations regarding politics. As we will see, there is a specific attitude that enhances the nature of the conversations and the ways individuals speak with one another. Habermas's discourse ethics draws heavily from what he refers to as the "lifeworld." This is a very complicated notion and will deserve a considerable amount of explication before examples of the kinds of conversations can be examined. The concept of lifeworld is closely tied to a technical element of philosophy—phenomenology. The next chapter will delve deeply into phenomenology so that readers will comprehend where it comes from, what it is, and how it helps define effective conversation in libraries. The background will lead us to sets of topics that can be fodder for discourse surrounding politics—conservative and liberal.

References

Alston, W. P. (1996). *A realist conception of truth.* Ithaca: Cornell University Press.

Austin, J. L. (1975). *How to do things with words.* Second edition. J. O. Urmson and M. Sbisà (Eds.). Cambridge, MA: Harvard University Press.

Austin, J. L. (1979). *Philosophical papers.* Third edition. J. O. Urmson and G. J. Warnock (Eds.). Oxford: Oxford University Press.

Barthes, R. (1967). *Writing degree zero and elements of semiology.* A. Lavers and C. Smith (Trans.). Boston: Beacon Press.

Benhabib, S. (2002). *The claims of culture: Equality and diversity in the global era.* Princeton: Princeton University Press.

Blackburn, S. (1984). *Spreading the word: Groundings in the philosophy of language.* Oxford: Oxford University Press.

Blackburn, S. (2005). *Truth: A guide.* Oxford: Oxford University Press.

Bourdieu, P. (1988). *Homo academicus.* P. Collier (Trans.). Stanford: Stanford University Press.

Bourdieu, P. (1991). *Language and symbolic power.* G. Raymond and M. Adamson (Trans.). Cambridge, MA: Harvard University Press.

Brown, G., and Yule, G. (1983). *Discourse analysis*. Cambridge: Cambridge University Press.
Budd, J. (2001). Information seeking in theory and practice: Rethinking public services in libraries. *Reference & User Services Quarterly* 40(3), 256–63.
Budd, J. M. (2006). Discourse analysis and the study of communication in LIS. *Library Trends* 55(1), 65–82.
Budd, J. M. (2011). Meaning, truth, and information: Prolegomena to a theory. *Journal of Documentation* 67(1), 56–74.
Burgess, A. G., and Burgess, J. P. (2011). *Truth*. Princeton: Princeton University Press.
Cooke, M. (1994). *Language and reason: A study of Habermas's pragmatism*. Cambridge, MA: MIT Press.
Dant, T. (1991). *Knowledge, ideology & discourse: A sociological perspective*. London: Routledge.
de Gramont, P. (1990). *Language and the distortion of meaning*. New York: New York University Press.
de Saussure, F. (1966). *Course in general linguistics*. W. Baskin (Trans.). New York: McGraw-Hill.
Devitt, M., and Sterelny, K. (1999). *Language and reality: An introduction to the philosophy of language*. Second edition. Cambridge, MA: MIT Press.
Dretske, F. I. (1981). *Knowledge and the flow of information*. Cambridge, MA: MIT Press.
Elbourne, P. (2011). *Meaning: A slim guide to semantics*. Oxford: Oxford University Press.
Fairclough, N. (1989). *Language and power*. London: Longman.
Fairclough, N. (2010). *Critical discourse analysis: The critical study of language*. Second edition. London: Routledge.
Foucault, M. (1970). *The order of things: An archaeology of the human sciences*. New York: Vintage Books.
Foucault, M. (1972). *The archaeology of knowledge and the discourse on language*. A. M. S. Smith (Trans.). New York: Pantheon.
Foucault, M. (1977). *Language, counter-memory, practice: Selected essays and interviews*. D. F. Bouchard and S. Simon (Trans.). Ithaca: Cornell University Press.
Gee, J. P. (1999). *An introduction to discourse analysis: Theory and method*. London: Routledge.
Goldman, A. I. (2002). *Pathways to knowledge: Private and public*. Oxford: Oxford University Press.
Guiraud, P. (1975). *Semiology*. G. Gross (Trans.). London: Routledge and Kegan Paul.
Gumperz, J. J. (1982). *Discourse strategies*. Cambridge: Cambridge University Press.
Habermas, J. (1984). *The theory of communicative action: Volume one: Reason and the rationalization of society*. T. McCarthy (Trans.). Boston: Beacon Press.

Habermas, J. (1990). *Moral consciousness and communicative action.* C. Lenhardt and S. W. Nicholsen (Trans.). Cambridge, MA: MIT Press.
Habermas, J. (1994). *Justification and application: Remarks on discourse ethics.* C. P. Cronin (Trans.). Cambridge, MA: MIT Press.
Habermas, J. (1998a). *On the pragmatics of communication.* M. Cooke (Ed.). Cambridge, MA: MIT Press.
Habermas, J. (1998b). *The inclusion of the other: Studies in political theory.* C. Cronin and P. De Greiff (Eds.). Cambridge, MA: MIT Press.
Hallett, G. L. (1988). *Language and truth.* New Haven: Yale University Press.
Harris, R. (1987). *Reading Saussure.* La Salle, IL: Open Court.
Hawkes, T. (1977). *Structuralism and semiotics.* Berkeley: University of California Press.
Heysse, T. (2020). Truth in democratic politics: An analysis of commitments. *Social Theory and Practice* 46(1), 55–88.
Holdcroft, D. (1991). *Saussure: Signs, system, and arbitrariness.* Cambridge: Cambridge University Press.
Howarth, D. (2000). *Discourse.* Buckingham: Open University Press.
James, W. (1909). *The meaning of truth.* Cambridge, MA: Harvard University Press.
Kearns, K. (2011). *Semantics.* Second edition. New York: Palgrave Macmillan.
Kelderman, E. (2021). Tenure under siege. *Chronicle of Higher Education* 67(13), 7.
Kincheloe, J. L., and Tobin, K. (2009). The much exaggerated death of positivism. *Cultural Studies of Science Education* 4(4), 513–28.
Kirkham, R. L. (1992). *Theories of truth: A critical introduction.* Cambridge, MA: MIT Press.
Labaree, R. V., and Scimeca, R. (2008). The philosophical problem of truth in librarianship. *Library Quarterly* 78(1), 43–70.
Lehrer, K. (1990). *Theory of knowledge.* Boulder, CO: Westview Press.
Lynch, M. P. (2005). *True to life: Why truth matters.* Cambridge, MA: MIT Press.
Lyotard, J.-F. (1984). *The postmodern condition: A report on knowledge.* G. Bennington and B. Massumi (Trans.). Minneapolis: University of Minnesota Press.
Macdonell, D. (1986). *Theories of discourse: An introduction.* Oxford: Basil Blackwell.
McCarthy, T. (1978). *The critical theory of Jürgen Habermas.* Cambridge, MA: MIT Press.
Mills, S. (1997). *Discourse.* London: Routledge.
Moon, J. D. (1995). Practical discourse and communicative ethics. In S. K. White (Ed.), *The Cambridge companion to Habermas* (pp. 143–64). Cambridge: Cambridge University Press.
Outhwaite, W. (1994). *Habermas: A critical introduction.* Stanford: Stanford University Press.
Palmer, R. E. (1969). *Hermeneutics.* Evanston, IL: Northwestern University Press.
Polanyi, M., and Prosch, H. (1975). *Meaning.* Chicago: University of Chicago Press.
Recanati, F. (2012). *Mental files.* Oxford: Oxford University Press.

Rorty, R. (1979). *Philosophy and the mirror of nature*. Princeton: Princeton University Press.
Schmitt, F. F. (1995). *Truth: A primer*. Boulder, CO: Westview Press.
Searle, J. R. (1969). *Speech acts: An essay in the philosophy of language*. Cambridge: Cambridge University Press.
Searle, J. R. (1979). *Expression and meaning: Studies in the theory of speech acts*. Cambridge: Cambridge University Press.
Searle, J. R. (1983). *Intentionality: An essay in the philosophy of mind*. Cambridge: Cambridge University Press.
Stubbs, M. (1983). *Discourse analysis: The sociolinguistic analysis of natural language*. Chicago: University of Chicago Press.
Sunstein, C. R. (2009). *On rumors: How falsehoods spread, why we believe them, what can be done*. New York: Farrar, Strauss and Giroux.
Tarski, A. (1944). The semantic conception of truth: And the foundations of semantics. *Philosophy and Phenomenological Research* 4(3), 341–76.
Thompson, J. B. (1984). *Ideology and modern culture*. Stanford: Stanford University Press.
Vološinov, V. V. (1986). *Marxism and the philosophy of language*. L. Matejka and I. R. Titunik (Trans.). Cambridge, MA: Harvard University Press.
Weinshall, M. (2003). Means, ends, and public ignorance in Habermas's theory of democracy. *Critical Review* 15(1/2), 23–58.
White, Stephen K. (1994). *The recent work of Jürgen Habermas: Reason, justice & modernity*. Cambridge: Cambridge University Press.
Wrenn, C. (2015). *Truth*. Cambridge: Polity Press.
Žižek, S. (1989). *The sublime object of ideology*. London: Verso.

CHAPTER THREE

What Conversations Can Take Place in Libraries (and in What Ways)?

As was promised in the last chapter, this one will begin by outlining in some detail the foundation of the attitude toward conversation in libraries about politics. One of the qualifications that even precedes discussion of a foundation is the need to think clearly and critically. Fortunately, Anthony Flew (1998) produces a blueprint, a set of tactics that can guide everyone as each person contemplates such things as politics. Throughout his book, Flew (1998) provides advice that give commonsense guidance to think about any claim that one is presented. Among the advice he offers is to be aware of the motive people may have for making a claim, to look for causes that can relate claims to the actual state of affairs, to learn how to sort facts from what he refers to as "bunk," to reason with others whenever possible, to avoid setting one's thoughts and opinions in concrete, and to assert, deny, propose, and refute when one is in conversation with others. Among the specifics of his advice, he (1998) says, "whenever and wherever I tolerate self-contradiction, then and there I make it evident, either that I do not care at all about truth, or that at any rate I do care about something else more" (pp. 16–17). Another bit that Flew (1998) suggests is, "Hypotheses are tested by deducing consequences which would follow if the hypothesis were true. When a hypothesis is tested and even one of its consequences is found in fact not to obtain, then that hypothesis, at least as originally formulated, is decisively demonstrated to have been false" (p. 36). One last observation will convey what Flew (1998) advises: "People may be persuaded by an abominable argument just as they may remain unconvinced by considerations which they certainly would accept if only they were more rational, or more honest, or both" (p. 62). This last passage is, of course, key to the idea of discursive practice that has been set forth here.

In the field of library and information studies there are some important works that are certainly pertinent to the purpose here. For example, Lankes, Silverstein, and Nicholson (2007) state, "Knowledge is created through conversation. Libraries are in the knowledge business. Therefore, libraries are in the conversation business" (p. 17). This syllogism captures precisely what I have been attempting to get across here. The authors (2007) continue: "If [conversation] theory is that conversation creates knowledge, the library community has added a corollary: the best knowledge comes from an optimal information environment, one in which the most diverse and complete information is available to the conversant(s)" (p. 18). The information proffered by libraries is definitely a major component of leading community members to develop their knowledge bases and to give shape to their beliefs. Lankes and colleagues (2007) also argue that technology plays a major role in developing and sustaining conversations. For example, they (2007) write, "An obvious example is libraries hosting blogs and wikis for their communities [as well as Twitter feeds and Facebook posts], creating virtual meeting spaces for individuals and groups" (p. 24). Existing and developing technologies render virtual meeting space possibilities more than merely possible; meetings *are* being held or sponsored now. Lankes et al. (2007) emphasize that the sponsorship and facilitation of meetings—in person or virtual—are essential means that can be used not only to reach but to involve community members.

There is one additional work that should be mentioned at the outset of this chapter. Beth Patin and colleagues (2021) present a particular concept relevant to social justice: "We argue epistemic injustices . . . occur in our field and cumulatively lead to epistemicide. . . . Epistemicide and its injustices present a complex, structural problem by impacting our fundamental capacity as knowers. If we are to be concerned with justice in society and within our field, it is critical we demand a paradigm shift to examine the epistemic injustices that harm one's capacity as a knower" (p. 1306). What does this mean? "We define epistemicide as the killing, silencing, annihilation, or devaluing of a knowledge system. . . . We believe epistemicide happens when several epistemic injustices occur that collectively reflect a structured and systemic oppression of particular ways of knowing" (Patin et al., 2021, p. 1307). Patin et al. borrow the idea from Bonaventura de Sousa Santos (2007), who said that epistemicide leads from one generation to the next, proliferating social and epistemic injustice. There are several harms that are created by epistemicide:

> The Primary Harm is to the individual. . . . After a person repeatedly experiences a Primary Harm, this may cause him [sic] to lose confidence in his beliefs and/or his justification for them. . . . The Secondary Harm [is to the larger society]. That concept of harm is important and emphasizes the loss to the here and now, but falls just short of acknowledging the loss of a potential knowledge legacy. . . . [There is a] *Third Harm*, which we define as a harm that is exponential in its potential to hurt, intergenerationally depriving not only the individual (primary) at this moment in time, and the current collective community (secondary), but addressing the scope of loss to the community. (Patin et al., 2021, p. 1312)

The present book actively recognizes the potential of epistemicide; this work is one effort to negate its deleterious efforts and potential.

The foundation for examination is phenomenology, and it will require quite a bit of background to describe it and to demonstrate just how it is foundational. A brief definition of phenomenology is "the study of human experience and of the ways things present themselves to us in and through such experience" (Sokolowski, 2000, p. 2). There are important aspects of phenomenology, which include the essence of things, intentionality, perception, intersubjectivity, and reason, among other things. The next section will explore what all this means for discursive practice and for libraries to operate as commons.

Phenomenology

It should be noted immediately that this coverage of phenomenology applies to all involved in the political conversation. This includes the discussants themselves—those who would engage one another in conversation—and those who would foster and structure the conversations. The latter group contains the librarians who provide the venue, the space, for the conversation, plus any who would serve as facilitators of conversations. Everything that follows is pertinent to the entire process of the discourse. It should be noted that this work will not cover the entirety of phenomenology; that would require multiple volumes. Some specific elements of phenomenology will be discussed as they relate to the purpose of this book. These elements will unfold in the coming pages.

The brief definition may not be sufficient to convey just what phenomenology is, and an understanding is central to what is to come. For example, as Jean-François Lyotard (1991) elaborates,

> The term signifies a study of "phenomena," that is to say, of that which appears to consciousness, that which is "given." It seeks to explore the given—"the thing itself" which one perceives, of which one thinks and speaks—without constructing hypotheses concerning either the relationship which binds this phenomena to the being of which it is phenomena, or the relationship which unites it with the I for which it is the phenomena. (pp. 32–33)

One of the characteristics of Lyotard's definition is the "presuppositionless" of the apprehension of phenomena. There are no a priori hypotheses, no beginning suppositions to taint or otherwise influence the perception of the given. Experience of the phenomena is key, and the experience is not limited to the physical senses. Stewart and Mickunas (1990) take this idea a bit further: "Basic to phenomenology is the contention that the world has no meaning apart from consciousness. But the relationship is reciprocal: consciousness has no meaning apart from the world" (p. 43). As Dermot Moran (2000) puts it, phenomenology "claims, first and foremost, to be a *radical* way of doing philosophy, a *practice* rather than a system. . . . Explanations are not to be imposed before the phenomena have been understood from within" (p. 4; emphasis in original).

Sokolowski (2000) expands upon his definition with considerably more detail:

> Phenomenology is the science that studies truth. It stands back from our rational involvement with things and marvels at the fact that there is disclosure, that things do appear, that the world can be understood, and that we in our life of thinking serve as datives for the manifestation of things. . . . Phenomenology also examines the limitations of truth: the inescapable "other ideas" that keep things from ever being fully disclosed, the errors and vagueness that accompany evidence, and the sedimentation that makes it necessary for us always to remember again the things we already know. (p. 185)

The requisite element of truth is extremely important to the very nature of phenomenology. Dan Zahavi (2003) emphasizes the role of truth in phenomenology: "Husserl now attempts to understand knowledge, justification, and truth on the basis of [a] model of justification. As long as we are making *signitive* claims, we are dealing with mere postulates. . . . When the object is intuitively given just as I intended it to be, my belief is justified and true; I am in possession of knowledge" (p. 31; emphasis in original). Zahavi (2003) continues, "Husserl also speaks of truth as the correlate of evidence, and one can also therefore also distinguish between two types of truth: Truth as a disclosure vs. truth as correctness [and also] true knowledge cannot simply be identified with the mere presence of an intuition" (p. 33). The connection of truth with evidence is vital; truth is ineluctably linked with evidence with the ends being justification and knowledge.

Walter Hopp (2020) also addresses the matter of truth. He (2020) says, "Propositions owe their truth or falsity solely to the obtaining or non-obtaining of the states of affairs that they represent. . . . This is plainly of realist theory of truth. In Husserl's hands, in his early work at least, it is a 'correspondence' theory" (p. 62). It should be noted that Husserl, in his later work, makes it clear that transcendental phenomenology is neither realist nor idealist but is some different that does embody some elements of both theories. There is a skepticism attached to naïve empiricism, just as there is a skepticism attached to, for example, Hegelian idealism. In fact, Peter Costello (2012) explains,

> In taking the path towards phenomenology, Husserl does not choose between the two possible options of realism and idealism, since he sees no compelling reason to attempt to reduce reflection to involvement, or vice versa. Rather, dissatisfied with both philosophical arguments and with the oppositions between them, he returns to the first position or assumption one makes in the natural attitude—namely, that things and the subject (or mind) *are*, and he asks whether that is the only way to relate to the question of being. (p. 15)

The question of being is a major issue for phenomenology.

Truth is related to meaning, although meaning has its own complexities that make it a concern all its own. J. N. Mohanty (1997) writes, "It becomes immediately clear that a meaning is a correlate of an act of meaning, so that it is not the detached meaning, reified into an ideal, self-existent entity, but rather the correlation between an act and its meaning, between what in the jargon of the school was called *noesis* and its *noema*, which is the proper theme for phenomenological investigation" (p. 2; emphasis in original). *Noesis* is the act in an intentional experience; *noema* is a meaning given to an intentional act. These definitions are actually as straightforward as they seem to be. The variable here is "intentional act." Moran (2000) quotes Edmund Husserl (1969) saying that consciousness is not a mere object:

> But experience is not an opening through which a world, existing prior to all experience, shines into a room of consciousness; it is not a mere taking of

something alien to consciousness into consciousness. . . . Experience is the performance in which for me, the experiencer, experienced being "is there," and is there *as what* it is, with the whole content and the mode of being that experience itself, by the performance going on in its intentionality, attributes to it. (§ 94, pp. 233–34; emphasis in original)

Experience is, then, a complex human action, *related* to consciousness but not a direct cause of it. One might say that experience is a contributary cause of consciousness—one among many things that lead us to be conscious of a phenomenon. In other words, experience can be a beginning of being conscious *of* something; it is a stage in intentionality. What is relevant here is that experience is not an end in itself; it is a component of a complex array of actions that lead to appreciation of what is. Husserl (1973) has something to say in support of this opinion: "If, therefore, we wish *to return to experience in the ultimately originated sense which is the object of our inquiry*, then it can only be to *the original experience of the life-world, an experience still unacquainted with any of these idealizations*" (§ 10, p. 45; emphasis in original).

Intentionality is a hallmark of all phenomenology, not just Husserl's. Zahavi (2019) clarifies what is meant by intentionality: "In being intentional, consciousness is not self-enclosed, but primarily occupied with objects and events that, by nature, are utterly different from consciousness itself" (p. 17). He (2019) continues, "It is customary to speak of intentionality as being aspectual or perspectival. One is never conscious of an object *simpliciter*, one is always conscious of an object in a particular way, be it from a certain perspective, or under a particular description" (p. 17; emphasis in original). A colloquial way to refer to the element of intentionality is to say that to be conscious is to be conscious *of* something. There is always the intended object or thought; consciousness is not empty. In short, intentionality "means the conscious relationship we have to an object" (Sokolowski, 2000, p. 8). Sokolowski (2000) adds, "By *phenomena* we mean, for example, pictures as opposed to simple objects, remembered events as opposed to anticipated ones, imagined objects as opposed to perceived, mathematical objects such as triangles and sets as opposed to living things, words as opposed to fossils, other people as opposed to nonhuman animals, political reality as opposed to the economic" (p. 13). In other words, the phenomena in question are not those of the natural sciences but are those of the human sciences.

Maurice Merleau-Ponty (1964) offers his own take on what phenomenology is:

> A phenomenology, therefore, has a double purpose. It will gather together all the concrete experiences of man which are found in history—not only those of knowledge but also those of life and of civilization. But at the same time it must discover in this unrolling of facts a spontaneous order, a meaning, an intrinsic truth, an orientation of such a kind that the different events do not appear as a mere succession. For a conception of this kind one comes to the spirit only by "the spirit of the phenomenon"—that is, the visible spirit before us not just the internal spirit which we grasp by reflection or by the *cogito*. This spirit is not only in us but spread far and wide in the events of history and in the human milieu. If it is true that [Edmund] Husserl sought by the study of phenomena to find the roots of reason in our experience, we should not be surprised that his phenomenology ended with the theory of a "reason hidden in history." (p. 52; emphasis in original)

The impact of history is not trivial; phenomenology embraces the past as well as the present; the past is also "given" to us as a reality that must be examined.

Merleau-Ponty rightly invokes Edmund Husserl; if there is a father of phenomenology, it is Husserl. Husserl began publishing notable works at the beginning of the twentieth century. Merleau-Ponty (1964) says,

> The crisis in science is attested by the many studies devoted to the value of science from 1900 to 1905 in France. . . . It was to be expected that Husserl, coming to philosophy from scientific disciplines (he began as a mathematician and his first work was a *Philosophy of Arithmetic*), should take very seriously this questioning of dogmatism concerning the foundations of geometry and physics. His desire to work out a new foundation for the sciences certainly weighed heavily in his decision to pursue a radical investigation in philosophy. (p. 43)

Merleau-Ponty (1964) continues, "Husserl, therefore, never agreed with a certain philosophical tradition in holding that philosophy could be a system of definitive results never requiring reexamination with the advance of experience," and, "As Husserl stated in his last years, the last subjectivity, philosophical, ultimate, radical subjectivity, which philosophers call *transcendental*, is an *intersubjectivity*" (p. 51, emphasis in original).

Intersubjectivity is vital to discursive practice of the sort talked about in the previous chapter. Peter Costello (2012), for example, points out that, "throughout his published works, Husserl sought to show how a rigorous description of human experience necessarily uncovers the fact that the object and the subject are always already united. This was the insight that Husserl labelled 'intentionality'" (p. 5). Costello expends the concept of intentionality—customarily, as we have seen, defined as being conscious *of* something—to illustrate that there is *always* a connection between subject and object. To put this into terms that are applicable here, intentionality is a force that helps to constitute *both* the apperception of what is said, written, and viewed, *and* the actions that may be taken with respect to others (we will return to the nature of the "other" shortly). The existence of the constitutive measure cannot be overstated. Consciousness is not merely an abstract mental experience; it carries with it the very purpose of action. For example, if a person becomes conscious of the content of a text (say, a book) that presents a liberal perspective on race, that consciousness is then contextualized within the totality of what the individual is conscious of. The totality of consciousness—by which I define intentionality—is the totality of intentionality. Within the totality, the person is called upon to reconcile and/or resolve agreements, contradictions, and aporias. This is a primary take for phenomenology. We will begin with a treatment of Edmund for a number of reasons, which will become clear shortly. A reason for such attention is provided by Dan Zahavi (2017): "In short, one way to argue for the continuing relevance of Husserl's phenomenology is by showing that there is still much to learn from his painstaking investigations of various concrete phenomena" (p. 1). He (2017) elaborates on his reasons for focusing on Husserl's legacy and continuing importance to all concerned with phenomenology:

> I will argue that Husserl was not a sophisticated introspectionist, not a phenomenalist, nor an internalist, nor a quietist when it comes to metaphysical issues, and not opposed to all forms of naturalism. On a more positive note, I will argue that a proper grasp of Husserl's transcendental idealism will reveal how fundamental a role he ascribed to embodiment and intersubjectivity. (p. 3)

We will examine Husserl's thought chronologically.

Early Husserl

At the start of the twentieth century Husserl began to move beyond his strictly scientific work and to explore what phenomenology could be. He did not abandon science altogether, but he concentrated more on logic and what that means for phenomenology. For example, he wrote (1970a),

> It is not therefore enough that the Ideas of logic, and the pure laws set up with them, should be given in such a manner. Our great task is now *to bring the Ideas of logic, the logical concepts and laws, to epistemological clarity and deficiencies.* Here *phenomenological analysis* must begin. Logical concepts, as valid thought-unities, must have their origin in intuition: they must arise out of an ideational intuition founded on certain experiences, and must admit of indefinite recon-

firmation, and of recognition of their self-identity, on the reperformance of such abstraction. (pp. 251–52; emphasis in original)

This marks the beginnings of his thoughts on what phenomenology is and what it can be. It is logic that governs the thinking and action. This is a part of the foundation of the beginnings of this thinking. The ideas of logic influence knowledge as well. He (1970a) also wrote, "We . . . conceive 'knowledge' in a wider, but not wholly loose sense: we separate it from *baseless opinion*, by pointing to some 'mark' of the presumed state of affairs or for the correctness of the judgement [sic] passed by us" (p. 61; emphasis added). The passage emphasized is absolutely vital to the thrust of the present work; what is needed is intuition and reflection in order to reach a state of knowledge about any phenomenon.

In fact, Husserl (1970a) expresses in clear terms what is needed for knowledge to obtain, as opposed to simple opinion. I should say here that for an individual to come down on the conservative or liberal (or other) side of a matter, Husserl's stricture's need to be remembered.

> We are concerned with discussions of a most general sort which cover the wider sphere of an objective *theory of knowledge* and, closely linked with this last, the *pure phenomenology of the experiences of thinking and knowing*. This phenomenology, like the most inclusive *pure phenomenology of experiences in general*, has, as its exclusive concern, experiences intuitively seizable and analysable [sic] in the pure generality of their essence, not experiences empirically perceived and treated as real facts, as experiences of human and animal experients in the phenomenal world that we posit as an empirical fact. (p. 249; emphasis in original)

This theme is one that carried forth throughout Husserl's thought and writings. The concept of knowledge, so expressed, is useful for all who would engage in conversation about political issues.

In this work, Husserl (1970a) affirms that actions should be free from presuppositions in order to function scientifically. He (1970a) writes, "An epistemological investigation that can seriously claim to be scientific must . . . satisfy the *principle of freedom from presuppositions*. . . . Every epistemological investigation that we carry out must have its pure foundation in phenomenology" (p. 263; emphasis in original). He (1970a) further states, "A purely phenomenological 'theory' of knowledge naturally has an application to all naturally developed, and (in good sense) 'naïve' science, which it transforms into 'philosophical' sciences" (p. 265). According to Moran (2000), the phenomenological science should not presume the results of any other science (p. 126). There should be an originality to the scientific application of phenomenology, and that consciousness helps to create an enlightened view of what constitutes human action. In a later work, Husserl (1999) went a bit further with his position: "All the various inferences proceed, as they must, according to guiding principles that are immanent, or 'innate,' in the pure ego" (p. 3). He (1999) goes further to say that any objectively valid results from inquiry signify "nothing but results that have been refined by mutual criticism and that now withstand every criticism" (p. 5). Zahavi (2003) explains what is meant by this position: "Our investigation should turn its attention toward the *givenness* or *appearance* or reality, that is, it should focus on the way in which reality is given to us in experience. We should, in other words, not let preconceived theories form our experience, but let our experience determine our theories" (p. 45). It comes down to what should come first, and Husserl's answer is that it should be experience, and that should lead all further thought and action to such things as theorizing.

In his early work, Husserl (1970a) details the importance of meaning and its sources and devises four points to illustrate what he intends:

1. It is part of the notion of an expression to have a meaning: this precisely differentiates an expression from the other signs. . . .
2. In meaning, a relation to an object is constituted. To use an expression significantly, and to refer expressively to an object (to form a presentation of it), are one and the same. . . .
3. If the meaning is identified with the objective correlate of an expression, a name like "golden mountain" is meaningless. . . .
4. If we ask what an expression means, we naturally recur to cases where it actually contributes to knowledge, or, what is the same, where its meaning-intention is intuitively fulfilled. (pp. 292–94)

Husserl rightly emphasizes the essential character and the importance of meaning. In some ways, the principles are a key to everything else he writes. The seeking of meaning is a primary act of human beings and human nature. And meaning is found in what is given to us, in what we are presented with. The idea of meaning reinforces the presuppositionless he has spoken of. It also reinforces the epistemological goal of phenomenology.

A reader may ask what the foregoing has to do with the message of this book. This concern deserves a reply (and a reply that will be reiterated down the line). As librarians approach providing a commons for conversation, the principles of phenomenology, including presuppositionless thinking, are vital to the effort. The efforts directed at discourse ethics presume *listening*. In order to listen effectively one must maintain an open mind and absorb the messages of others (and this will be addressed momentarily). Being open to the given is one way to accomplish the goal of an essential commons. Likewise, the participants in the conversations must adopt a similar stance. The premise of discourse ethics applies here as well. The openness to the given applies equally to the conversants. It is by these tenets that the effectiveness of the commons can be accomplished. Moreover, what follows will be essential to the establishment and maintenance of a space where political discourse can be shared, heard, and acted upon.

To return to Husserl, it is a matter of philosophical import that acts have potentially multiple aspects. He (1970b) says, "*Each concretely concrete objectifying act has three components: its quality, its matter, and its representative content. To the extent that this content functions as a purely signitive or purely intuitive representative, or as both together, the act is a purely signitive, a purely intuitive or a mixed act*" (p. 242; emphasis in original). Regarding the kind of communication we are speaking of here, the act is likely to be mixed. There is representative content that has a signitive (that is, related to signs and symbols) element *and* the intuitive (conscious, or present to us) element. Political speech contains both of these elements and is communicative in both ways. This is an important factor for Husserl because the act of perceiving an object is a complex act. He (1970b) states, "We therefore call the *phenomenological union of matter with representative content*, in so far as it lends the latter its representative character, the *form of representation*, and the *whole* engendered by these two moments the representation *pure and simple*" (p. 243; emphasis in original). The first portion of the quotation may be the most notable; there is the connection of matter/object with the representation that is essential to the totality of perception.

Another of the many roots of phenomenology is truth, which has been mentioned here. Husserl (1970b) discusses this aspect also:

1. If we keep to the notion of truth . . . , *truth* as the correlate of an identifying act is a *state of affairs* (*Sachverhalt*), as the correlate of a coincident identity it is an *identity: the full agreement* of what is meant with what is *given as such*. . . .
2. A second concept of truth concerns the *ideal relationship* which obtains in the unity of confidence which we defined as self-evidence, *among the epistemic essences of the coinciding acts*. . . .
3. We also experience in self-evidence, from the side of the act which furnishes "fulness," *the object given in the manner of the object meant*: so

given, the object of fulness itself. This object can also be called being, truth. . . .
4. Lastly, considered from the standpoint of intention, the notion of the relationship of self-evidence yields us truth as the *rightness of our intention* (and especially that of our judgement [sic]), its adequacy to its true object, or *the rightness of the intention's epistemic essence in specie*. . . . (pp. 263–64; emphasis in original)

When Husserl speaks of self-evidence he intends to relate it to the element of being in truth. There is also the obvious connection to knowledge, which is inextricably tied to truth. As Zahavi (2003) explains, truth lies between the meant and the given (p. 31). Truth, as is evident from Husserl's explanation, is also inextricably connected to the *given*, and perception is a component of the connection. Husserl (1970b) writes,

> In the sense of the *narrower, "sensuous" perception*, an object is directly apprehended or is itself present, if it set up in an act of perception *in a straightforward (schlichter) manner*. What this means is this: that the object is also an *immediately given object* in the sense that, *as this object perceived with this definite objective content*, it is not *constituted* in relational, connective, or otherwise articulated acts, *acts founded on other acts which bring other objects to perception*. (p. 282; emphasis in original)

Husserl's Middle Period

In 1913 Husserl articulated one of his most complete and influential statements about phenomenology. This work was unique at the time and guided the early thought of Martin Heidegger (although Heidegger later departed from Husserl on several important points) and Jean-Paul Sartre. It also set the stage for many of Husserl's later works (which, for reasons of space and efficiency, will not be treated at length here), providing some core ideas about the substance of his phenomenological thought. In this work, Husserl (1962) laid some groundwork for his conception of the science of phenomenology:

> Sciences of experience are *sciences of "fact."* The acts of cognition which underlie our experiencing posit the Real in *individual* form, posit it as having patio-temporal existence, as something existing in *this* time-spot, having this particular duration of its own and a real content which in its essence could just as well have been present in any other time-spot; posits it, moreover, as something which is present at this place in this particular physical shape (or is there given united to a body of this shape), where yet the same real being might just as well, so far as its own essence is concerned, be present in any

other place, and in any other form, and might likewise change whilst remaining in fact unchanged, or change otherwise than the way in which it actually does. (§2, pp. 46–47)

What do Husserl's words mean for us? For one thing, he is expressing the belief that science is a realist endeavor. This carries the implication that our perceptions, our experiences, and our discourse are all *real*; they are not fantasies or figments of our imagination. For one thing, our conversations have a reality that is the same as our experiences of the natural world. This is because *we* are part of that world. For another thing, the discourse in which we engage carries meaning; that meaning is also real. As we speak with one another we have to remember that the meaning—and the truth of what we say—can be determined. It is imperative for us to remember these facts about the phenomenology of our lives.

The realism of Husserl's conception neither ignores nor contradicts the presuppositionless of his thought. In order to adopt the position Husserl advocates, there is the necessity that one takes the world as given. As Edo Pivčevič (1970) states, "We do not have to deny the existence of the fact-world; in fact, we do not have to deny anything at all. All we have to do is to refrain from making any judgements [sic] concerning the 'things out there' in their spatio-temporal existence. This is the gist of his *epochē*" (p. 70). *Epochē* refers to the bracketing that is involved in the suspension of judgment until a phenomenological analysis can be performed. In fact, this process is integral to the distinction between two attitudes, or ways of being—the natural and the phenomenological.

In *Ideas* Husserl introduces at some length the difference between the attitudes. The natural attitude is just that, the less examined way of looking at the world around us—and at ourselves—that comes naturally in a simplistic empirical manner. He (1962) writes,

That which we have submitted towards the characterization of what is given to us from the natural standpoint, and thereby of the natural standpoint itself, was a piece of pure description *prior to all "theory."* In these studies we stand bodily aloof from all theories, and by "theories" here we mean anticipatory ideas of every kind. Only as facts of our environment, not as agencies for uniting facts validly together, do theories concern us at all. (§30, p. 95; emphasis in original)

Husserl (1962) continues, "This 'fact-world,' as the world already tells us, I find to *be out there*, and also *take it just as it gives itself to me as something that exists out there*. All doubting and rejecting of the data of the natural world leaves standing the *general thesis of the natural standpoint*" (§30, p. 96; emphasis in original). Some things have changed since Husserl articulated the nature of the natural attitude. The major alteration is that the digital/electronic world has joined the natural world of naïve empiricism. People absorb, for example, social media in much the same way they do the "fact-world." This is an important development, and it will be discussed near the end of this chapter.

The most complete commentary on the natural attitude is provided by Sokolowski (2000). He describes just how individuals perceive the world as it can be seen by empirical means. He (2000) also contrasts the natural attitude with the phenomenological attitude, which "is the focus we have when we reflect upon the natural attitude and all the intentionalities that occur within it" (p. 42). Sokolowski (2000) elaborates on what the phenomenological attitude is constituted of: "All human beings, all selves, do this sort of reflective philosophical analysis from time to time, but when most people enter into this kind of life they are usually very confused about what they are doing" (pp. 48–49). Enter phenomenology as a method of perceiving and of being. There must be an apperception of what the attitude is, how it manifests itself, and how people can make productive use of it. As Sokolowski (2000) says,

> The turn to the phenomenological attitude is called the *phenomenological reduction*, a term that signifies the "leading way" from the natural targets of our concern, "back" to what seems to be a more restricted viewpoint, one that simply targets the intentionalities themselves. Reduction, with the Latin root *re-ducere*, is a leading back, a withholding or a withdrawal. . . . When we enter into the phenomenological attitude, we suspend our beliefs, and we *bracket* the world and all the things in the world. We put the world and the things in it "into brackets" or "into parentheses." (p. 49; emphasis in original)

The bracketing is an act of reflection, an act that necessitates a certain kind of examination that transcends the "fact-world," or the naïve empirical world. There is something deeper to what is perceivable, and it is through the phenomenological attitude that the depth is achieved. Husserl himself makes the point that adoption of the phenomenological attitude does not negate the natural attitude or relegate it to insignificance. The world is still there and the givenness of the world must be accepted. What is possible and necessary is taking that givenness and *adding* the reflection of the phenomenological attitude so that the bracketing and the *epoché* will be an augmentation to the natural attitude. It is vital to remember that, for the phenomenological method to obtain, both attitudes must be exercised.

The acceptance of the natural and phenomenological attitudes is vital to the essence of the thrust of this present work. If individuals are going to converse with one another in honest, ethical, and complete ways, the truth of the natural attitude and the givenness of the fact-based world are necessary. As Zahavi (2017) points out, the positive sciences "operate on the basis of a natural (and necessary) naivety, namely the tacit belief in the existence of a mind-independent reality. This realist assumption is so fundamental and deeply rooted that it is not only accepted by the positive sciences, it also permeates our daily pre-theoretical life" (p. 56). This is something of a condemnation of the natural attitude, but it is a starting point for a *theoretical* attitude toward the world. It is thus necessary, but it is by no means sufficient. Zahavi (2017) also says, "Phenomenological reflection does not only target experiential structures. It also investigates the object of experience, and the correlational a priori that holds between the experienced object and the different modes of givenness" (p. 26). Husserl (1999) himself lays out the results of the adoption of the phenomenological attitude: "Once we have laid hold of the phenomenological task of describing consciousness concretely, veritable infinities of facts—never explored prior to phenomenology—become disclosed. They can all be characterized as *facts of synthetic structure*" (p. 41; emphasis in original).

It behooves all involved in the discursive practice of speaking (and listening) about the political world to transcend the natural attitude and to move to the phenomenological attitude. If librarians, for instance, can achieve this transcendence they will be in a position to guide the conversations. This will require librarians to attend to this section of the present work. They will have to familiarize themselves with the key elements of phenomenology (which we will continue to discuss) and what those elements mean for action. Moreover, it is the responsibility of the conversants to accept the transcendence of the positive sciences and the natural attitude. In short, all involved with the process need to be familiar with what has gone before (and what will follow).

Late Husserl

In his last published work, Husserl (1970c) summarized many of the points he made in earlier writings. For example, early on, he (1970c) writes, "Merely fact-minded sciences make merely fact-minded people" (p. 6). This is, of course, pertinent to the conception of the natural attitude. It displays his commitment to the phenomenological attitude; it may unnecessarily denigrate the natural attitude, which (as is noted earlier) is a vital step along the way to achieving the phenomenological attitude. Facts about the world should be apprehended as a means of transcending the naïve givenness of the natural world. That said, it is incumbent upon us all to make that transcendence and to reach a phenomenological attitude, complete with appreciation of intentionality, bracketing, and all other features of the attitude (including those we will explore that are articulated by others). In making his point, Husserl (1970c) states, "This new philosophy seeks nothing less than to encompass, in the unity of a theoretical system, all meaningful questions in a rigorous scientific manner, with an apodictically intelligible methodology, in an unending but rationally ordered progress of inquiry" (pp. 8–9).

We reach a point here where we must ask the question whether, and to what extent, librarians and discussants should be philosophers. Granted, there has been quite a lot of philosophy presented here to this point. This has been deliberate because it is the claim here that the professions in general, and librarianship included, need to have some philosophical foundations. One of the things we have been dealing with is knowledge, for instance. The development of knowledge and evaluation of knowledge claims necessitate attention to epistemology. There is also the assessment of the world as it appears to us and the world as it can be interpreted for meaning, which introduces metaphysics into the mix. As is evident at this point, I believe that phenomenology combines some vital philosophical insights and applies, I argue, directly to the discourse on politics and political life at this time in our history (as well as of history in general). Therefore, I do agree with Husserl's (1970c) specific assertion, "anyone who seriously seeks to be a philosopher, begin with a sort of *radical skeptical epochē* which places in question all his hitherto existing convictions, which forbids in advance any judgmental use of them, forbids taking any position as to their validity or invalidity" (p. 76).

We can turn to another work by Husserl for guidance as to what to apply and how to think about these complex questions. For example, he (1999) states, "*Reason is not an accidental de facto ability*, not a title for possible accidental matters of fact, but rather a title for an *all-embracing essentially necessary structural form belonging to all transcendental subjectivity*" (p. 57). Reason is to be applied; it is not an abstract entity or exercise. It allows us, for example, to examine what passes for evidence and enables us to make ultimate judgments. Because we begin without presuppositions, conclusions must be reached by some means. Reason and the apprehension and evaluation of evidence enable us to reach conclusions. Husserl (1999) tells us, "In the broadest sense, evidence denotes a universal primal phenomenon of intentional life, namely . . . the quite pre-eminent mode of consciousness that consists in the *self-appearance, the self-exhibiting, the self-giving*, of an affair . . . , a universality, a value, or other objectivity" (p. 57; emphasis in original).

He (1999) elaborates, "The evidence pertaining to particular Objects in a real Objective world is '*external* experience.' . . . [A]s a matter of essential necessity, external experience alone can verify objects of external experience, though, to be sure, it does so only as long as the (passively or actively) continuing experience has the form of a *harmonious* synthesis" (pp. 61–62; emphasis in original).

In summary (for this section), Husserl advocates for a stable and almost unanimous thought related to phenomenology over time—lifeworld. This is the totality of lived experience of the individual, the *ego cogito*. It encompasses what is perceived of the fact-world *and* the interpretation as part of the phenomenological attitude. It embraces all that we put into living our lives in a philosophical manner. Therefore, it is necessary to the conversations regarding political life that are at the heart of this book. Husserl (1970c) expresses the importance of lifeworld: "The life-world, for us who wakingly live in it, is always already there, existing in advance for us, the 'ground' of all praxis whether theoretical or extratheoretical. The world is pregiven to us, the waking, always somehow practically interested subjects, not occasionally but always and necessarily as the universal field of all actual and possible praxis, as horizon" (p. 142). Husserl then turns to the limitations of the natural attitude and contrasts it with a fully realized lifeworld. This is one of Husserl's most adopted ideas, although some, such as Martin Heidegger, take different turns on its meaning. Suffice it to say here that the conception and realization of lifeworld is necessary to the application of conversation of political themes that is at the heart of this work.

Other Phenomenologists

Maurice Merleau-Ponty

Maurice Merleau-Ponty, unfortunately, died quite young (in his early fifties), just as he was making some of the most significant contributions to phenomenology, particularly in the areas of perception and behavior. His focus of attention brought people's thinking into new arenas, and his work has been noted for decades because of the novelty of his approach and the profundity of his thinking. He (1962) addresses the question of what phenomenology is and arrives at his own version of an answer:

> It is a transcendental philosophy which places in abeyance the assertions arising out of the natural attitude, the better to understand them; but it is also a philosophy for which the world is always "already there" before reflection begins—as an inalienable presence; and all its efforts are concentrated upon

re-achieving a direct and primitive contact with the world, and endowing that contact with a philosophical status. (p. vii)

Merleau-Ponty's debt to Husserl is evident in his definition; they begin at roughly the same place. His (1962) debt extends, as is evident, to the givenness of the world: "The world is there before any possible analysis of mine, and it would be artificial to make it the outcome of a series of syntheses which link, in the first place sensations, then aspects of the objects corresponding to different perspectives, when both are nothing but products of analysis, with no sort of prior reality" (p. x).

Merleau-Ponty also accepts intentionality (in part because, if one is to buy into phenomenology, one *cannot* do anything other than to accept it; it is a hallmark of the philosophy). He (1962) writes,

> To "understand" is to take in the total intention—not only what these things are for representation (the "properties" of the thing perceived, the mass of "historical facts," the "ideas" introduced by the doctrine)—but the unique mode of existing expressed in the properties of the pebble, the glass or the piece of wax, in all the events of a revolution, in all the thoughts of a philosopher. (p. xviii)

Here we see Merleau-Ponty affirming what Husserl has said, plus going beyond Husserl in some important ways. The "mode of existing" is key to Merleau-Ponty's thinking and he emphasizes it throughout his works. In commenting on this element of Merleau-Ponty's thought, Gary Brent Madison (1981) comments, "Human existence is thus a structure. But this structure includes a duality; it is dialectical, and this means that it is composed of two terms which imply each other, which stand out against one another, and which exist only in this constant reference to one another" (p. 13). The recognition of the dialectic is not something that often occurs in critiques of Merleau-Ponty's phenomenology. This and other aspects of his thought do put the agreed-upon components of phenomenology into relief. Madison (1981) adds, "It can therefore be seen that the dialectic which constitutes human behavior is a *dialectic of transcendence* and that the structure is a vertical circularity" (p. 13; emphasis in original). His remark should not be understated.

To return to Merleau-Ponty, his take on intentionality is one way by which he demonstrates the originality of his thought:

> All consciousness is consciousness of something. Nor is this "something" necessarily an identifiable object. There are two ways of being mistaken about quality: one is to make it into an element of consciousness, when in fact it

is an object *for* consciousness, to treat it as an incommunicable impression, whereas it always has a meaning; the other is to think that this meaning and this object, at the level of quality, are fully developed and determinate. (p. 5; emphasis in original)

When he says an object (which need not be identifiable) can be an object for consciousness Merleau-Ponty adds a dimension to phenomenology. For example, the nonidentifiable object may be a thought, a conception that will eventually require a more complete realization; there may need to be a rendering of the nascent thought into an object of thought, although that is not the beginning stage. Moreover, there is an imposition upon consciousness, a requirement that consciousness *expend effort* on achieving the aforementioned rendering. In the context of the present work, this can be seen as exerting cognitive work to do the rendering of the concept into a fully realized conscious idea. A political statement may not be immediately open to full consciousness without the exerting of the work. Once that effort has been made, the cognizer may be able to subject the idea to the phenomenological attitude (which may require passing through and transcending the natural attitude).

One of the claims that Merleau-Ponty can make is the nature of alterity, the recognition of "otherness." This otherness is, as is the case with objects of consciousness, an external experience that is *given* to us. He (1962) explains,

Our task will be . . . to rediscover phenomena, the layer of living experience through which other people and things are first given to us, the system "Self-others-things" as it comes into being; to re-awaken perception and foil its trick of allowing us to forget it as a fact and as perception in the interest of the object which it presents to us and the rational tradition to which it gives rise. (p. 57)

It should interest us that he refers to the "rational tradition." This, again, is a paean to Husserl, who stressed the importance of reason as a means to become enlightened about what we can become conscious of. It also helps us now to place reason and rationality into the conversations and discursive practice that we can endeavor to achieve. The systemic notion is captured by Madison (1981) as he writes, "Thus between one's own lived body and the body of the other there is a circularity such that these two bodies together form a *single system*, just as, between consciousness and the body and between the lived body and the perceived world, there are internal relations which make it be that all these elements are moments of a single circular structure" (p. 40).

One additional passage from Merleau-Ponty's work brings home the choices we have as we approach our relationships with what is given to us:

> To revert with Descartes from things to thought about things is to take one of two courses: it is either to reduce experience to a collection of psychological events, of which the *I* is merely the overall name or the hypothetical cause, in which case it is not clear how my existence is more certain than that of any thing, since it is no longer immediate, save at a fleeting instant; or else it is to recognize as anterior to events a field and a system of thoughts which is subject neither to time nor to any other limitation, a mode of existence owing nothing to the event and which is existence as consciousness, a spiritual act which grasps at a distance and compresses into itself everything at which it aims, an "I think" which is, by itself and without any adjunct, an "I am." (p. 372; emphasis in original)

The ultimate reaching of "I am" is, in some ways, a culmination of the phenomenological philosophy. Husserl also turned to Descartes as a starting place and as a justification for referring to each of us as an *ego cogito*.

Emmanuel Levinas

Levinas, who lived most of his life in France, may be best known in phenomenological circles for his examination of what constitutes the relationship between self and other. He (1969) writes in one work, "To be I is, over and beyond any individuation that can be derived from a system of references, to have identity as one's content. The I is not a being that always remains the same, but is the being whose existing consists in identifying itself, in recovering its identity throughout all that happens to it" (p. 36). It is perhaps most important to emphasize that the self does not always remain the same. Each of us changes throughout our lives; this means that ideas can change, commitments can change, experiences can prompt change, and living persons' being can alter over time. He refers to experiences, as does Husserl, but stresses that existence is not static. This observation carries for the other as an "other" self, and other identity.

How do we relate to the other (or as Levinas refers, the absolute Other)? He (1969) writes, "Conversation, from the very fact that it maintains the distance between me and the Other, the radical separation asserted in transcendence which prevents the reconstitution of totality, cannot renounce the egoism of its existence; but the very fact of being in a conversation consists in recognizing in the Other a *right* over this egoism, and hence in justifying oneself" (p. 40; emphasis in original). For Levinas, the conversation that people engage in helps to maintain distance as it seems to create sharing.

Levinas, throughout his life, made the point that self and Other are distinct; we cannot say that the Other is nothing more than another self. There are distinctions, in part because of the unique experiences that each individual, each *ego cogito*, lives with and through. The challenge that remains is how to live, how to exist as a self among Others. Much of his writing aims to broach this challenge. One way this is met is through speech.

Levinas, in part, states that history is more than the past because it is a past of which we can speak. The speaking helps to define relationships, including the self and Other as they are now *and* as they are with the memory and the conversations in which the past is interpreted (interpretation will be revisited in the discussion of Paul Ricoeur). In addressing speech, Levinas (1969) observes,

> Rhetoric, absent from no discourse, and which philosophical discourse seeks to overcome, resists discourse (or leads to it: pedagogy, demagogy, psychagogy). It approaches the other not to face him, but obliquely—not, to be sure, as a thing, since rhetoric remains conversation, and across all its artifices goes unto the Other, solicits his yes. But the specific nature of rhetoric (of propaganda, flattery, diplomacy, etc.) consists in corrupting this freedom. (p. 70)

Levinas's passage can be taken as a warning; if rhetoric is defined in terms of such things as propaganda, and not as honest persuasion, there will be dysfunctional discursive practice. The ethical may be missing from the conversation, and it is the ethical that is absolutely vital to the kind of communicative action being spoken of in the present work.

Levinas sometimes takes issue with Husserl's phenomenology, but at one point he finds reason to praise it:

> The Husserlian thesis of the primacy of the objectifying act . . . leads to transcendental philosophy, to the affirmation (so surprising after the realist themes the idea of intentionality seemed to approach) that the object of consciousness, while distinct from consciousness, is as it were a product of consciousness, being a "meaning" endowed by consciousness, the result of *Sinngebung* [giving meaning to]. The object of representation is to be distinguished from the act of representation—this is the fundamental and most fecund affirmation of Husserl's phenomenology, to which a realist import is hastily given. (p. 123)

We have seen that Husserl insists upon a realism, a recognition of the "fact-world" as given to us. This is, as Levinas tells us, an act of consciousness *and* a product of consciousness.

As is the case with Husserl, thinking about what is outside ourselves is something that strikes Levinas as extremely important. Levinas (1998) writes,

> Thought begins the very moment consciousness becomes consciousness of its particularity, that is to say, that encloses it; when thought becomes conscious of itself and at the same time conscious of the exteriority that goes beyond its nature, when it becomes metaphysical. Thought establishes a relationship with an unassumed exteriority. As thinking being, man is the one for whom the exterior world exists. From now on, his so-called biological life, his strictly interior life, is illuminated by thought. (p. 15)

The fact-world is perceived by human beings first as part of the natural attitude, then evolving into the phenomenological attitude. This is something with which Levinas can agree. As he (1998) says, "Thought begins with the possibility of conceiving a freedom exterior to my own. To think a freedom exterior to my own is the first thought. It marks my very presence in the world" (p. 17).

Moreover, Levinas (1998) acknowledges the conversational activity in which people engage *as I and other*: "The *I* is ineffable because it is speaking par excellence; respondent, responsible. The other as pure interlocutor is not a known, qualified content, apprehensible on the basis of some general idea. He faces things, in reference only to himself. Only with speech between singular beings is the interindividual meaning of beings and things, that is, universally constituted" (p. 26). He recognizes that the other is not I; he sees, in contrast to some other phenomenologists, that the self, while able to perceive the exterior world, is *not* the other. One cannot see the other in the same terms as one sees the self. Yet there is an ethical relationship between self and other, manifest largely through conversation. Levinas (1998) says,

> The face to face of language admits of a more radical phenomenological analysis. To respect cannot mean to subject oneself, and yet the other commands me. I am commanded, that is, recognized as capable of a work. To respect is to bow down not before the law, but before a being who commands a work from me. But's for this commandment to entail no humiliation—which would deprive me of the very possibility of respecting—the commandment I receive must also be the commandment to command the one who commands me. It consists in commanding a being to command me. This reference of a commandment for a commandment is the fact of saying We, of constituting a party. By reason of this reference of one commandment to the other, We is not the plural of I. (p. 35)

Levinas's conception of I and Other is unique, even among phenomenologists, in some ways. This illustrates some ways in which the distinction is manifest, but he says even more about his idea of the Other. He (2003) expresses his own viewpoint:

> The Other is present in a cultural whole, illuminated by that whole just a text by its context. The manifestation of the whole endures its presence. It is illuminated by the light of the world. The Other gives itself in the concrete of the totality to which it is immanent and that . . . our cultural initiative—artistic, linguist, or corporal gesture—expresses and unveils. (p. 31)

His observation that the light of the world illuminates the cultural whole is one that is largely shared by the philosophers discussed here. Each of us is affected by the state of the world that we perceive. This includes the perception of the self and the perception of the Other, even though there may be differences between them. He maintains that the Other comes to the self through the context of perception of the world, but by himself/herself alone. That is, the self interacts with the Other through the constitution of mediation but also through an extra-mediated relationship. Self and Other can come together by means of both natural and phenomenological attitudes but also by means of one self confronting another self. This is undoubtedly a complex relationship, and we can turn to another philosopher for a somewhat different view, but one that is influenced by Levinas.

Paul Ricoeur

Paul Ricoeur was something of a polymath, writing on many topics throughout his very long career. He did, though, pay attention to a number of phenomenological issues. For example, he (1991) says, "A reflexive philosophy considers the most radical philosophical problems to those that concern the possibility of *self-understanding* as the subject of the operations of knowing, willing, evaluating, and so on" (p. 12; emphasis in original). Ricoeur appears to be sensitive to questions asked by Dan Zahavi (2005): "What is the relation between (phenomenal) consciousness and the self? . . . What is the relation between self-awareness and the self? . . . Finally, what is the relation between consciousness and self-awareness?" (p. 2). It would seem that the relation between consciousness and self-awareness is a prelude to the matter of self-understanding. Ricoeur (1991) unites the matter to intentionality: "That is to say, in the least technical sense, the priority of the consciousness *of something* over self-consciousness. . . . In its rigorous sense, intentionality signifies the *act* of intending something is accomplished only through the identifiable and reidentifiable unity of intended *sense*" (p. 13; emphasis in original).

Ricoeur (1991) continues on the theme:

> The most important consequence of all this is that an end is put once and for all to the Cartesian and Fichtean—and to an extent Husserlian—ideal of the subject's transparence to itself. To understand oneself is to understand oneself as one confronts the text and to receive from it the conditions for a self other than that which first undertakes the reading. (p. 17)

Ricoeur is speaking of reading texts, but his words apply, as he indicates, to individuals comprehending the self in the midst of others. Zahavi (2005) has something to say about this also:

> We are never conscious of an object *simpliciter*, but always of the object as appearing in a certain way; as judged, seen, described, feared, remembered, smelled, anticipated, tasted, and so on. We cannot be conscious of an object . . . unless we are aware of the experience through which this object is made to appear. . . . The object is given through the experience; if there is no awareness of the experience, the object does not appear at all. (p. 121; emphasis in original)

Ricoeur disagrees to some extent with Husserl and the idea of presuppositionless positioning. He (1991) says, "In what sense is the development of all understanding in interpretation opposed to the Husserlian project of *ultimate foundation*? Essentially in the sense that all interpretation places the interpreter in medias res and never at the beginning or the end" (pp. 32–33; emphasis in original). Ricoeur's point is well taken, but, as Husserl maintains, one can omit the extant interpretation and avoid presuppositions; Habermas appears to agree with this in his program of discourse ethics.

Ricoeur (1991) does agree with Husserl on some other phenomenological issues: "In thus linking explication to the clarification of horizons, phenomenology seeks to go beyond a static description of experience, a mere geography of the layers of meaning. The processes of transferring from the self to the other, then toward objective nature, and finally toward history, realize a progressive constitution—indeed ultimately a 'universal genesis'—of what we naively experience as the 'life-world'" (p. 51). The complexity of the phenomenological process is captured well by Ricoeur. There is a complex relationship between self and other, keeping in mind that these entities are separate and not the same, that presents to the self a challenge of understanding *and* self-understanding. There is a real object to be apprehending and interpreted by the self (and is also interpreted by the other) that exists and becomes a component of experience (primarily external experience). And there is an understanding of history (and this is a matter of self-understanding as well as the broader understanding of external and personal history). This is something of a summary of what we have to address as part of this book. If there are to be conversations, the foregoing components of phenomenology come into play.

Ricoeur also addresses discourse and its practice. This is an act that cries for interpretation and his work demands that interpretation be taken seriously. He (1991) tackles the issue directly:

> I propose to organize this problematic around five themes: (1) the realization of language as *discourse*; (2) the realization of discourse as a *structured work*; (3) the relation of *speaking to writing* in discourse and in the works of discourse; (4) the work of discourse as the *projection of a world*; (5) discourse and the work of discourse as the *mediation of self-understanding*. Taken together, these features constitute the criteria of textuality. (p. 76; emphasis in original)

We must keep in mind that the conversations are likely to be grounded in texts and textuality (in what individuals read and interpret prior to the discursive acts and prior to the setting aside of presuppositions). The entirety of the actions of those involved constitute events in which the individuals are involved. Ricoeur (1991) recognizes this added complexity and says, "What are we to understand by 'event'? To say that discourse is an event is to say, first, that discourse is realized *temporally* and in the *present*" (p. 77; emphasis added). All this takes place within a system of language that, if discourse is to be successful and effective, must be shared. There is not space here to address this vital matter, but the conversations that can take place in libraries depend upon shared language. This is by no means a trivial concern; absence of a shared language creates challenges on a monumental scale.

In another work, Ricoeur (1992) affirms the efficacy of the Other: "*Oneself as Another* suggests from the outset that the selfhood thought of without the other, that instead one passes into the other" (p. 3). As he says, self and other must be considered together, they are ineluctably linked though human action. That action carries consequences for both self and other and must be interpreted as such. He insinuates ethics into the relationship and into the life of the self. "Let us define 'ethical intention' as *aiming at the 'good life' with and for others, in just institutions*" (Ricoeur, 1992, p. 172). These words cannot be understated; in fact, they can be emblematic for the present work. The components of the statement provide direction for the discursive practices related to politics. There is, undeniably, an ethical element to the discourse and to the conversations that are centered on persons' ideas *and* the writings and speech upon which those ideas are based. The ethical can never be ignored or diminished, as Habermas pointed out and has been emphasized here.

Ricoeur (1992) elaborates on some of what he intends. Related to "with and for others," he says,

> My thesis is that solicitude is not something added on to self-esteem from outside that it unfolds the dialogic dimension of self-esteem, which up to now has been passed over in silence. By unfolding, as has already been stated in another context, I mean, of course, a break in life and in discourse that creates the conditions for a second-order continuity, such that self-esteem and solicitude cannot be experienced or reflected upon one without the other. (p. 180)

There is much to consider in his commentary, including the dialogic nature of the relationship between self and other. While there are differences between *I* and *thou*, there is the possibility of communicative action aimed at understanding. With greater understanding, differences do not disappear but can be diminished. The self-experience that comes with the demand to recognize the Other can be a powerful motivator to continue the living with and for others. Also, the *for* can be stressed as oneself acknowledges the Other and transcends merely living *with* others.

Ricoeur also states that the *places* in which we live and interact with others are an essential aspect of life. He (1992) notes that "living well is not limited to interpersonal relations but extends to the life of *institutions*. . . . What fundamentally characterizes the idea of institution is the bond of common mores and not that of constraining rules. In this, we are carried back to the ēthos from which ethics takes its name" (p. 194; emphasis in original). Living well is not an individual thing because people must interact and live together, especially in institutions. If we take the broadest possible view, the political life is, itself, an institution. We can each ensure that this (and other institutions) is ethically driven. Ricoeur recognizes that people live both individual *and* collective lives. We exist on our own and develop individual identities, but we do so within a larger context of living together. This includes sharing portions of life through, for example, work. Imagine a school or university; such a place requires justice as Ricoeur envisions it (that is, an ethical institution where the people do live with and for others). It is a simple matter to extend this example to other workplaces.

Ricoeur also sees the dynamic of discursive practice within his maxim. He (1992) writes, "What I am criticizing in the ethics of argumentation is not the invitation to look for the best argument in all circumstances and in all discussions but the reconstruction under the title of a strategy of *purification*, taken from Kant, that makes impossible the contextual mediation without which the ethics of communication loses its actual hold on reality" (p. 286; emphasis in original). The ethical element is thus unavoidable and the process of argumentation ceases to be a matter of *winning* but embraces understanding through dialogue. He (1992) continues, "What has to be questioned is the antagonism between argumentation and convention, substituting for it a subtle dialectic between *argumentation* and *conviction*, which has no theoretical outcome but only the practical outcome of the arbitration of moral judgment in situation" (p. 287; emphasis in original).

Phenomenology and Discourse

The foregoing is intended to supply us all with the wherewithal to carry out conversations on political issues in a civil manner. All of the mentioned tenets of phenomenology can, and should, be adopted by discussants—not so that each person changes her mind, but so that everyone can listen and speak ethically about matters that are extremely important and that affect our daily lives. We have explored meaning and its sources in semantics; Hopp (2020) connects meaning to intentionality in order to display the actual ways we communicate and comprehend:

> Propositions and concepts . . . do not owe their semantic or syntactic features to any conventions. If a word *changes meaning* that does not mean that the concept it expresses is such that *it* changes; rather, it means that the word expresses a different concept than it did before. . . . Similarly, when a person changes their opinion away from liberalism and towards conservatism, liberalism does not change into conservatism. (pp. 56–57; emphasis in original)

Hopp (2020) further links the gist of intentionality (consciousness is consciousness *of* something) with logic: "Logic is about something, namely the ontological form of the world. . . . In accepting *logical* laws, one is doing a lot more than agreeing to use symbols in accordance with certain conditions. One is accepting that reality must, could, and could not be certain ways" (p. 63; emphasis in original). So Husserl is at the very least a weak realist. Likewise, we should adopt a form of realism as part of our view of the world and the ways we speak about it.

There are some necessary realizations that need to occur if the objectives is of achieving a commons among libraries. David Woodruff Smith (2004) tells us, "Both phenomenology and ontology are crucial to a unified system of knowledge—of a unified world. And both carry us beyond naturalism: their results should be consistent with natural sciences, but the proper results of phenomenology and ontology are not simply amassed in empirical investigation in the natural sciences alone" (p. 15). The two together are necessary for our understanding both of the natural world and of the reflection on that world that must take place. Smith (2004) takes the ontological necessity further and his system is important to us here; there are three aspects that give the ontology its shape:

1. The *form* of an entity is how or what it is: its whatness or quiddity—the kinds, properties, relations that make it what it is.
2. The *appearance* of an entity is how it is known or apprehended: how it looks if perceptible (its appearance in the everyday sense), but also how it is conceived if conceivable, how it is used if utilizable—how it is experienced or "intended" as thus and so.
3. The *substrate* of a thing is how it is founded or originated: how it comes to be, where it comes from, its history or genetic origin if temporal, its composition or material origin if material, phylogenetic origin if biological, its cultural origin if a cultural artifact—in short, its ecological origin in a wide sense, and ultimately its ontological origin in basic categories or modes of being. (pp. 17–18; emphasis in original)

The three facets are illustrative of the ways things appear to us and the ways we act according to the facets.

Smith (2004) emphasizes the distinctions that occur in our apprehensions of what is presented to us:

A. Perception   B. Thought   C. Volition/Action

1. Sentient-Motor Activity
2. Indexical Awareness
3. Conceptual Intentionality
4. Symbolic Intentionality

As phenomenology describes human experience, the phenomenology of action describes the experience of *acting* or *doing* something, especially doing something consciously and intentionally, or volitionally. (pp. 114, 123; emphasis in original)

Intentionality once again comes to the fore.

To reiterate, intentionality means that consciousness is consciousness *of* something. This sounds very simple, but its application is more complicated. With reference to libraries as commons, this implies that the discussants be conscious/aware/reflective of the topic of discussion. For librarians, this requires that they be conscious of any and all of the political topics (pertinent here) that people may be invited to discuss. This does not require librarians to be expert on all topics, but it does mean that they be aware of multiple serious, evidence-based points of view. This puts a considerable burden on librarians who would, for example, facilitate the conversations that would take place. I maintain here that this is a necessary burden for libraries to fulfill the promise that has been mentioned earlier. Librarians should represent the political issues to themselves and to one another and should reflect upon the meaning of the political issues that might be discussed. It is possible that, in larger library systems, not all staff need to adopt the intentionality that Husserl and others speak of. In smaller libraries, however, everyone may have to adopt intentionality if they are to enable their libraries to serve as commons. And all should keep in mind that serious, thoughtful writings on topics are those on which to concentrate.

There may be a need, for libraries to act fully as commons, that conversations require facilitation. Facilitators of debate and discourse are frequently trained, and trained facilitators may well be needed for the commons to be realized. It is possible that some librarians may seek such training and become facilitators. If this is the case, then there should be time allowed for the training and, ideally, some reward for becoming a facilitator and acting as such during conversations among community members within the library. This is a burden that has to be recognized by administrators and, to be most successful, library board members. The facilitators' jobs include keeping discussion on topic, ensuring that conversation remain civil, and (this may be most important) in keeping with discourse ethics. The essential character of discourse ethics cannot be overstated. Quite a lot of attention has been paid to discourse ethics; this needs to be a component of the phenomenological attitude that librarians should aspire to. The preceding chapter provides rudimentary information about discourse ethics. If the ethical element is foremost (and is communicated to the discussants at the outset), there is potential for the goals of the commons to be achieved.

What will follow in the present chapter is an array of examples of topics that can be fodder for conversations in libraries working as commons. These certainly do not exhaust the possibilities for conversations, but they are issues that are on people's minds and can be treated to both the natural and the phenomenological attitudes. They are essential topics and they are difficult; they challenge discussants to listen as well as speak. The materials that are included in each instance are selected intentionally to represent serious thought regarding the issues and they also are intended to represent serious conservative and liberal points of view. The objective here is that these examples can provide bases for the kinds of conversations that can occur in libraries, among serious discussants (meaning those who seek to learn and share and are committed *not* to disrupt the conversation with ideological or polemical points), with the facilitation of those who are qualified to make certain that intentionality reigns and that discourse ethical behavior is the rule of the day.

Sample Conversations

Populism

Populism is, without a doubt, a complex concept. Definition is one of the complexities. Cas Mudde and Cristóbal Rovira Kaltwasser (2017) claim, "We position populism first and foremost within the context of liberal democracy. . . . Theoretically, populism is most fundamentally juxtaposed to liberal democracy rather than to democracy per se or to any other model of democracy" (pp. 1–2). In contrast, Jan-Werner Müller (2016) says, "In addition to being anti-elitist, populists are always *antipluralist*. Populists claim that they, and they alone, represent the people" (p. 3; emphasis in original). Paul Taggart (2000) offers another view:

> The phenomena which observers and participants describe as populist are unlike movements which form parties, develop programmes [sic] and policies and lead relatively stable and patterned political lives. Populist movements have systems of belief which are diffuse; they are inherently difficult to control and organize; they lack consistency; and their activity waxes and wanes with a bewildering frequency. (pp. 1–2)

We can see the challenge in these different viewpoints. That said, there is a perception that populism not only exists but is a commonplace even in the United States. Populism has a considerable history (see the previous authors' works), but only the present will be discussed here.

Mudde and Kaltwasser (2017) simplify their definition by saying, "A more recent approach considers populism, first and foremost, as a political strategy employed by a specific type of leader which seeks to govern based on direct and unmediated support from their followers" (p. 4). The talk about a politician's "base" is typical of this way of thinking. There are many people who believe in this definition. A substantial portion of the population strongly believes that the leader should turn first to the people in order to govern. Is there something wrong with this belief? Not necessarily. People believe in their own interests and will vote and support candidates accordingly. Steve Hilton (2018) supports such an idea as he begins his book: "This is an invitation for you to participate in the next revolution: the return of power back to the people, just as the Constitution intended. . . . But why a *populist* revolution? Why must it return *power to the people*? The case I'll make to you in this book is that the institutions and policies that shape today's economy, society, and government overwhelmingly benefit those at the top" (p. 1). His position is decidedly anti-elitist. He (2018) says, "The people's anger has horrified the elites on all sides. And no wonder: the technocrats, bureaucrats, and corporations from Wall Street to Silicon Valley, from Brussels to Davos and back to Washington, DC, sense a threat to their power" (p. 3).

Hilton (2018) further defines his position:

> Here's what Positive Populism means in practical terms. It is a pro-worker economic agenda designed to lift the living standards and reduce the economic anxiety of the majority of working families whose incomes fell as economic power was concentrated in the hands of the elite. It is a social policy agenda that aims to repair our torn social fabric, focusing in particular on the breakdown of family and community. (p. 7)

He (2018) continues, "There's something else that's significant about Positive Populism as a political philosophy. It is pragmatic, not ideological; inclusive, not tribal. Its aim is to solve problems using the methods that are more likely to work, whether or not they offend 'true believers' in America's two old parties" (p. 10). For a position such as Positive Populism, there is simultaneously a hope and a skepticism, the adherents would claim. There is the hope that the people could seize economic power from elites, thus ensuring that the gains that might be possible could be shared by all individuals and families (and not be limited to the very wealthy). The skepticism centers on a doubt of the established political parties who (it is perceived) have an interest in retaining the status quo. Messages from politicians that the status quo is wrong and should be changed resonate with many people, especially people who identify with the side that is not among the economic and political elite. In short, those who believe in "people power" are more likely to gravitate toward the kind of program that Hilton advocates.

Those who would find Positive Populism attractive are likely to agree with Hilton's diagnosis. For example, they may also articulate what he (2018) says about the causes of the problem: "Our illogical and unjust system is not a random accident. It is the result of deliberate policy choices. It is an elitist system because it has been designed to favor employers rather than employees, the owners of businesses rather than the workers" (p. 35). On the surface, such a diagnosis might seem to suggest that socialism is a possible solution to the problem. However, the believers in Positive Populism would point to the failures of Communist regimes and the totalitarian results of a turn to Communism of the form of the Soviet Union or the People's Republic of China. The adherents would reject socialism and argue for a more traditional form of democracy to solve the identified problems. To turn to Hilton again, he says, "the transformation we're seeing in our economy is set to dramatically sharpen the divide between the well educated and everyone else.... Unless we radically reshape it, education will become opportunity's enemy: imprisoning people with useless knowledge and out-of-date tools" (pp. 54–55). This might be a controversial viewpoint on which not everyone will agree. (One sample conversation will be "education," and such a position will be discussed.)

When it comes to what to do next, to how we should change, Hilton (2018) has some advice; he denies that all politics is local and claims

> that's why the positive populist is, at heart, a devolutionist. We want to keep power in the hands of the people, to decentralize it whenever possible. Going in the other direction, ceding power to a higher and inevitably more distant authority, should only happen when necessary—after a high burden of proof has been demonstrated. That's what a populist means by "limited government." Local, close to the people. That's the kind of agreement we need. (p. 167)

Hilton's idea, according to him, is positive; it seeks to remedy problems and to answer challenges. According to him it is also inclusive and seeks to create room for *all* people. As he (2018) concludes, "My populism is positive, open, and productive. It is patriotic and generous. I cannot bear to see it highjacked by a hateful few. Populism doesn't equal racism, or xenophobia, or bigotry—and rightly so" (p. 2018). This discourse concentrates on a positive message, but it is not necessarily the only assessment of populism.

For instance, Mudde and Kaltwasser (2017) write, "We define populism as *a thin-centered ideology that considers society to be ultimately separated into two homogeneous and antagonistic groups, 'the pure people' versus 'the corrupt elite,' and which argues that politics should be an expressions of the* volonté Générale *(general will) of the people*" (pp. 5–6; emphasis in original). It may seem, at first blush, that there is not much difference between their vision and that of Hilton, but the "pure people" are not as easily defined, nor do they constitute a unanimous population. They (2017) further state that "populism can be merged completely with nationalism, when the distinction between the people and the elite is both moral and ethnic" (p. 14). When it comes to the general will of the people, they (2017) say, "Rather than a rational process constructed via the public sphere, the populist notion of the general will is based on the notion of 'common sense'" (p. 18). Mudde and Kaltwasser (2017) deter from the thought of the likes of Hilton by claiming, "populism also has a dark side. Whatever its manifestation, the monist core of populism, and especially its notion of a 'general will,' may well lead to the support of authoritarian tendencies" (p. 18).

Mudde and Kaltwasser (2017) conclude, "Populism is part of democracy. Rather than the mirror image of democracy, however, populism is the (bad) conscience of liberal democracy. In a world that is dominated by democracy and liberalism, populism has essentially become an illiberal democratic response to undemocratic liberalism" (p. 116). Note that they do not say that populism is *undemocratic*; rather it is by nature democratic, but it is not the most effective response to the challenge of inequalities among citizens— inequality that may be structural. Taking up the party element, Taggart (2000) offers, "the *new* populism illustrates most clearly the anti-constitutional politics of populism in general. The attack on political parties . . . clearly [has] something to tell us about the state of contemporary party politics in the widest possible sense" (p. 73; emphasis added). Some populists, while affiliated with a political part, simultaneously distance themselves from party policy in an effort to distinguish themselves from the very parties that helped place them in office. That is, an individual may claim affiliation with an extra-party group as a means of uniting with a populist voter base. Affiliates of the Tea Party can be seen as examples of these kinds of populists.

Taggart (2000) also notes,

> In practice, populists are often more sure of who they are not than of who they are. The demonization of social groups, and particularly the antipathy towards the elite, provides populists with an enemy, but it is also a crucial component of the attempt to construct an identity. The new populism is a very conspicuous attempt to fashion an identity for what is otherwise an amorphous and heterogenous mass by singling out particular groups. (p. 94)

One might take what has been said about populism, in particular definitions of the "elite," as problematic within the context of the relationship between self and Other. It calls into question both identity and the nature of the Other, with the very definition of *ego cogito* called into question. Is this unavoidable? The answer depends on how people *act* with regard to populism. Müller (2016) suggests, "The crucial promise, simply put, is that the people can rule. At least in theory, populists claim that the people as a whole not only have a common and coherent will but also can rule in the sense that the right representatives can implement what the people have demanded in the form of an imperative mandate" (p. 76). There may be a basis for serious conversation that includes agreement and civil disagreement.

Nationalism
Nationalism, like populism, takes multiple forms, and writers have adopted many points of view in describing and analyzing it. Steven Grosby (2005) says, "Distinctive of nationalism is the belief that the nation is the only goal worthy of pursuit—an assertion that often leads to the belief that the nation demands unquestioned and uncompromising loyalty. When such a belief about the nation becomes predominant, it can threaten individual liberty" (p. 5). Of course there is the contrasting view of nationalism—it is positive, but it is incumbent upon every citizen to ensure that the nation optimize its liberty- and ethics-causing power. Grosby (2005) adds a further observation: "Nations emerge over time as a result of numerous historical processes. As a consequence, it is a pointless undertaking to attempt to locate a precise moment when any particular nation came into existence, as if it were a manufactured product designed by an engineer" (pp. 7–8). There is an evolutionary and complicated process by which nations emerge, even when geopolitical powers attempt to "create" nations (such as Yugoslavia in the twentieth century).

It may be useful to conceive of nationalism as an *idea* as much as a geographical and political entity. For example, Yoram Hazony (2018) suggests, "The *nationalism* I grew up with is a principled standpoint that regards the world as governed best when nations are able to chart their own independent course, cultivating their own traditions and pursuing their own interests without interference. This is opposed to *imperialism*" (p. 5; emphasis in original). The opposition is an important one; the self-determination of nations is a powerful idea, and an attractive one. Hazony (2018) continues this line of thought: "The individual's desire to protect his life, personal freedom, and property [which is a Lockean concept]. Each of us in fact wants and needs something else in addition, which I suggest we call *collective self-determination*:

the freedom of the family, tribe, or nation" (p. 9; emphasis in original). He claims that the rise of modernity has lessened these desires and argues throughout his book that they are forceful and enduring.

Rich Lowry (2019), adopting an avowedly conservative viewpoint, says, "Nationalism should rightly be infused with a country's ideals and its sense of mission; it should be a unifying force hostile to racism and all invidious distinctions that play into sub-national loyalties and identity politics; it should be respectful of the prerogatives of other nations, even as it is jealous of its own" (p. 15). In defending his definition of nationalism, Lowry (2019) states, "Of course, nation-states can be bumptious and aggressive, but a constant source of war throughout history isn't nationalism but its opposite: the quest for domination, the drive not to govern ourselves but govern others" (p. 49). If we look, for instance, at World War II, it is apparent that some "nations" did seek to take over other countries, to control and dominate. Germany did invade other countries and attempt to impose an ideology and a rule over those dominated. In this respect, Lowry is correct. He (2019) also praises Brexit as Great Britain's effort to reclaim its national identity in the face of the European Union's moves to dissipate the impact of nations and the cultural distinctions that the nations should embrace.

Hazony (2018) addresses a more conceptual matter:

> We see that political philosophy is naturally divided into two subjects, one more fundamental than the other. One subject is the *philosophy of government*, which seeks to determine the best form of government, given the existence of a state with a high degree of internal unity and independence. Prior to this is the *philosophy of political order*, which seeks to understand the causes of political order, and on the basis of this understanding, to determine what are the different forms of political order available to us and which of them is the best. (p. 59; emphasis in original)

He sees political order as the concern of the first order. Political order is the product of argumentation and reflection and not a knee-jerk reaction in favor of independence. That said, in the aftermath of the argumentation (in the Aristotelean sense) and reflection, independence and unity are likely to emerge. The difference is that the emergence is based upon reason and not a deference to something that might be taken to be self-evident in any event. So first comes reason, then the end product of nationalism arises.

Hazony (2018) also recognizes that a geopolitical area may be composed of difference and that unity may be difficult to come by. He says,

> By a *nation*, I mean a number of tribes with a shared heritage, usually including a common language [but not necessarily] or religious traditions [again, not necessarily], and a past history of joining together against *common* enemies—characteristics that permit tribes so united to understand themselves as a community distinct from other such communities that are their neighbors. By a *national state*, I mean a nation whose disparate tribes have come together under a single standing government, independent of all other governments. (p. 109; emphasis in original)

His definitions follow directly from his statement of philosophy. It is reason, deliberation, and argumentation that bring disparate tribes together under one government. The United States is something of an anomaly in Hazony's vision, with its commitment to states' rights and the limitations placed on the central government. History (and the present time) illustrates the tensions that the United States experiences in this structure. Nonetheless, the United States would be considered a national state by Hazony.

He (2018) goes further to offer that global security and peace can be realized through the acknowledgment of "an order of independent national states" (p. 168). He goes on:

> By definition, an order of national states—understood as distinct from a tribal or feudal order—involves the aggregation and mutual cohesion of many such tribes and clans, which have given up their supposed right to govern themselves, conduct foreign policy, and wage war, in order to for larger, independent national states whose tribes are internally at peace. The principle of collective self-determination, if transformed into a universal right of independence for every tribe and clan that asserts it, is just the opposite of such an order of national states. (pp. 169–70)

His outlook is optimistic, and there are instances around the globe where the tribal and clan interests are in opposition to the national states; the far-reaching consequences of dispute form one of the most existential challenges faced by all nations today.

Yael Tamir (2019) is aware of the challenge just mentioned:

> Present-day nationalism appears in two different forms, both grounded in the weakness of the state: the first, . . . represents the desire of national groups, concentrated in distinct territories, to capture the opportunity and demand self-rule. . . . The second kind of nationalism is the nationalism of the less well-off, those left defenseless by the process of hyperglobalization. The vulnerable revoke national feelings in order to convince the elites to come back home from their global voyage and put their nation first. (pp. 8–9)

Yet Tamir defends nationalism conditionally. She (2019) writes, "In the developed world two related processes transformed the social and political landscape: the political pendulum swung too far to the individualist pole . . . while the economic balance tilted too far to the free-market side. . . . These transformations raise new challenges and call for new responses" (p. 24). Tamir is undeniably optimistic, even in the face of some reactionary and populist examples of nationalism. Yet she claims that anger should be given a voice within the nation state, and there should be a move in favor of the benefit of the many rather than the few. She also states that "a borderless world is far from ideal; it can be neither democratic not just" (p. 34).

When it comes to the United States, it may be best to give Jill Lepore (2019) the final word because her diagnosis is grounded in something of a balance of concerns. She writes that there exist a good nationalism and a bad nationalism: "By good nationalism, they usually mean liberal or civic nationalism, an attachment to a set of civic ideals. By bad nationalism, they usually mean illiberal or ethnic nationalism, nativism, racism, and recourse to aggression. American nationalism is often figured as one or the other, but really it's almost always been both" (p. 58). "Nativism" usually refers to the concentration on the native born, with hostility to the Other, frequently in the form of immigrants. This can indeed lead to conflict, which unfortunately runs to the extreme. The phenomenological attitude can be the counter to what Lepore calls "bad nationalism," but this depends on a willingness of people to transcend the natural attitude and to accept the ethical imperative of "good nationalism."

Capitalism
At this point in history in Western nations, capitalism *is*. This is the case even though there are some socialistic elements in some places, such as nationalized medicine in Canada and the United Kingdom. It must be noted that capitalism is more than an economic phenomenon; it is just about as much political as it is economic. This aspect was recognized some time ago by Milton Friedman. He (2002) observes, "First, the scope of government must be limited. Its major function must be to protect our freedom both from the enemies outside our gates and from our fellow-citizens: to preserve law and order, to enforce private contracts, to foster competitive markets" (p. 2). He (2002) continues, "The second broad principle is that government power must be dispersed. If government is to exercise power, better in the county than the state, better in the state than in Washington" (p. 3). For Friedman, who was a student of Ayn Rand, capitalism is the foremost tenet of political economy. It ensures both economic and political freedom for all citizens; it

is the fairest mechanism for both the economic and political health of the nation.

According to Friedman (2002), "Economic arrangements play a dual role in the promotion of a free society. On the one hand, freedom in economic arrangements is itself a component of freedom broadly understood, so economic freedom is an end in itself. In the second place, economic freedom is also an indispensable means toward the achievement of political freedom" (p. 8). One might ask what, precisely, "economic freedom" is. If it signifies that there is to be self-determination with regard to one's economic state, then it can be interpreted as a necessary character of life. If it contributes to political freedom, it is likewise essential to a good life. Friedman suggests that competitive capitalism contributes directly to both forms of freedom and so is also a necessary good. Power is dispersed when there is competition and that contributes to a political state where there is far less likely to be an intrusive dominating power.

One might also wonder how businesses could contribute to the freedom and well-being of people. Friedman (2002) offers a response to that potential conundrum:

> The view has been gaining widespread acceptance that corporate officials and labor leaders have a "social responsibility" that goes beyond serving the interest of their stockholders or their members. This view shows a fundamental misconception of the character and nature of a free economy. In such an economy, there is one and only one social responsibility of business—to use its resources and engage in activities designed to increase its profits so long as it stays within the rules of the game, which is to say, engages in open and free competition, without deception or fraud. (p. 133)

With respect to workers, Friedman (2002) says, "I believe strongly that the color of a man's skin or the religion of his parents is, by itself, no reason to treat him differently; that a man should be judged by what he is and what he does and not by these external characteristics" (p. 111). Yet he also believes that there should be no laws prohibiting discrimination in employment because that would violate the "voluntary" contracts into which people engage. In short, freedom, for Friedman, exists within a purely capitalist structure; that freedom *should* lead to political and personal freedom.

Daniel Bell (1996) takes another view of capitalism, even if from a fundamentally conservative point of view: "Twentieth-century capitalism wrought in some ways an even more startling sociological transformation—the shift from production to consumption as the fulcrum of capitalism. This was the rise of consumer durables. . . . And all this created the revolution in retailing, particularly . . . the invention of the installment plan" (p. 293). Bell claims that this development runs counter to the Protestant ethic that Max Weber saw as the heart of capitalism's rise. Bell (1996) observes, "Capitalism today is the predominant mode of production. But it is primarily a socioeconomic system, and both the political order and the culture—I speak here of high art, not the commodities of consumer culture—are not shaped by capitalism. Democracy, as a political form, is anterior to capitalism, and the desires for liberty and equality . . . lie deep in men's conception of justice" (p. 330). If we take the viewpoints of Friedman and of Bell we may still yearn for a definition of capitalism and its place in the lives of people.

While he does not offer a definition of capital, Branko Milanovic (2019) says, "A rising share of capital in total income also affects interpersonal income distribution because typically, (1) people who draw a large share of income from capital are rich, and (2) capital income is concentrated in relatively few hands. These two factors result almost automatically in greater income inequality between individuals" (p. 15). We will discuss inequality shortly, but Milanovic's observation deserves comment. Most people earn a living by making salaries or wages and saving relatively little of those earnings. There is little opportunity for the vast majority of households to invest, beyond a company pension (sometimes in the form of a 401k investment). The wealthiest of the US population may have substantial investments, frequently exceeding the money earned by working. If that is so, the individuals and households may be paying more capital gains taxes than income taxes. Thus, a minority of the population controls the capital that is held and invested. As Milanovic (2019) further states, "Asset classes held by the rich are also more valuable because they tend to be taxed less than asset classes held by the middle class. Thus capital gains and, in the United States, carried interest (income received by investment fund managers) are, in most cases, taxed at lower rates than interest from savings accounts" (p. 33).

Milanovic (2019) notes the difference between democratic capitalism (the ideal) and political capitalism (which does exist in a number of countries). He observes, "Corruption is endemic to political capitalism. Any system that requires discretionary decision-making must have endemic corruption. The problem with corruption, from the point of view of the elite, is that, taken too far, it tends to undermine the integrity of bureaucracy and the ability to conduct economic policies that produce high growth" (p. 94). Continuing the diagnosis, he (2019) says, "The system is always in precarious equilibrium. If corruption gets out of hand, the system may collapse. But if the rule of law is fully implemented, then the system changes radically and moves from the control of one party or one elite to a system of elite competition. . . . China and Vietnam are the paradigmatic examples of political capitalism" (pp. 95–96).

He (2019) asks a question that may occur to many people:

> Doesn't it follow that we should ditch the world of hypercommercialized capitalism in favor of an alternative system? The problem with this otherwise sensible argument is that we lack any viable alternative to hypercommecialized capitalism. The alternatives the world has tried have proved worse—some of them much worse. On top of that, discarding the competitive and acquisitive spirit is hardwired into capitalism would lead to a decline in our incomes, increased poverty, deceleration or reversion of technological progress, and the loss of other advantages (such as goods and services that have become an integral part of our lives) the hypercommercialized capitalism provides. (p. 185)

Milanovic is obviously a critic of capitalism as it is, but he is still optimistic regarding the future of capitalism, provided some reforms can be implemented, such as a tax advantage for the middle class, improvements in schools and schooling, and limitations for the funding of political campaigns (as a means of limiting the influence of capital in elections and the avoidance of political capitalism). These kinds of moves can help the United States and the world achieve *liberal* capitalism.

A discussion of capitalism would be incomplete without some mention of the work of Thomas Piketty. His book is massive and is data driven; he presents numerous analyses as a means of reaching his conclusions. One of his (2014) findings is, "the ideal policy for avoiding an endless inegalitarian spiral and regaining control over the dynamics of accumulation would be a progressive global tax on capital. Such a tax would also have another virtue: it would expose wealth to democratic scrutiny, which is a necessary condition for effective regulation of the banking system and international capital flows" (p. 471). His point is that there needs to be less concentration of capital and a greater distribution of wealth that is based in capital accumulation. As he indicates, such a tax would reduce the power of private interest over the general interest. All this said, Piketty doubts if this ideal is realistic in the world as it is today. A genuine global adoption of such a tax is unlikely, although selective adoption by some nations may be possible. He (2014) echoes Milanovic to some extent when he argues, "A progressive tax on capital is a more suitable instrument for responding to the challenges of the twenty-first century than a progressive income tax, which was designed for the twentieth century" (p. 473). For the reasons expressed earlier, a progressive capital gains tax would result in greater national income than the present maximum rate of 20 percent for long-term capital gains.

Early in his book, Piketty (2014) summarizes his conclusions:

> The first is that one should be wary of any economic determinism in regard to inequalities of wealth and income. The history of the distribution of wealth has always been deeply political, and it cannot be reduced to purely economic mechanisms. In particular, the reduction of inequality that took place in most developed countries between 1910 and 1950 was above all a consequence of war and of policies adopted to cope with the shocks of war. Similarly, the resurgence of inequality after 1980 is due largely to the political shifts of the past several decades, especially in regard to taxation and finance. The history of inequality is shaped by the way economic, social, and political actors view what is just and what is not, as well as by the relative power of those actors and the collective choices that result. It is the joint product of all relevant actors combined. (p. 20)

It is starkly evident that the discourse on capitalism embodies very different ideas of what capitalism is and its dynamics in society. There are views that capitalism is a "liberal" structure that enables the movement of money through the economic system and that can result in benefits for everyone involved in the economy. In other words, there is a perceived benevolence ensconced in the system of capitalism, as Friedman demonstrates. Others present a different viewpoint wherein there is the possibility for concentration of capital and political power. It is up to every thinker to read the discourse carefully and to examine evidence (as Husserl advocates) as a way to develop a perception of capitalism that encompasses all possible conceptions. Discourse ethics may be nowhere more important than in conversations about capitalism and the future of capital in the United States and globally.

Inequality

This topic was introduced earlier, but it deserves its own discussion for several reasons. One reason is that the issue carries with it a body of data that can be analyzed. The primary reason is that inequality strikes at the heart of the republic; numerous people are affected and there are discussions relating to what the proper response would be. Let us begin with a report sponsored by the Cato Institute. John Early (2018) begins his examination by stating, "The usual statistics invoked to support [the claim that poverty persists at high levels], however, are misleading. Those statistics exclude about $1 trillion in annual transfer payments to lower-income households and do not account for the effects of taxes" (p. 1). He (2018) presents a set of factors that are usually excluded from, say, census income data:

- The Earned Income Tax Credit (EITC)
- The monetary value of benefits from the Supplemental Nutrition Assistance Program (SNAP), more commonly known as food stamps
- Free or subsidized medical care such as Medicaid and the Children's Health Insurance Program (CHIP)
- Free, subsidized, or controlled rent or other "affordable housing" schemes
- Heating subsidies
- Free or reduced-fee social services such as daycare, tax preparation, or meal services. (p. 2)

Early (2018) also notes, "Official income statistics make no adjustments for taxes paid. Taxes reduce spendable income at every income level" (p. 2). While that observation is true, it is not a simple dynamic. For example, in a high-cost area (where such things as rent, gasoline, other transportation costs, time to get to the workplace, and other elements increase costs), those at the lowest two quintiles of income may be disadvantaged. Even in affordable communities, the cost of living may be placing a strain on the available income of millions of people. For those in the top two quintiles of income the pressures to make ends meet may well be lessened. He (2018) adds, "The net effect is that pretax data overstate the true income of upper-income households by as much as 50 percent, and missing transfers understate the true income of lower-income households by a factor of two or more" (p. 2). A household would probably have to be in the top quintile for the factor of 50 percent to be the case. Moreover, some aid, such as Medicaid, is determined by individual states and so can be variable.

The data presented by Early must be taken in a larger context. While the claims made are not inaccurate, there are some missing factors. Among the missing is the cost of living. What that means is, for instance, the percentage of disposable income that has to be dedicated to housing, calculated by the amount of rent/mortgage payments relative to after-tax income. Other variables include the percentage of food and clothing and their rates relative to disposable income. It is one thing to present data in order to support claims and conclusions; it is another thing to present a genuine dialogic set of data that can anticipate questions or disputes. Discourse ethics enters here, as does Husserl's ideas about what science can do, and the need for ethical presentation in these contested political issues is great.

One factor that can be analyzed is income distribution by racial group. Dedrick Asante-Muhhamad et al. (2019) investigate this issue and find disparities. Among their findings are that, as of 2019, the median family wealth of White families was $147,000, while that for Latino families was $6,600 and for Black families was $3,600 (p. 2). It should be noted that "wealth" constitutes more than income; it includes property owned, savings, investments, and other things. The authors further observe that, since the 1980s, the wealth of White families has grown, while that for Latino and Black families has been stagnant. They (2019) write, "Between 1983 and 2016, the median Black family saw their wealth drop by more than half after adjusting for inflation, compared to a 33 percent increase for the median White household. Over that same period, the number of households with $10 million or more skyrocketed by 856 percent" (p. 3). They (2019) also observe, "Black families are about 20 times more likely to have zero or negative wealth (37 percent) than they are to have $1 million in assets (1.9 percent). . . . White families are equally likely to have zero or negative wealth (about 15 percent) as they are likely to be a millionaire (15 percent)" (p. 3).

Race aside, the authors (2019) note, "The median American family saw their wealth drop 3 percent between 1983 and 2016, while the richest 0.1 percent have seen their wealth jump 133 percent" (p. 4). Granted, the authors do not mention tax rates (defined here as rates actually paid rather than hypothetical income tax rates) or subsidies for low-income families. These factors make some differences and they should be calculated in a complete examination of wealth, assets, and disposable income. The authors (2019) conclude, "Despite aspirant and sensationalized media stories, the racial wealth divide has not improved over the last three decades" (p. 6).

When it comes to the rhetorical responses to inequality, there is some variation. For example, Harry Frankfurt (2015) says, "To focus on inequality, which is not in itself objectionable, is to misconstrue the challenge we actually face. . . . Economic equality is not a morally compelling ideal. The primary goal of our efforts must be to repair a society in which many have far too little, while others have the comfort and influence that go with having more than enough" (p. 5). Frankfurt's position deserves some attention. He appears to be opposed to people going wanting, but he does *not* argue for equality. He could be interpreted as being opposed to a socialism where there would be a mass redistribution of wealth so as to result in a kind of flat line when it comes to individual or household assets. He restates his viewpoint: "In my opinion [approaching an egalitarian ideal] is a mistake. Economic equality is not, as such, of any particular moral importance; and by the same token, economic inequality is not in itself morally objectionable. . . . I shall call [my] alternative to egalitarianism the 'doctrine of sufficiency'—that is, the doctrine that what is morally important with regard to money is that everyone should have enough" (p. 7).

It is curious that he does not see a moral reason to support egalitarianism. This is not to say that there are not reasons to make the argument *against* egalitarianism. For one thing, talents and abilities vary; some people are more intelligent than others, for example. Those with enhanced talents are likely to succeed materially. That said, extremes of economic inequality could be seen as morally objectionable. Someone without talent or notable ability should not have to live on the edge. Society could be seen to have a responsibility to all citizens who put forth the effort to work and earn a living to be able to do just that. If someone's ability is in building maintenance, should that person have a sufficient living, based on the work done? Frankfurt may claim that this is constructing a straw man, but he opens a door he may not have intended to by saying that inequality is *not* morally objectionable.

Piketty (2020) adopts a different starting point:

> Every human society must justify its inequalities; unless reasons for them are found, the whole political and social edifice stands in danger of collapse. Every epoch therefore develops a range of contradictory discourses and ideologies for the purpose of legitimizing the inequality that already exists or that people believe should exist. From these discourse emerge certain economic, social, and political rules, which people then use to make sense of the ambient social structure. (p. 1)

There certainly may be inequalities, but there are reasons, as has just been stated, for the inequalities. If some among the populace are intentionally or structurally economically disadvantaged, then those people are not in any way to blame for their plight. It behooves society to examine who makes the economic and political rules, who constructs the fundamental structure. Is there a moral imperative designed into that system? That can be the question on which a conversation is grounded.

Robert Dahl (2006) examines the issue from the point of view of politics. He provides a standard for an ideal democracy:

- Effective participation
- Equality in voting
- Gaining enlightened understanding
- Final control of the agenda
- Inclusion. (p. 9)

If these elements are indeed mandatory, there are means that must be in place so that they can be achieved. If the means are absent or missing, there will be an essential inequality within society. That inequality may or may not be associated with other inequalities. For whatever reason, Dahl (2006) sees equality as a moral necessity. He (2006) does not ignore economic inequality though:

> First, without regulation—and even with it—a market economy inevitably and almost constantly inflicts harm on some people, and at times on many. . . . Second, a market economy—a capitalist market economy, at any rate—inevitably generates a vast inequality in resources among its citizens. These inequalities extend not merely to incomes and wealth but, directly and indirectly, to information, status, education, access to political elites, and many others. (pp. 65–66; emphasis in original)

The discourse that emerges from consideration of inequality is, as is the case with some other topics, based in reason and evidence, but it also raises ethical matters. The conversation, to be effective, will have to embrace the range of issues in order to achieve some agreement, if not consensus.

Education
This is a large topic, but the conversation example will focus briefly on education in general and then on higher education. While there may be a number of critiques (positive and negative) of education, the words of Charles Murray will be concentrated on here because he expressed opinions that are quite widely held. He (2008) states at the outset, "This book calls for a transformation of American education—a transformation not just of means, but of ends" (p. 11). He (2008) then sums up his four basic observations that form the bulk of his book:

- Ability varies
- Half of the children are below average
- Too many people are going to college
- America's future depends on how we educate the academically gifted. (pp. 12–13)

The majority of the book is spent on these four observations, along with Murray's remedies for the future of education.

His first point should not be controversial; not all students have equal academic and intellectual abilities, just as not all people have equal athletic abilities. That said, there remains the question of what to do about the variance of abilities. His second observation is closely related to the first: half of the children are below the median in ability and intelligence (measured in a variety of ways). Murray (2008) writes, "Only for linguistic and logical-mathematical ability are we told that we can expect everyone to do well. . . . Children in the lower half of the distribution are just not smart enough to read or calculate at a level of fluency that most of the rest of us take for granted" (p. 44). He (2008) quickly adds, "Recognition of this truth does not mean callousness or indifference. It does not mean spending less effort on the education of some children than of others. But it does mean that we must jettison glib rhetoric that makes us feel good. No more talk about leaving no child behind" (p. 45). What is missing from Murray's diagnosis is how to spend the time educating all children. Some of high ability may require considerable time spent challenging them so that they can achieve at the highest level. Those not at the highest level may require time to reach a *higher* level of achievement so that they can perform well in occupations of their choosing and can participate in the political process.

Regarding his third observation, Murray (2008) states, "a lot fewer than 1.5 million [high school graduates attending four-year colleges in 2005] should be going to a *four-year residential institution* and trying to get a [bachelor's degree]" (p. 67; emphasis added). Again, this may not seem to be controversial. However, he (2008) also says, "No more than 20 percent of students have [the] level of academic ability [to attend a four-year college], and 10 percent is a more realistic estimate" (p. 67). He does not address why, say, the top half of graduates could attend a four-year college. For one thing, high school graduation is itself an instrument of selection; those who drop out of high school may be at the lower end of the ability scale (although that dynamic needs its own investigation). The figure is offered as an opinion. Another opinion Murray offers relates to the future of the traditional institution. He (2008) claims,

> A *brick-and-mortar campus is increasingly obsolete.* The physical infrastructure of the college used to make sense for three reasons. First, a good library was essential to higher learning and only a college faculty and student body provided the economies of scale that made good libraries affordable. Second, scholarship flourishes through colleagueships, and the college campus made it possible to put scholars in physical proximity to each other. Third, the best teaching requires interaction between teachers and students, and physical proximity was the only way to get it. All three rationales for the brick-and-mortar campus are fading fast. (p. 88; emphasis in original)

This set of claims, perhaps more than any others that Murray makes, warrants close scrutiny. As is evident from the material presented in the first chapter of this book, a library is much more than a building. Further, access to information is very, and increasingly, expensive, and not all information is available online. What Murray calls colleagueship is indeed important to learning, and the jury is still out as to the best way to provide for it. Further, student-teacher relationships, while perhaps possible in online environments, still require study. The relationships are, without question, essential, but the best mode by which to provide them is open to inquiry. Murray's opinions are held by a number of individuals, including by policy makers. But they are opinions, held with a minimum of reasoning and evidence. They are presented here because they must be attended to.

Numerous writers have offered diagnoses of higher education, and the vast majority find something wanting. Some see colleges and universities as being neoliberal institutions, bent on behaving like businesses. By way of background, David Harvey (2005) delineates some features of neoliberalism:

1. *Privatization and commodification.*
2. *Financialization.*
3. *The management and manipulation of crises.*
4. *State redistributions.* (pp. 160–63; emphasis in original)

Christopher Newfield (2016) accepts the definitions and says, "Turning universities into private businesses not the cure for the college cost problem, but rather its cause" (p. 26). There are estimates that the current student loan debt total approaches $1.7 trillion. If that figure is even close to being correct, college is out of the price range of many people who otherwise might succeed at learning and achievement. As James Kwak (2017) observes, "Competitive markets can be a wonderful thing. The problem is that the popular case for free markets is too often applied unthinkingly to the entire sphere of social interaction, with little or no regard for the complexity of the real world" (p. 15). Newfield and others claim that higher education is a major component of the complexity of the real world. What happens if qualified potential students cannot afford to further their educations?

Greg Lukianoff and Jonathan Haidt offer some epigrams they claim will suit people for success in higher education. They (2018) write,

1. Prepare the child for the road, not the road for the child
2. Your worst enemy cannot harm you as much as your own thoughts, unguarded
3. The line dividing good and evil cuts through the heart of every human being

176 ～ Chapter Three

    4. Help schools to oppose the great untruths
    5. Limit and refine device time
    6. Support a new national norm: service or work before college. (pp. 237–50)

The authors believe that institutions can be wiser if they support academic freedom, make freedom of inquiry a priority, and seek truth. They are optimistic about the possibilities for positive change in higher education. (For a considerably broader and deeper consideration of higher education, see Budd, 2018, pp. 39–72.)

Climate Change
There are many climate change deniers, but a majority of them do so for ideological and/or unreasoned excuses. Heather Cann and Leigh Raymond (2018) identify documents denying climate change emanating from the Heartland Institute; their results suggest that the framing of denial is moving toward ad hominem attacks on the scientists working on climate change. That said, there are some skeptics who examine data to reach their conclusions. One such individual is Steven Koonin, who served as the undersecretary for science at the US Department of Energy in the Obama administration. The title of his book, *Unsettled?*, presents his position.

Koonin is not a climate change denier, but he wonders if the changes are human caused or if they are a product of cyclical change. He does refer to a great amount of data to make his point. Early in his book, Koonin (2021) says,

> Here are three [climate facts] that might surprise you, drawn directly from recent published research or the latest assessments of climate science published by the US government and the UN:
>
> - Humans have had no detectable impact on hurricanes over the past century.
> - Greenland's ice sheet isn't shrinking any more rapidly today than it was eighty years ago.
> - The net economic impact of human-induced climate change will be minimal through at least the end of this century. (pp. 1–2)

He (2021) offers some more points related to climate science:

> - Humans exert a growing, but physically small, warming influence on the climate. . . .

- The results from the multitude of climate models disagree with, or even contradict, each other and many kinds of observations. . . .
- Government and UN press releases and summaries do not accurately reflect the reports themselves. . . .
- In short, the science is insufficient to make useful projections about how the climate will change over the coming decades, much less what effect our actions will have on it. (p. 4)

Koonin (2021) suggests that "trillion-dollar decisions about reducing human influences on the climate are, in the end, about values; risk tolerance, intergenerational and geographical equities, and a balance among economic development, environmental impact, and energy cost, availability, and reliability" (p. 6). His point from the outset is that people should look closely at data and reports on the climate before they make up their minds about seeming causes of changes. He repeatedly makes the point that climate is not the same as weather, so the perceptions of a seasonal weather change (or even change lasting a few years) may not signal long-term climate change. He also states that the United States is not the largest polluter on the globe and that any alterations to industry, transportation, agriculture, and deforestation must be examined on a global basis, and policy must likewise be global.

When he (2021) turns his attention to possible solutions to climate change, he mentions,

> For greenhouse gas emissions to decrease enough (and at a sufficiently rapid pace) to stabilize human influences on the climate in the foreseeable future, there would have to be dramatic changes in policies—the rules under which the energy system is created and operated. One possibility is outright regulation: *Coal-fired plants shall cease operation within a decade* or *New gasoline-powered cars cannot be sold after 2035*. (p. 230; emphasis in original)

He does question the technical practicality of such regulations and fuel-related rules. There would be a cost to such large-scale regulations, and the economic aspects would have to be considered before draconian measures would be taken. With all this said, Koonin (2021) concludes, "Solar Radiation Management merits serious research, and in fact the US Congress has recently provided funds for exploratory work" (pp. 241–42).

Michael Mann has studied climate and climate change for more than two decades. His work is largely based on data (sometimes proxy data for more than 200 years ago, composed of ice cores, tree rings, coral, and other sources). Recent data has been based on empirical measurements, including ocean temperatures. He reaches a different conclusion than does Koonin. Mann (2007) writes, "It is generally believed that modern (e.g., nineteenth to twenty-first century) climate change is due primarily to anthropogenic factors, including increased greenhouse gas concentrations owing to fossil fuel burning and the more regionally limited offsetting cooling influence of anthropocentric tropospheric aerosols" (p. 112). He (2007) applies what is called the "climate field reconstruction" method to measure recent changes to the climate. His earlier work found a measurable correlation between 112 indicators and temperature change annually ($r = 0.41$). He (2007) presents the annual changes graphically (p. 121), and they demonstrate warming from 1900 to 2000. He presents graphically another figure in which the measurements of multiple research teams likewise demonstrate warming, this time from 1800 to 2000 (p. 127). In conclusion Mann (2007) states, "Forced changes in large-scale atmospheric circulation, such as the NAO [North Atlantic Oscillation], and internal dynamics related to El Niño may play an important role in explaining regional patterns of variability and change" (p. 131). For further research, he (2007) urges, "Future efforts at large-scale climate reconstruction methods should address the reconstruction of fields other then surface temperature (e.g., measures of atmospheric circulation, such as sea level pressure, and hydroclimatic variables, such as precipitation and drought)" (p. 131).

In a more recent paper, of which Mann is a coauthor, Cheng et al. (2021) say, "The most recent data indicate that the OHC [ocean heating content] in the upper 2000 m layer of the world's oceans has increased with a mean rate of 5.7 ± 1.0 ZJ yr^{-1} for the 1958-2020 period" (p. 524). ZJ is the symbol for zettajoule, which is 10^{21} joules (1° C equals 2.2 ZJ). The calculation can be interpreted as meaning that the warming is substantial.

Other sources addressing climate change employ rhetorical means to argue their positions. Some of these are not immune to hyperbole. Christiana Figueres and Tom Rivett-Carnac (2020) state, "The world is on fire, from the Amazon to California, from Australia to the Siberian Arctic. The hour is late, and the moment of consequence, so long delayed, is now upon us. Do we watch the world burn, or do we choose to do what is necessary to achieve a different future" (p. xv)? Such language may not advance the conversation about climate change. The authors (2020) offer ten actions that could be considered, though, as part of active discourse:

ACTION 1: *Let Go of the Old World*
ACTION 2: *Face Your Grief but Hold a Vision of the Future*
ACTION 3: *Defend the Truth*

What Conversations Can Take Place in Libraries (and in What Ways)? 179

ACTION 4: *See Yourself as a Citizen—Not as a Consumer*
ACTION 5: *Move Beyond Fossil Fuels*
ACTION 6: *Reforest the Earth*
ACTION 7: *Invest in a Clean Economy*
ACTION 8: *Use Technology Responsibly*
ACTION 9: *Build Gender Equality*
ACTION 10: *Engage in Politics.* (pp. 89–150)

Each of the action items require interpretation, which the authors present but which may be questioned. What we see here is a complex topic, with a plethora of data attached to it. Some readings of the data vary, but even Koonin recognizes that there is some climate change; the issue to be determined (according to him) is the degree to which it has a human origin. Denial of climate change on purely ideological (in the pejorative sense) bases does not have a place in the conversation, but there are firm grounds for conversation.

COVID-19

At the time of this writing there have been more than 44.8 million cases of COVID-19 and more than 723,000 deaths in the United States (October 19, 2021). It is evident that this pandemic has resulted in sadness and pain for many citizens, yet there is still controversy relating to the disease. There are deniers and anti-vaxxers (people opposed to vaccination). It is challenging to write this while the pandemic is still active, but this is a topic that cries for a civil conversation. There are resources to which we can turn to find serious discourse about the disease.

Nicole Saphier is a physician, author, and commentator who has written a recent book on COVID-19. She (2021) is critical of the media in her work and writes,

> The information driving the crisis response and that which is being conveyed on television by reputable reporters and contributors is largely based on preprints, observational studies, and opinion pieces. As a result, it's difficult for the public to understand the difference between legitimate, data-driven science and that which is equivalent to anecdotal reports informed merely by a desire to share preliminary knowledge or, regrettably, to make a sensation. (p. xvi)

She (2021) continues, "We must not politicize the science. . . . And to that end, we need experts and politicians to explain their reasoning—not just tell us what to do" (p. xvii). Along the same lines, though, she (2021) says, "Unfortunately, it's nearly impossible to change a conspiracy theorist's mind because their philosophies have become solidified and self-referential" (pp. 5–6). Her words should be heeded, and they make the beginnings of an argument.

She addresses the social unrest resulting from lockdowns and the closures of many businesses, and she acknowledges what she calls "erratic information and the politicization of science" (p. 15). As a physician, Saphier recognizes the need to take preventative steps to reduce the spread of the disease. She (2021) mentions, "The primary reason to wear a face is to protect others from asymptomatic and presymptomatic transmission, but growing evidence is showing a level of protection for the wearer as well. While wearing a mask may not unequivocally prevent someone from contracting the virus, it can also decrease the viral load, leading to less severe symptoms" (p. 33). She (2021) also notes that "eight of the ten states with the highest new cases per capita during the winter holiday months [2020–2021] did not have a widespread mask mandate" (p. 38). There are, then, means people could and can employ to mitigate the spread of the disease, according to someone in the know.

Saphier is critical of media and observes a number of instances in which television and other outlets were, at times, hypocritical. For example, she mentions the negative press related to Republican political and campaign gatherings where there was little or no mask wearing or social distancing, while at the same time the press tended to praise the protests related to the police killings of black citizens. However, she (2021) also relates,

> High-ranking Fox News anchor Neil Cavuto . . . immediately warned viewers on his program of the documented risks associated with taking hydroxychloroquine, saying it could kill people who are in certain health risk populations. "The fact of the matter is, though, when the president said 'what have you got to lose?' a number of studies, those certain vulnerable population [sic] have one thing to lose: their lives," Cavuto said. Not long after that, Cavuto's next guest, an urgent care doctor in New York City, Janette Nesheiwat, conversely said that she thought the president's choice to use the drug as a preventive measure was "very smart." (p. 70)

Saphier, while critical of the media, offers grounds for discussion and begins a conversation that needs to continue.

A perspective from a different political point of view is presented by Andy Slavitt. Slavitt is very critical of the Trump administration, but he also offers a number of apolitical observations as well. For example, he (2021) says, "Responding to a public health crisis requires decisive action, near unity, and a readiness to adapt as we learn about what causes the disease to spread and about what actions can effectively mitigate that spread" (p. 4). He

(2021) also notes that the virus took many by surprise and that there were few individuals who saw the warning signs early on: "Mike [Osterholm; a physician] was one of a number of people who had been warning in the early days of the pandemic. . . . So were Bill Gates; Bill Joy, the co-founder of Sun Microsystems; the Pulitzer Prize-winning journalist Laurie Garrett; and Larry Brilliant, the epidemiologist who was part of the successful effort to eradicate smallpox. They were the Cassandras of our era" (p. 29). He tweeted that the direst predictions were not inevitable; quick action could lead to an effective response.

Slavitt (2021) reports on the conversation he had with his son, Zach (a high school student focusing on mathematics), about the exponential mathematics related to infectiousness. If it were the case that one person infects 2.3 other people, there could be as many as 4,142 individuals infected within 50 days (p. 34). That rate, Slavitt maintains, should be alarming and should lead to measures to limit exposure to infected people. In another tweet he (2021) writes, "I'm told the virus spreads from Trump supporter to Biden supporter to Bernie [Sanders] supporter and back. There are too many problems—and indeed solutions—to fight each other" (p. 54). Slavitt does express some partisan views at times, but even with that bias he makes points that should be a part of a serious conversation. When he asks, for instance, how many people might die from the virus (and estimates extended early on to well over one million people), he confesses that he did not put much stock in the worst-case scenarios. Few policy makers or advisors did believe the highest numbers.

Slavitt (2021) proves himself somewhat prescient when he states, "Saving lives from COVID-19 came with other costs. Mental health issues and addiction, already at crisis levels before the pandemic, exploded" (pp. 71–72). Recent data affirm his observation; deaths from overdose rose by more than 29 percent in 2020 (AHA News, 2021). When people were prevented from leaving home—with the exceptions of "essential" workers and necessary purposes—many turned to some form of self-medication to deal with the stress. Moreover, some people with non-COVID-19 illnesses and emergencies found themselves in difficulty at times getting needed health care. Slavitt (2021) points out that other matters, such as inequality, are affected by the pandemic: "While millions were getting infected, hundreds of thousands were dying, and millions more were losing employment, the system wasn't failing everybody. Between March and September 2020, the nation's billionaires grew $845 billion richer" (p. 172).

For a less partisan account of the origins and progress of the virus, there is Lawrence Wright's account (2021). He takes a chronological approach to this matter, and he reports from as many sources as possible where the virus originated and how it spread, seemingly first to Italy, then beyond (including to the United States). In the earliest days of COVID-19, according to Wright (2021), there was little or no data that supported any of the reports of the first diagnoses and the existence of a "Patient 0." The physicians were stymied by what was about to hit, and there was concern about the potential impact on the economy; both concerns were warranted (p. 43). Wright (2021) reports,

> More than a month had passed [it was then early February 2020] since the first known patient arrived in the U.S., and in that time the CDC [Centers for Disease Control] had conducted fewer than 500 tests. South Korea, which had its first case one day before the U.S., had already tested 65,000 people. China was reportedly testing 1.6 million per week. The United States remained blind to the spread of the contagion, unable to fight what it couldn't see. (pp. 63–64)

Wright's chronicle is one that should be read as possibly the least biased account of the pandemic and the US response to it.

As was stated earlier, and as is noted by the authors cited here, it is very challenging to write about something we are in the middle of. Also at the time of this writing, tens of millions of people have not been vaccinated and the nonvaccinated comprise the majority of new cases. That factor needs to be a component of the conversation on the pandemic. This may be the most complex and difficult discourse facing serious conversations at this time. The various factors involved in COVID-19 render discussion problematic because of the difficulty of getting reliable information and recommendations for action and of misinformation being spread widely. The conversation requires close attention to what is being said and the sources of those remarks that are being made.

Epilogue

The purpose of this chapter is twofold: the suggestion that there is a philosophical approach that has very practical application and that can inform the conduct of civil conversation and the facilitation of this conversation and the presentation of example topics that may be fodder for conversation. The intended end is the pursuit of truth and knowledge by means of ethical and serious discourse. That end is in line with Jonathan Rauch's (2021) observation of Plato's report of Socrates's last words in his dialogue with Theaetetus: "Let us meet here again." Rauch (2021) adds, "Acquiring knowledge is a conversation, not a destination. It is a process, a journey—a journey we take together, not alone. Others are always involved. Knowledge is not just something I have; more fundamentally, it is some *we* have" (p. 3; emphasis in original). This describes the understanding that is presented throughout the present work.

We can wrap up this chapter by remembering some things that have taken place in the recent past and how those events can be interpreted. Bruno Latour (2018) says that the period of the early 1990s

> was initially by what is called "deregulation," a term that has given the word "globalization" an increasingly pejorative cast. The same period witnessed, everywhere at once, that start of an increasingly vertiginous explosion of inequalities. The two phenomena coincided with a third that is less often stressed: the beginning of a systematic effort to deny the existence of climate change. (p. 1)

Latour seeks to develop a different way of thinking about the world and our relation to it. This effort requires developing a different political attitude: "It is really a question of 'getting out of the Left/Right opposition.' . . . Given the intensity of the passions into question always arouses, we must not confuse it with a new center, a new swamp, a new 'soft belly'" (p. 48).

How do we get to the point Latour describes? He (2018) further says,

> It is hard to see, at least for the moment, how to get along with such affect-laden terms [as left and right, conservative and liberal]. Public action must be oriented toward a recognizable goal. However open to dispute the word "progressive" may be, it is highly unlikely that anyone can be mobilized by a call to "regress." With the "end of progress," the prospect of living less well than one's parents, the project of learning to shrivel up slowly is hardly going to electrify crowds. (p. 49)

Latour maintains the idea of "progressive" is composed of elements of both left and right, that it looks forward to the progress of everyone in the state, regardless of what some "progressives" claim is their aim. The melding of left and right, the absorption of the most productive thoughts and actions of both sides, may be a reasonable goal for all who would participate in political discourse today. Conversing so that each side sees the valid points of the other may be the best way to cross political lines and to proceed toward truth and knowledge.

I readily recognize that the changing of minds is very challenging and that each of us resists this strenuously. Rauch (2021) also recognizes this phenomenon and says, "When we care about a proposition, changing our mind about it will be difficult. Contrary facts will be rationalized away, or their source discounted, or their implications rejected, or their veracity denied altogether" (p. 30). He (2021) advocates the Constitution of Knowledge (similar in spirit to the US Constitution), which has two rules:

> ***The fallibilist rule: No one gets the final say.*** *You may claim that a statement is established as knowledge only if it can be debunked, in principle, and only insofar as it withstands attempts to debunk it. That is, you are entitled to claim that a statement is objectively true only insofar as it is both checkable and has stood up to checking, and not otherwise.*
>
> ***The empirical rule: No one has personal authority.*** *You may claim that a statement has been established as knowledge only insofar as the method used to check it gives the same result regardless of the identity of the checker, and regardless of the source of the statement.* (pp. 88–89; emphasis in original)

Rauch's rules apply here as well. They are in keeping with discourse ethics and the quest for truth. In short, I endorse them as applicable to the development of conversations that can take place in libraries.

Rauch (2021) also emphasizes the problems presented by today's (and possibly tomorrow's) social media. He says that

> First, it hacked our brains. . . .
> Second, digital media splintered reality. . . .
> The main idea of the Constitution of Knowledge . . . is that reality is what *we* know, not what you or I know. . . . The Constitution of Knowledge does not require [members of the reality-based community] to see the world the same way or to agree on facts. In fact, it only works where people see the world differently and disagree on facts, so that they can test their ideas and surmount their biases. . . .
> Third, digital media ran liberal science in reverse. It inverted the social incentives which the reality-based community depends on. . . .
> Finally, misinformation acquired a business model. (pp. 126–35)

Again, I agree with Rauch. Digital social media can spread misinformation at least as quickly and as widely as it can spread valid information. This must be recognized as a challenge to the present agenda set forth in this book. Participation in conversations can be squelched by the rapid dissemination of lies and misinformation, which may be believed if individuals believe the claims and take them to be factual.

The primary drive behind this present book is to accomplish goals of *creating* community around the search for truth and at least some measure of agreement. This can be achieved through the means Rauch establishes as the Constitution of Knowledge. It is a challenge, but I believe it is achievable. This book is a work of optimism: the building of conversations of difficult topics, based on serious discussion of those topics. If what has been presented here *works*, we may transform the communities that engage in the conversations. And libraries can be at the center of the transformation.

References

AHA News. (July 14, 2021). CDC: Drug overdose deaths up 29.4% in 2020. https://www.aha.org/news/headline/2021-07-14-cdc-drug-overdose-deaths-294-2020.

Asante-Muhhamad, D., Collins, C., Hoxie, J., and Terry, S. (January 14, 2019). Dreams deferred: How enriching the 1% widens the racial wealth divide. *Blogging Our Great Divide*, 1–7.

Bell, D. (1996). *The cultural contradictions of capitalism.* New York: Basic Books.

Budd, J. M. (2018). *The changing academic library: Operations, culture, environments.* Third edition. Chicago: Association of College and Research Libraries.

Cann, H. W., and Raymond, L. (2018). Does climate denialism still matter? The prevalence of alternative frames in opposition to climate policy. *Environmental Policy* 27(3), 433–54.

Cheng, L., et al. (2021). Upper ocean temperatures hit record high in 2020. *Advances in Atmospheric Sciences* 38(April), 523–30.

Costello, P. R. (2012). *Layers in Husserl's phenomenology: On meaning and intersubjectivity.* Toronto: University of Toronto Press.

Dahl, R. A. (2006). *On political equality.* New Haven: Yale University Press.

de Sousa Santos, B. (2007). Beyond abyssal thinking: From global lines to ecologies of knowledges. *Review Fernand Braudel Center* 30(1), 45–89.

Early, J. F. (April 24, 2018). Reassessing the facts about inequality, poverty, and redistribution. *Policy Analysis No. 839*, 1–23.

Figueres, C., and Rivett-Carnac, T. (2020). *The future we choose: Surviving the climate crisis.* New York: Alfred A. Knopf.

Flew, A. (1998). *How to think straight: An introduction to critical reasoning.* Amherst, NY: Prometheus Books.

Frankfurt, H. G. (2015). *On inequality.* Princeton: Princeton University Press.

Friedman, M. (2002). *Capitalism and freedom.* Chicago: University of Chicago Press.

Grosby, S. (2005). *Nationalism: A very short introduction.* Oxford: Oxford University Press.

Harvey, D. (2005). *A brief history of neoliberalism.* Oxford: Oxford University Press.

Hazony, Y. (2018). *The virtue of nationalism.* New York: Basic Books.

Hilton, S. (2018). *Positive populism: Revolutionary ideas to rebuild economic security, family, and community in America.* New York: Crown Forum.

Hopp, W. (2020). *Phenomenology: A contemporary introduction.* London: Routledge.

Husserl, E. (1962). *Ideas: General introduction to pure phenomenology*. W. R. B. Gibson (Trans.). New York: Collier Books.
Husserl, E. (1969). *Formal and transcendental logic*. D. Cairns (Trans.). The Hague: Martinus Nijhoff.
Husserl, E. (1970a). *Logical investigations*, vol. 1. J. N. Findlay (Trans.). London: Routledge and Kegan Paul.
Husserl, E. (1970b). *Logical investigations*, vol. 2. J. N. Findlay (Trans.). London: Routledge.
Husserl, E. (1970c). *The crisis of the European sciences and transcendental phenomenology*. D. Carr (Trans.). Evanston, IL: Northwestern University Press.
Husserl, E. (1973). *Experience and judgment: Investigations in a genealogy of logic*. J. S. Churchill and K. Ameriks (Trans.). Evanston, IL: Northwestern University Press.
Husserl, E. (1999). *Cartesian meditations: An introduction to phenomenology*. D. Cairns (Trans.). Dordrecht, Netherlands: Kluwer Academic Publishers.
Koonin, S. E. (2021). *Unsettled? What climate science tells us, what it doesn't, and why it matters*. Dallas: BenBella Books.
Kwak, J. (2017). *Economism: Bad economics and the rise of inequality*. New York: Pantheon Books.
Lankes, R. D., Silverstein, J., and Nicholson, S. (2007). Participatory networks: The library as conversation. *Information Technology and Libraries* 26(4), 17–33.
Latour, B. (2018). *Down to earth: Politics in the new climatic regime*. London: Polity.
Lepore, J. (2019). *This America: The case for the nation*. New York: Liveright.
Levinas, E. (1969). *Totality and infinity: An essay on exteriority*. A. Lingis (Trans.). Pittsburgh: Dusquene University Press.
Levinas, E. (1998). *Entre nous: On thinking-of-the-other*. M. B. Smith and B. Harshav (Trans.). New York: Columbia University Press.
Levinas, E. (2003). *Humanism of the other*. N. Poller (Trans.). Urbana: University of Illinois Press.
Lowry, R. (2019). *The case for nationalism: How it made us powerful, united, and free*. New York: Broadside Books.
Lukianoff, G., and Haidt, J. (2018). *The coddling of the American mind: How good intentions and bad ideas are setting up a generation for failure*. New York: Penguin Press.
Lyotard, J.-F. (1991). *Phenomenology*. B. Beakley (Trans.). Albany, NY: SUNY Press.
Madison, G. B. (1981). *The phenomenology of Merleau-Ponty*. Athens: Ohio University Press.
Mann, M. E. (2007). Climate over the past two millennia. *Annual Review of Earth and Planetary Sciences* 35, 111–36.
Merleau-Ponty, M. (1962). *The phenomenology of perception*. C. Smith (Trans.). London: Routledge.
Merleau-Ponty, M. (1964). *The primacy of perception*. Evanston, IL: Northwestern University Press.
Milanovic, B. (2019). *Capitalism, alone: The future of the system that rules the world*. Cambridge, MA: Belknap Press of Harvard University Press.

Mohanty, J. N. (1997). *Phenomenology: Between essentialism and transcendental philosophy*. Evanston, IL: Northwestern University Press.
Moran, D. (2000). *Introduction to phenomenology*. London: Routledge.
Mudde, C., and Kaltwasser, C. R. (2017). *Populism: A very short introduction*. Oxford: Oxford University Press.
Müller, J.-W. (2016). *What is populism?* Philadelphia: University of Pennsylvania Press.
Murray, C. (2008). *Real education: Four simple truths for bringing America's schools back to reality*. New York: Three Rivers Press.
Newfield, C. (2016). *The great mistake: How we wrecked public universities and how we can fix them*. Baltimore: Johns Hopkins University Press.
Patin, B., Sebastian, M., Yeon, J., Bertolini, D., and Grimm, A. (2021). Interrupting epistemicide: A practical framework for naming, identifying, and ending epistemic injustice in the information professions. *Journal of the Association of Information Science and Technology* 72(10), 1306–18.
Piketty, T. (2014). *Capital in the twenty-first century*. A. Goldhammer (Trans.). Cambridge, MA: Belknap Press of Harvard University Press.
Piketty, T. (2020). *Capital and ideology*. A. Goldhammer (Trans.). Cambridge, MA: Belknap Press of Harvard University Press.
Pivčevič, E. (1970). *Husserl and phenomenology*. London: Hutchinson University Library.
Rauch, J. (2021). *The constitution of knowledge: A defense of truth*. Washington, DC: Brookings Institution Press.
Ricoeur, P. (1991). *From text to action: Essays in hermeneutics, II*. K. Blamey and J. B. Thompson (Trans.). Evanston, IL: Northwestern University Press.
Ricoeur, P. (1992). *Oneself as another*. K. Blamey (Trans.). Chicago: University of Chicago Press.
Saphier, N. (2021). *Panic attack: Playing politics with science in the fight against COVID-19*. New York: Broadside Books.
Slavitt, A. (2021). *Preventable: The inside story of how leadership failures, politics, and selfishness doomed the U.S. coronavirus response*. New York: St. Martin's Press.
Smith, D. W. (2004). *Mind world: Essays in phenomenology and ontology*. Cambridge: Cambridge University Press.
Sokolowski, R. (2000). *Introduction to phenomenology*. Cambridge: Cambridge University Press.
Stewart, D., and Mickunas, A. (1990). *Exploring phenomenology: A guide to the field and its literature*. Second edition. Athens: Ohio University Press.
Taggart, P. (2000). *Populism*. Buckingham: Open University Press.
Tamir, Y. (2019). *Why nationalism*. Princeton: Princeton University Press.
Wright, L. (2021). *The plague year: America in the time of COVID*. New York: Alfred Knopf.
Zahavi, D. (2003). *Husserl's phenomenology*. Stanford: Stanford University Press.

Zahavi, D. (2005). *Subjectivity and selfhood: Investigating the first-person perspective.* Cambridge, MA: MIT Press.

Zahavi, D. (2017). *Husserl's legacy: Phenomenology, metaphysics, and transcendental philosophy.* Oxford: Oxford University Press.

Zahavi, D. (2019). *Phenomenology: The basics.* London: Routledge.

Index

activism, 54–61, 76
ALA. *See* American Library Association
American Library Association, vi, 34, 37–38, 45–47, 55–62
Association of American Universities, 39
authors, 1, 5, 8, 12, 24, 41–42, 47, 51, 55, 67, 74, 76–78, 130, 158, 171, 176, 179, 182

BEL. *See* Board of Education for Librarianship
Berlin, Isaiah, 14–15
Board of Education for Librarianship, 39
book, 3–9, 11, 21–24, 27, 29–36, 41–42, 44–52, 79–80, 111, 136
Brennan, Jason, vi, 15–16
Burke, Edmund, 11

Callinicos, Alex, 11
Carnegie, Andrew. *See* Carnegie libraries
Carnegie Foundation. *See* Carnegie libraries

Carnegie libraries, 10, 35–36, 38–39
cataloguing. *See* classification
censorship, 14, 43–53, 79, 109–110
Chiarizio, Matthew, 3
civil discourse (political), vi, 1, 11, 102
Civil War, 14, 23, 25
classification, 38
coeducation, 23
collection development, 42, 56, 72, 78
Cold War, 26
communication, vi, 7, 20, 43, 51, 53, 59, 70–71, 77, 89–90, 95–99, 101, 103–104, 106, 110–111, 114, 119, 125, 139, 155
communicative action, 98–102, 107, 110, 114, 118–119, 121–123, 125, 149, 154
Communism, 45–49, 160
Critical Theory, 75–76
conservativism, vi, 11, 20, 43–44, 94, 109, 125, 137, 158, 163, 167, 183
Constitution of the United States, 13, 51, 78, 159, 161, 184
Coulter, Ann, 12

Deneen, Patrick, 13–14
democracy, vi, 3, 7, 15–17, 19, 33, 41, 56–57, 116, 121, 158, 160–161, 167, 172; liberal, 16–17, 158; in collections, 42
democracy (deliberative), 19
democratic institutions, vi, 10–11, 58
de Saussure, Ferdinand, 96–97
de Tocqueville, Alexis, 16
Dewey, Melvil, 37–38, 74
digital age, 5
digital books. *See* electronic books
Dillon, Dennis, 2–4
disinformation, 114
discourse, v–vi, 4–5, 20, 55, 75–76, 80–81, 89, 102–107, 110–111, 118–119, 122, 125, 131, 141, 149, 157, 160, 169, 172 173, 179, 182–183; civil discourse, 1, 5, 11, 102, 153; discourse (political), 12, 15–16, 102, 125, 139, 144, 155, 184
discourse ethics, vi, 2, 93, 102, 119–125, 138–139, 152, 154–155, 157–158, 170, 184
discursive action, 121
Dworkin, Ronald, 15

e-books. *See* electronic books
egalitarianism, 172
electronic books, 3–7
Epstein, Richard, 19

fake news, 7
Fernbach, Philip, 11–12
First Amendment, 50–51, 53
French Revolution, 14
Franklin, Benjamin, 30, 33
Fuller, 42

gatekeeping, 51–52
Goldman, Alvin, 42, 67, 117, 119
Google, 5, 72
Great Depression, 27–28

Great War. *See* World War I
Guinness, Os, 14
Gutmann, Amy, 15

Habermas, Jürgen, 81, 98–103, 119–121, 123–125, 152, 154
Hamlin, Arthur T., 22–24, 26–27
Hardy, Thomas, 24
Harvard, John, 21
hate speech, 53–54
hermeneutics, 68, 101–102
Herring, James E., 4–5
higher education, 6, 23, 25–28, 173, 175–176; history, 21–26
humanities, 6
Hume, David, 12

identity politics, 15, 163
ideology, 3, 11, 16–17, 40, 56, 72, 74, 75–76, 107–109, 161, 163
information literacy, 4, 8, 27, 76
intellectual freedom, 47, 51, 57, 59–61, 74
intelligent populace, 32–34
Internet, 2, 6, 43, 51

Jones, Wayne, 7

Kaltwasser, Cristóbal Rovira, 16, 158–159, 161
Kanopy, 5, 6
Klinenberg, Eric, 7–9, 20
knowledge, 6, 10–12, 16, 25, 30, 36–37, 41, 44, 51, 54–55, 62, 64–67, 69, 73, 76, 81, 89–92, 99, 106, 108–112, 118, 124, 130–133, 137–138, 140, 144, 150, 156, 160, 180, 183–185

language, 23, 55, 70, 71, 89–91, 93–98, 104–109, 111, 119, 150, 153, 164, 179

left (political), 12, 14, 19, 25, 47–48, 183–184
liberals, 11, 19, 24, 60, 94, 109, 125, 136–137, 158, 169, 183
liberalism, vi, 11, 13, 16–17, 19–20, 82, 155, 161
liberty, 13–14, 19, 94–95, 109–110, 162, 167
library/libraries, vi, 1–5, 7, 9–10, 13, 19–22, 24–25, 27–36, 41–53, 56, 60, 72–76, 78–80, 111–112, 130, 157, 174–175; as social infrastructure (or third space), 4, 9, 20, 30–32, 34; history, 21–30; subscription, 30–31, 33
librarianship, vi, 2, 5, 10, 19, 20, 23, 27, 35–41, 47, 54–57, 60–64, 67–68, 74–75, 79–80, 144; education for, 27, 38–40, 68, 118; gender, 32, 38, 56
librarians, 1–2, 4–5, 7, 10–11, 14, 19, 21, 23–24, 34, 37, 39, 47–48, 50–51, 53–58, 61, 63, 67–68, 72–79, 131, 143–144, 147; faculty as, 23; as teachers, 4–5, 27
libraries (academic, college and university), 6, 7, 21–27, 42, 52
libraries (public), 3–5, 7, 9–10, 19, 24–25, 28–38, 42–45, 48, 50, 52, 60, 73
libraries (school), 4–5, 49–50, 52
Library Bill of Rights, 45–48, 52–54, 60
library catalog, 21, 25–26
Library of Congress, 48
library users, 31, 42, 56, 61
Library Company of Philadelphia, 30
linguistics, 96–97
literacy, 4, 7, 27, 76
literary societies, 24
Lukacs, John, 16

Marinett, Filippo Tommaso, 2–3
Merleau-Ponty, Maurice, 69, 134–135, 145–148
Mill, John Stuart, 13, 19

misinformation, 114, 182, 184
Mudde, Cas, 16, 158–159, 161

Neoliberalism, 55, 72, 175
news, 3, 7–8, 12, 41, 51, 53, 75, 180
neutrality, 1, 47–48, 60, 76, 79, 109
Nichols, Jack, 12

outreach, 34

phenomenology, 2, 7, 68–69, 71, 120, 125, 131–149, 152–153, 155–156
philanthropy, 21, 35–36, 45
Pinker, Susan, 20
Plato, 15, 183
populism, 16–17, 158–162
positivism, 16, 68, 90
printing, 3, 22; age of, 3
propaganda, 44, 52, 149
public sphere, 51, 80–81, 161
publishing, 5, 65, 110, 135

queer theory, 54–55, 78–79

reader, 7, 9–10, 13, 34–35, 65, 74, 98, 106, 111–112, 125, 138
research funding, 26–27
rhetoric, vi, 6, 22, 33, 60, 82, 111, 149, 171, 174, 178
right (political), 11–12, 14, 19, 183–184

Sandel, Michael, 11
semiotics, 96, 106
Sloman, Steven, 11–12
Smith, George, 19
social epistemology, 41–42
social media, 3, 7–9, 142, 184–185
social practices, 97, 104
Southworth, E. D. E. N. (Emma Dorothy Eliza Nevitte), 43–44

STEM disciplines (science, technology, engineering, and math), 6
Stoddard, Solomon, 21

Taggart, Paul, 17, 158, 161
taxation, 10, 34, 36, 169
technology, 3, 6–7, 27–28, 72, 74, 76, 130, 179
Thompson, John, 3–4, 107
transcendence, 11, 143–144, 146, 148
Trump, Donald J., 12, 181
truth, 11, 58–59, 89, 91, 94, 101, 109, 112–121, 129, 132–133, 135, 140–141, 143, 174, 176, 179, 183–185
United States Capitol attack 2021, v

United States Bureau of Education, 24
utopia, 2, 10, 14

Walters, William H., 6
web. *See* world wide web
Weber, Max, 81, 167
Wiegand, Wayne, 20, 30–31, 37, 44, 46–47
World War I, 34, 36, 44
World War II, 27–28, 46–47, 163
world wide web, 2, 8

Zastrow, Jan, 6

About the Author

John M. Budd is professor emeritus with the School of Information Science and Learning Technologies of the University of Missouri. He has also been on the faculties of the University of Arizona and Louisiana State University. He has been very active in the American Library Association, the Association for Library and Information Science Education, and the Association of Information Science and Technology. He is the author of about 125 refereed journal articles and a number of books, including *Six Issues Facing Libraries Today: Critical Perspectives* (Rowman & Littlefield, 2017) and *Democracy, Economics, and the Public Good: Informational Failures and Potential* (Palgrave Macmillan, 2015).